Tom Kubiak

Insights to Performance Excellence 1999

Also Available from ASQ Quality Press:

Perspectives in Total Quality
Michael J. Stahl, editor

Principles and Practices of Organizational Performance Excellence
Thomas J. Cartin

Critical SHIFT: The Future of Quality in Organizational Performance
Lori Silverman with Annabeth L. Propst

Business Process Improvement Toolbox
Bjørn Andersen

The Toolbox for the Mind: Finding and Implementing Creative Solutions in the Workplace
D. Keith Denton

Success through Quality: Support Guide for the Journey to Continuous Improvement
Timothy J. Clark

101 Good Ideas: How to Improve Just About Any Process
Karen Bemowski and Brad Stratton, editors

Principles of Quality Costs: Principles, Implementation and Use, Third Edition
ASQ Quality Costs Committee - Jack Campanella, editor

Managing Quality Fads: How American Business Learned to Play the Quality Game
Robert Cole

To request a complimentary catalog of ASQ Quality Press publications,
call 800-248-1946.

Insights to Performance Excellence 1999

An Inside Look at the 1999 Baldrige Award Criteria

Mark L. Blazey

ASQ Quality Press
Milwaukee, Wisconsin

Insights to Performance Excellence 1999: An Inside Look at the 1999 Baldrige Award Criteria
Mark L. Blazey

10 9 8 7 6 5 4 3 2 1

ISBN 0-87389-461-8

Acquisitions Editor: Ken Zielske
Project Editor: Annemieke Koudstaal
Production Coordinator: Shawn Dohogne

ASQ Mission: The American Society for Quality advances individual and organizational performance excellence worldwide by providing opportunities for learning, quality improvement, and knowledge exchange.

Attention: Bookstores, Wholesalers, Schools and Corporations:
ASQ Quality Press books, videotapes, audiotapes, and software are available at quantity discounts with bulk purchases for business, educational, or instructional use. For information, please contact ASQ Quality Press at 800-248-1946, or write to ASQ Quality Press, P.O. Box 3005, Milwaukee, WI 53201-3005.
To place orders or to request a free copy of the ASQ Quality Press Publications Catalog, including ASQ membership information, call 800-248-1946. Visit our web site at http://www.asq.org.

Printed in the United States of America

Printed on acid-free paper

American Society for Quality
ASQ

Quality Press
611 East Wisconsin Avenue
Milwaukee, Wisconsin 53202
Call toll free 800-248-1946
http://www.asq.org
http://standardsgroup.asq.org

This book is dedicated to the memory of my father, who taught me the value of continuous improvement, and to my family, who provide support for the continuous search for quality: my mother, Ann Marrer Blazey; my brothers Scott, Brian, and Brent; my children Elizabeth and Mark; and most of all, my lifelong partner and loving wife Karen.

Contents

Preface

A substantial portion of my professional life has been spent helping people understand the power and benefits of this integrated management system and become quality award examiners. These people come from all types of organizations and from all levels within those organizations. Participants include corporate quality directors, state organization chiefs, small business owners, heads of hospitals, and school superintendents, to name a few. This book was originally developed for them. It was used as a teaching text to guide their decisions and deliberations as they provided feedback to organizations that documented their continuous improvement efforts using Baldrige Award-type management systems. Many examiners who used this text asked me to publish it in a stand-alone format. They wanted to use it to help their own organizations, customers, and suppliers guide and assess their continuous improvement efforts.

These two groups of readers—examiners of quality systems and leaders of high performing organizations—can gain a competitive edge by understanding not only the parts of a high performance management system, but how these parts connect and align. My goal for this book is that readers will understand fully what each area of the quality system means for organizations and find the synergy within the seven major parts of the system: leadership, strategic planning, customer and market focus, information and analysis, human resource focus, process management, and business results.

Organization leaders have reported that this book has been valuable as a step-by-step approach to help identify and put in place continuous improvement systems. As this progresses, improvement efforts in one area will lead to improvements in other areas. This process is similar to experiences we have all encountered as we carry out home improvement: Improve one area, and many other areas needing improvement become apparent. This book will help identify areas that need immediate improvement as well as areas that are less urgent but, nevertheless, vitally linked to overall improvement.

Acknowledgments

Curt Reimann, Harry Hertz, and the dedicated staff of the Malcolm Baldrige National Quality Award office have provided long-standing support and guidance in promoting quality excellence. The book would not be possible in a timely fashion without the design and layout expertise, dedication, and commitment of Enterprise Design and Publishing, and the substantive contribution of Russell Buyse of R. Buyse & Associates, Inc. In addition, several others have helped shape my thinking about performance excellence and refine this book, including John Lawrence, Mary Gamble, Karen Davison, Jeff Martin, Sharon Miletich, Maryann Brennan, John A. Pieno Jr., Dione Geiger, Don Tornberg, Mike Grant, Mike Brown, Ed Hare, April Mitchell, George Bureau, Dan MacIntosh, Debra Danziger-Barron, Skip Coggins, Jim Shipley, Karen Hoffman, Tom Kubiak, Pat Billings, Wendy Brennan, Gerald Brown, Anne O'Brien, Wendy Steager, Hugh Smith, Steve Hoisington, Gary Floss, Jack Evans, Arnie Weimerskirch, Paul Grizzell, Olga Striltschuk, Dale Misczynski, Don Anderson, and Dennis Sester. I also appreciate the typing assistance and proofreading of Heather Lupinsky. The chapter on site visits, the criteria model, the supplemental scoring guidelines, and some of the information pertaining to changes from the 1998 Criteria are used with permission of Quantum Performance Group, Inc. The core values, Criteria, selected glossary terms, and background information in this book are drawn from the *Malcolm Baldrige National Quality Award 1999 Criteria for Performance Excellence.* Portions of the Organizational Assessment Survey are used with permission from the National Council for Performance Excellence. Kevin Hendricks and Vinod Singhal provided research results that were used in this book from their extensive study of financial performance. Data from the Foundation for the Malcolm Baldrige National Quality Award regarding the perception of chief executive officers from over 300 United States organizations were also included in this book.

—*Mark Blazey*

Introduction

The *Malcolm Baldrige National Quality Award 1999 Criteria for Performance Excellence* and scoring guidelines are powerful assessment instruments that help leaders identify organizational strengths and key areas for improvement. The primary task of leaders is then to use the information to achieve higher levels of performance.

Building an effective management system capable of driving performance improvement is an ongoing challenge because of the intricate web of complex relationships among management, labor, customers, stakeholders, partners, and suppliers. The best organizations have a management system that improves its work processes continually. They measure every key facet of business activity and closely monitor organizational performance. Leaders of these organizations set high expectations, value employees and their input, communicate clear directions, and align the work of everyone to achieve organizational goals and optimize performance.

Unfortunately, because of the complexity of modern management systems, the criteria used to examine them are also complex and difficult to understand. *Insights to Performance Excellence 1999* helps performance excellence examiners and organization improvement practitioners clearly understand the 1999 Baldrige Performance Excellence Criteria and the linkages and relationships between the items.

Five types of information are provided in this book for each of the 19 items that comprise the Criteria.

- **The actual language of each item, including notes.**
- **A *plain English* explanation of the essence of the item** with some suggestions about meeting key requirements.
- **A summary of the requirements of the item in flowchart form.** The flowcharts capture the essence of each item and isolate the requirements of each item to help organizations focus on the key points the item is assessing. Note that most boxes in the flowcharts contain an item reference in brackets [ ]. This indicates that the criteria require the action. If there is no item reference in brackets, it means the action is suggested but not required. Occasionally a reference to "[scoring guidelines]" is included in a box. This means that, according to the scoring guidelines, the requirement to evaluate and refine a process is required to score above the 50 percent level.

- **The key linkages between each item and the other items.** The major or primary linkages are designated using a solid arrow (———►). The secondary linkages are designated using a dashed arrow (- - - - ►).
- **Examples of effective practices that some organizations have developed and followed.** These samples present some ideas about how to meet requirements. Examiners should not take these sample effective practices and convert them into requirements for organizations they are examining.

Several changes have been made to this 1999 edition.

- A few significant changes in this edition were required by changes in the Baldrige Criteria. Changes have been made in the flow diagrams and the linkages between the items.
- An explanation of the changes in the Criteria between 1998 and 1999 is provided in this edition.
- Primary and secondary linkages between the items have been defined.
- The first section of the book has been expanded to include a broader rationale for using the Baldrige Criteria to improve organization performance, as well as more lessons learned from using the Criteria.
- A revised section has been added to guide organizations through a streamlined self-assessment process.

Taken together, *Insights to Performance Excellence 1999* will strengthen your understanding of the Criteria and provide insight on analyzing your organization, improving performance, and applying for the award.

Insights to Performance Excellence

This section provides information for leaders who are transforming their organizations to achieve performance excellence. This section:

- Presents a business case for using the Baldrige Criteria to improve organizational performance;
- Describes the core values that drive organizational change to high levels of performance and underlie the Baldrige Criteria; and
- Provides practical insights and lessons learned—ideas on transition strategies to put high performance systems in place and promote organizational learning.

This section emphasizes themes driven by the 1999 Criteria and core values. It also includes suggestions about how to start down the path to systematic organizational improvement, as well as lessons learned from those who chose paths that led nowhere or proved futile despite their best efforts.

The Business Case for Using the Baldrige Performance Excellence Criteria

All leaders know that change is not easy. They will be asked and perhaps tempted to turn back many times. They may not even be aware of these temptations or of the backsliding that occurs when their peers and subordinates sense their commitment is wavering. Those leaders who are dedicated to achieving high performance appreciate examples of success from organizations that are ahead of them on the journey. These are organizations that have held the course despite nagging doubts, organizational turbulence, and attempts at sabotage.

The following section of the book:

- Summarizes perceptions and predictions about business trends and the value of the Malcolm Baldrige Award, based on survey responses of Chief Executive Officers from 308 major United States organizations. (This survey was conducted by the Foundation for the Malcolm Baldrige National Quality Award, April 1998.)
- Summarizes research on financial performance of approximately 400 firms that were recognized by local, state, or national award for Quality Management practices. (Research results are reported with permission of Dr. Vinod R. Singhal. Research was conducted by Kevin B. Hendricks and Vinod R. Singhal.)

- Describes public and private sector organizations that have gained ground and made rapid strides forward on their journeys, having achieved recognition as winners of the Malcolm Baldrige National Quality Award. It then identifies the core values that have guided these organizations to achieve high levels of performance excellence.

Value of Baldrige Criteria and Awards

In a report entitled The Nation's CEOs Look to the Future[1], 308 CEOs from large, small and several non-corporate organizations described what they believe lies ahead for business in the U.S. and the value of the Baldrige Criteria and Award. These trends relate in many ways to the 1999 Criteria and will be considered each year as the Criteria are revised to reflect the current business environment and the most effective management practices for that environment.

The vast majority (67 percent to 79 percent) of the CEOs believe that the Baldrige Criteria and awards are very or extremely valuable in stimulating improvements in quality and competitiveness in U.S. businesses. Given the trends and business environment they describe in the survey, and how they see U.S. businesses keeping pace, the Criteria provide a valuable competitive advantage.

Major Trends

More than 70 percent of the CEOs reported the trends listed below as major ones that will be likely to effect the business environment significantly in the coming years ahead:

- Globalization. This trend, identified as critical by 94 percent of respondents, has implications for all Categories, but particularly Strategic Planning, where global competition and alliances must be included in planning and for Customer and Market Focus where building and maintaining customer relationships is critical;
- Improving Knowledge Management. This trend, identified as critical by 88 percent of respondents, means that knowledge acquisition management is and will continue to be a significant competitive advantage. How Information and Analysis as well as training, education, and sharing of best practices is managed will be key to performance excellence.
- Cost and Cycle Time Reduction. This trend, identified as critical by 79 percent of respondents, is particularly relevant to Process Management. Organizations that effectively manage key product and service design

1 The Nation's CEOs Look to the Future: A Survey Conducted for the Foundation for the Malcolm Baldrige National Quality Award. Data collection: February–April 1998. Results tabulated and analyzed by Louis Harris & Associates, Inc.

and delivery processes will have a competitive edge in the global marketplace.

- Improving Supply Chains Globally. This trend, identified as critical by 78 percent of respondents, is a companion to the trend already described as Globalization. As business is increasingly taking place on the global stage, supply chain management needs to improve—either with direct suppliers and partners or beyond to partnerships and alliances. These requirements are particularly important to Process Management.
- Manufacturing at Multiple Locations in Many Countries. This trend, identified as critical by 76 percent of respondents, again relates to Globalization and also to Improving Supply Chain Management. To be successful at multiple country manufacturing, one needs to use a systems approach involving all Categories from Strategic Planning to Process Management with a strong focus on Customers and Markets as well as Human Resources.
- Managing the Use of More Part-Time, Temporary, and Contract Workers. This trend, identified as critical by 71 percent of respondents, reflects the rapidly changing environment that businesses operate within. The "hot" skills and technologies of today become out of date quickly. The product and service focus of today is tomorrow's throw away. Organizations must manage successfully with a more flexible and contingent workforce. Yet they must still manage that workforce effectively; the workforce still need the right skills and knowledge, motivation and incentives, and satisfaction from work. This trend is a major challenge particularly relevant to the Human Resource Focus Category.

Other Major Trends

More than 51 percent of the CEOs reported the trends listed below as major ones that will be likely to effect business in the years ahead. These include (from most cited, 69 percent, to least cited, 52 percent):

- Developing new employee relationships based on performance;
- Improving human resources management;
- Improving the execution of strategic plans;
- Developing more appropriate strategic plans;
- Ongoing measurement and analysis of organizational processes;
- Developing a consistent global corporate culture;
- Outsourcing of manufacturing; and
- Creating a learning organization.

These trends, together with the ones listed above, present a picture of what CEOs predict will be major business trends in the coming decade. The case for using the Baldrige Criteria as a way to manage effectively is validated and strengthened by the specific trends, their close relationship to the Criteria, and also by the next section in which the same CEOs rate the competencies major U.S. industries must possess to take advantage of these trends as a competitive advantage. CEOs report a huge gap between current state competency and future/desired state competency for many major trends. For example:

- Almost all of the CEOs report Globalization as a major trend, but only 18 percent rate major U.S. organization competency as excellent. Seventy percent rated the competency as only fair;
- Improving Knowledge Management was cited by 88 percent of CEO respondents as a major trend, but only 23 percent see U.S. organization competency as excellent. Fifty-five percent rate the competency level as only fair; and
- Competency in Cost and Cycle time reduction was rated as excellent by 31 percent and only fair by 52 percent.

These are a sample of competency gaps cited by CEOs in the survey. They reiterate the need to use proven management practices to close these gaps and ensure that U.S. organizations remain or become leaders in the global marketplace to sustain our quality of life.

CEO Skills Needing Improvement

CEOs were asked as part of the survey to reflect on their skills and their peer group's skills and to report on which skills were most in need of improvement. The skills cited below were thought by more than 50 percent to need "a great deal" of improvement. They are key to addressing the major business trends reported earlier in this section. The skills include:

- The ability to think globally and execute strategies successfully;
- Flexibility in a changing world;
- The ability to develop appropriate strategies and rapidly redefine their business; and
- The understanding of new technologies.

Another 40 to 50 percent of CEOs believe that these skills also need to improve "a great deal." Skills needing improvement include the ability:

- To work well with different stakeholders;
- To create a learning organization;
- To make the right bets about the future;
- To be a visible, articulate, charismatic leader; and
- To be a strong enough leader to overcome opposition.

Stakeholders and Interests That Are Becoming More Important

The majority of CEOs (75 percent or more) think that International Customers, Consumers, and Employees are becoming more important to business success. Over 60 percent believe that Suppliers, Outside Board Directors, and Institutional Shareholders are also becoming more important. Addressing requirements of the Customer and Market Focus Category and Employee Focus categories is increasing in importance according to the CEOs surveyed.

Execution of Strategies Is Critical

When asked which required more improvement—the development or execution of appropriate strategies—CEOs selected "Execution" by about a three-to-one margin. This means that alignment and realistic action plans need to be improved along with accountability. If the organization is pulling in different directions to accomplish individual unit or division priorities, energies and resources are being drained. Execution is flawed and results are suboptimized.

Expanding Market Size Is Critical

When asked which is more important, to increase market share or expand market size, CEOs selected "Expanding Market Size" by over a four-to-one margin. This will require improved Leadership, Strategic Planning, and Customer and Market Focus, particularly in the global economy. It will also require a more skilled and diverse workforce and more effective work processes.

The Competition Ahead

CEOs had various ideas about where the most serious competition to their businesses will come from in the next decade. Only a small number (12 percent) thought the toughest competition would come from other Fortune 500 companies. About 33 percent thought it was most likely to come from U.S. companies not yet on the Fortune 500 list. About 30 percent thought their toughest competitors were most likely to be foreign companies. Some saw start-up, entrepreneurial businesses as being the most serious competition. Comparing services and products to the competition and determining what the competition is doing to satisfy its customers is central to Baldrige-based assessments.

It is interesting though that most CEOs did not see the most serious competitors as being the major Fortune 500 companies of today. Perhaps this, more than any other CEO opinion, presents a compelling case for using the Baldrige Criteria—the fast and relentless pace of business change where companies on top today are not likely to be on top tomorrow without corresponding changes and improvements in their business.

Research Supports the Business Case

Two researchers were interested in quality award winners and to what extent (if any) quality management impacted financial performance. The research of Dr. Kevin B. Hendricks from the College of William and Mary School of Business and Vinod R. Singhal from the Georgia Institute of Technology, Dupree College of Management is the basis for the following piece of evidence that supports the use of the Baldrige Criteria.[2]

Their research looked beyond "hype and the popular press" to the real impact of quality management and examined the facts surrounding performance excellence. The research was based on about 600 recipients of various quality awards and similar recognition. The recognition provided to these organizations was based upon similar core values and concepts. Companies were mostly manufacturing firms (75 percent). All were publicly traded companies. Although they did not find that quality management turned "straw into gold" their research added significantly to the business case for using the Criteria as a tool to enhance performance.

Hendricks and Singhal examined the following efficiency or growth measures to examine:

- Percent change in sales;
- Stock price performance;
- Percent change in total assets;
- Percent change in number of employees;
- Percent change in return on sales; and
- Percent change in return on assets.

2 This research is described in the following papers: K.B. Hendricks and V.R. Singhal, "Quality Awards and the Market Value of the Firm; An Empirical Investigation." *Management Science,* 42:3, 1996, pp. 415-436; K.B. Hendricks and V.R. Singhal, "Does Implementing an Effective TQM Program Actually Improve Operating Performance? Empirical Evidence From Firms that Have won Quality Awards." *Management Science,* 43:9, 1997, pp. 1258-1274; K.B. Hendricks and V.R. Singhal, "The Long-Run Stock Price Performance of Firms with Effective TQM Programs." Working paper, Georgia Institute of Technology and The College of William and Mary, 1998.

Implementation Costs Do Not Negatively Impact the Bottom Line

The research examined two five-year periods during the quality management implementation cycle. The first period can be called beginning implementation. This period started six years before and ended one year before the receipt of their first award. During this period, organizations are implementing quality management and incurring associated costs of implementation such as training, communications and production, and design changes. The researchers found no significant differences in financial measures between these companies (winners) and the control group of companies (non-winners but similar in other respects) for this period. This is important because of the costs (both direct and indirect) associated with implementing quality management systems. The research suggests that the significant cost savings identified during this period of intensified focus on cycle time, time to market, and other factors pay for the implementation costs.

Improved Financial Results Can Be Expected with Successful Implementation

The study then examined results of companies from one year before winning the award to four years after the award was given. This period can be called mature implementation, and it is in this period that one would expect the improved management to bear fruit. This was the case with this research. There were significant differences in financial performance between award winners and controls (non-winners). For example, the growth in operating income averaged 91 percent for winners contrasted to 43 percent for non-award winners. Award winning companies reported 69 percent growth in sales compared with 32 percent for the control group. The total assets of the winning companies increased 79 percent compared to 37 percent for the controls. Winners had significantly better results than the control group.

Stock Price Performance of Winners Is Significantly Better

Consistent with other efficiency and financial findings, the winners outperformed the S&P 500 Index by 114 percent to 80 percent. In actual dollars, the better performance would be worth $669 million for the average award winner. They also outperformed other benchmark composites from the New York, American, and NASDAQ stock exchanges. It is important to note here that most of the "winners" did not also win the Baldrige Award. Baldrige recipients performed two to three times better than the S&P 500 index.

Quality Management Is a Long-Term Solution

Companies that expect immediate gains from quality management systems are likely to be disappointed. It took years to create the culture you have today; it can take years to change it. Nevertheless, this research, combined with other results makes a solid business case for using Baldrige-based management Criteria as the way to run the successful business of the future.

High Performing Organizations

High performing organizations outrun their competition by delivering value to stakeholders through an unwavering focus on customers and improved organizational capabilities. Examples of improved capabilities have occurred in all sectors of the economy, not just the private sector. These results range from time and cost savings to customer retention and loyalty.

Many examples of significant improvements are evident from using the Baldrige-based management system.

- Boeing Airlift and Tanker, a 1998 Baldrige winner, designs, develops, and produces military transport aircraft. They targeted 50 key processes for improvement and cut cycle time by over 80 percent. Return on net assets is seven times greater than the next best competitor. Net asset turnover improved sevenfold since 1994 while the return on sales improved threefold. Empowered employee teams have produced a 60 percent improvement in productivity.
- Texas Nameplate Company, Inc., a 1998 winner, makes identification labels. Their market share in Texas increased from 69 percent to 93 percent and almost doubled nationally. A gain-sharing program augments wages by 11 percent and has helped double net profit as a percent of sales in the last four years. Gross profit as a percent of sales is 59 percent.
- Xerox Business Services (XBS), a 1997 Baldrige winner, provides document services throughout the world. XBS increased revenues more than 30 percent annually, growing into a $2 billion business in less than five years.
- ADAC Laboratories of California, a 1996 Baldrige Award winner, designs, manufactures, markets and supports products for health care customers. Customer retention increased from 70 to 90 percent during the past five years. Since 1990, average cycle time declined from 56 hours to 17 hours and revenue tripled.
- For the past two years, Trident Precision Manufacturing, another 1996 Baldrige Award winner, has experienced zero defects in its custom products. Trident's quality rating for its major customers (based on customer reports) is higher than 99.8 percent.
- Wainwright Industries, a 1994 Baldrige winner, cut the time for mak-

ing one of its principal extruded products from 8.75 days to 15 minutes, and reduced defect rates tenfold.

- Cadillac, a 1990 winner, reduced the time for die changes in its stamping plant from eight hours to four minutes by redesigning the entire process.
- Corning Telecommunications Products Division, a 1995 Baldrige Award winner, has become the world market leader and the low-cost provider, and has earned the highest customer satisfaction ratings in the industry by far.
- In five years, Solectron Corporation, a 1991 and 1997 Baldrige winner, experienced a sales increase from $130 million to $3.7 billion, representing a 2,800 percent improvement. Net profits soared more than tenfold. Market share doubled since 1992. The stock price went up sixty fold since 1989.
- At Federal Express, a 1989 Baldrige winner, cost per package was cut by more than 40 percent.
- Globe Metallurgical, Inc., a 1988 Baldrige winner, experienced a 60 percent increase in revenues and a 40 percent increase in profits since 1992.
- Ames Rubber Corporation, a 1993 Baldrige winner, achieved a 99.9 percent quality and on-time delivery status through sharing quality techniques with suppliers.
- AT&T Consumer Communications, a 1994 Baldrige winner, listened to its customers and received its largest customer response ever in a short time frame to its "True" marketing program.
- AT&T Transmission Sales Business Unit, a 1992 winner, achieved a tenfold improvement in equipment quality and a 50 percent reduction in cycle time that saved $400 million over six years.

Similar findings are appearing throughout the world as organizations use the Baldrige performance excellence Criteria to manage their businesses.

In summary, as expected, organizations using the Baldrige Criteria to enhance performance do better on the stock market—a lot better! The Baldrige Award office in the U.S. Department of Commerce found similar results in recent studies.

- They "invested" a hypothetical sum of money in each of the publicly traded whole companies that won the Baldrige Award since 1988. They tracked the investment from the first business day of the month following the announcement of the Baldrige winners' award (or the date they began trading publicly), to December 1, 1997. Adjustments were made for stock splits. The results continue to show that the publicly traded Baldrige-winning companies outperformed the S&P 500 by a substantial margin, achieving a 394.5 percent return on investment compared to 146.9 percent for the S&P 500.

- The Baldrige Award office also tracked a similar investment for the 52 publicly traded applicants that received Baldrige Award site visits. As a group, they outperformed the S&P 500 by approximately 80 percent, achieving a 216.0 percent return compared to 118.7 percent for the S&P 500.

The Core Values to Achieve Performance Excellence

Today, approximately 46 states and dozens of countries worldwide use the Baldrige Criteria to identify performance excellence in businesses, schools, health care facilities, and government agencies. These organizations find that the performance excellence Criteria help guide them through difficult management decisions on their endless journeys. Their actions and policies are driven by a consistent set of core values.

The Baldrige performance excellence Criteria are built on a powerful set of common values that characterize high performing organizations. This section identifies the 11 core values that underlie the Criteria. These values bind an organization together and yield high performance. High performing organizations deliver ever-increasing value to stakeholders by improving organizational capabilities.

These core values are critical for successful organizations of any size and in any sector—from small mom-and-pop shops to hospitals, government agencies, public utilities, schools, and businesses.

By adopting these values, organizations can optimize their performance. As competition gets tougher, nothing less than optimization will do. No organization will be immune from the ravages of poor quality, suboptimization, and failing to satisfy customers.

The first value is a passion for **customer-driven quality.** Without this, little else matters. Customers are the final judges of how well the organization did its job, and what they say counts. It is their perception of the service and product that will determine whether they remain loyal or constantly seek better providers.

- The organization must focus on systematically listening to customers and acting quickly on what they say.
  The organization must build positive relationships with its customers through focusing on accessibility and management of complaints.

- Dissatisfied customers must be heeded most closely, for they often deliver the most valuable information.
- If only satisfied and loyal customers (those who continue to do business with us no matter what) are paid attention, the organization will be led astray. The most successful organizations keep an eye on customers who are not satisfied and work to understand their preferences and meet their demands.

Customer-Driven Quality

Quality is judged by customers. Thus, quality must take into account all product and service features and characteristics that contribute value to customers and lead to customer satisfaction, preference, and retention.

Value and satisfaction may be influenced by many factors throughout the customer's overall purchase, ownership, and service experiences. These factors include the organization's relationship with customers that helps build trust, confidence, and loyalty.

Customer-driven quality addresses not only the product and service characteristics that meet basic customer requirements, but also includes those features and characteristics that differentiate products and services from competing offerings. Such differentiation may be based upon new or modified offerings, combinations of product and service offerings, customization of offerings, rapid response, or special relationships.

Customer-driven quality is thus a strategic concept. It is directed toward customer retention, market share gain, and growth. It demands constant sensitivity to changing and emerging customer and market requirements, and the factors that drive customer satisfaction and retention. Customer-driven quality also demands awareness of developments in technology and of competitors' offerings, and rapid and flexible response to customer and market requirements.

Customer-driven quality means much more than defect and error reduction, merely meeting specifications, or reducing complaints. Nevertheless, defect and error reduction and elimination of causes of dissatisfaction contribute to the customers' view of quality and are thus also important parts of customer-driven quality. In addition, the organization's success in recovering from defects and mistakes ("making things right for the customer") is crucial to building customer relationships and to customer retention.

The most potent value is **continuous improvement and learning.** High performing organizations are learning organizations—they create a culture of seeking to evaluate and improve everything they do. They strive to get better at getting better.

- A culture of continuous improvement is essential to maintaining and sustaining true competitive advantage.
- Without systematic improvement and ongoing learning, organizations will ultimately face extinction.
- With systematic continuous improvement, time becomes a powerful ally. As time passes, the organization grows stronger and smarter.

Continuous Improvement and Learning

Achieving the highest levels of performance requires a well-executed approach to continuous improvement and learning. The term "continuous improvement" refers to both incremental and "breakthrough" improvement. The term "learning" refers to adaptation to change, leading to new goals and/or approaches. Improvement and learning need to be "embedded" in the way the organization operates. The term embedded means that improvement and learning: (1) are a regular part of daily work; (2) are practiced at individual, work unit, and organizational levels; (3) seek to eliminate problems at their source; and (4) are driven by opportunities to innovate and do better, as well as by problems that must be corrected. Sources of improvement and learning include: employee ideas; R&D; customer input; best practice sharing; and benchmarking.

Improvement and learning include: (1) enhancing value to customers through new and improved products and services; (2) developing new business opportunities; (3) reducing errors, defects, waste, and related costs; (4) improving responsiveness and cycle time performance; (5) increasing productivity and effectiveness in the use of all resources; and (6) enhancing the organization's performance in fulfilling its public responsibilities and service as a good citizen.

Thus, improvement and learning are directed not only toward better products and services but also toward being more responsive, adaptive, and efficient—giving the organization additional marketplace and performance advantages.

Management by fact is the cornerstone value for effective planning, operational decision making at all levels, employee involvement and empowerment, and leadership.

- Everyone makes decisions every day. However, without data, the basis for decision making is intuition—gut feel.
- Most drivers decide when to fill their fuel tanks based on data from the fuel gauge and get very uncomfortable if the gauge is broken. Yet peo-

ple routinely make decisions of enormous consequence about customers, strategies, goals, and employees with little or no data. This is a recipe for disaster, not one designed to ensure optimization.

Management by Fact

Businesses depend upon the measurement and analysis of performance. Such measurements must derive from the organization's strategy and provide critical data and information about key processes, outputs, and results. Many types of data and information are needed for performance measurement and improvement. Performance areas included are: customer, product, and service; operations, market, and competitive comparisons; and supplier, employee, and cost and financial.

Analysis refers to extracting larger meaning from data and information to support evaluation, decision making, and operational improvement within the organization. Analysis entails using data to determine trends, projections, and cause and effect—that might not be evident without analysis. Data and analysis support a variety of purposes, such as planning, reviewing overall performance, improving operations, and comparing performance with competitors or with "best practices" benchmarks.

A major consideration in performance improvement involves the selection and use of performance measures or indicators. *The measures or indicators selected should best represent the factors that lead to improved customer, operational, and financial performance. A comprehensive set of measures or indicators tied to customer and/or organizational performance requirements represents a clear basis for aligning all activities with the organization's goals.* Through the analysis of data from the tracking processes, the measures or indicators themselves may be evaluated and changed to better support such goals.

Organizations must invest in their people to ensure they have the skills for today and for the future. This core value has broadened from employee participation and development to **valuing employees.** In high performing organizations, the people who do the work of the organization should make most of the decisions about how the work is done. However, a significant barrier exists that limits employee decision making—access to data and poor data-based decision-making skills.

- Leaders are unwilling to let subordinates make decisions based on intuition—they reserve that type of decision for themselves.
- Therefore, access to data and developing skills to manage by fact is a prerequisite for optimizing employee contributions to the organization's success.

- Organizations cannot effectively push decision making down to the level where most of the work is done unless those doing the work have access to the necessary data and are skilled at making fact-based decisions.

Valuing Employees

An organization's success depends increasingly on the knowledge, skills, innovative creativity, and motivation of its workforce. Employee success depends increasingly on having opportunities to learn and to practice new skills. Organizations need to invest in the development of the workforce through education, training, and opportunities for continuing growth. Opportunities might include job rotation and increased pay for demonstrated knowledge and skills. On-the-job training offers a cost effective way to train and to better link training to work processes. Education and training programs may need to utilize advanced technologies, such as computer-based learning and satellite broadcasts. Increasingly, training, development, and work units need to be tailored to a diverse workforce and to more flexible, high performance work practices.

Major challenges in the area of valuing employees include: (1) integrating human resource practices—selection, performance, recognition, training, and career advancement; (2) developing, cultivating, and sharing the organization's knowledge that is possessed by its employees; and (3) aligning human resource management with strategic change processes. Addressing these challenges requires use of employee-related data on knowledge, skills, satisfaction, motivation, safety, and well-being. Such data need to be tied to indicators of organizational or unit performance, such as customer satisfaction, customer retention, and productivity. Through this approach, employee contributions may be better integrated and aligned with business directions.

Fast response is a value usually driven by customer requirements and the desire to improve operating efficiency and lower costs.

- Except for a few pleasurable experiences, everyone wants things faster.
- Organizations that develop the capacity to respond faster by eliminating activities and tasks that do not add value, find that productivity increases, costs go down, and customers are more loyal.
- Analyzing and improving work processes enables organizations to perform better, faster, and cheaper.
- To improve work processes, organizations need to focus on improving design quality and preventing problems. The cost of preventing problems and building quality into products and services is significantly less than the cost of taking corrective action later.

- It is critical to emphasize capturing learning from other design projects.
- Use information concerning customer preference, competitors' products, cost and pricing, marketplace profiles, and research and development (R&D) to optimize the process from the start.
- Public responsibility issues and factors including environmental demands must be included in the design stage.

> ***Fast Response***
>
> Success in globally competitive markets demands ever-shorter cycles for introductions of new or improved products and services. Also, faster and more flexible response to customers is now a more critical requirement. Major improvements in response time often require simplification of work units and processes. To accomplish this, the time performance of work processes should be among the key process measures. Other important benefits can be derived from this focus on time: time improvements often drive simultaneous improvements in organization, quality, cost, and productivity. Hence, it is beneficial to integrate response time, quality, and productivity objectives.

To remain competitive, every organization must be guided by a common set of **measurable goals** and **a long-range view of the future.**

- These measurable goals, which emerge from the strategic planning process, serve to align the work of everyone in the organization.
- Measurable goals allow everyone to know where they are going and when they deviate from their path.
- Without measurable goals, everyone still works hard, but they go in different directions—suboptimizing the success of the organization.

> ***Long-range View of the Future***
>
> Pursuit of market leadership requires a strong future orientation and a willingness to make long-term commitments to key stakeholders—customers, employees, suppliers, stockholders, the public, and the community. Organizations should anticipate many factors in their strategic planning efforts, such as customers' expectations, new business opportunities, the increasingly global marketplace, technological developments, new customer and market segments, evolving regulatory requirements, community/societal expectations, and strategic changes by competitors. Short- and long-term plans, strategic objectives, and resource allocations need to reflect these influences. Major components of such a long-term commitment include developing employees and suppliers and fulfilling public responsibilities.

Achieving long-range goals is increasingly difficult without internal and external **partnership development.**

- Internal partnership agreements with workers, including labor unions and other units as appropriate, must be created and strengthened.
- External alliances and strategic partnerships are key to enhancing overall capabilities quickly. Such partnerships characterize high performing organizations that think strategically about maximizing performance for their customers.

Partnership Development

Organizations need to build internal and external partnerships to better accomplish their overall goals.

Internal partnerships might include labor-management cooperation, such as agreements with unions. Agreements might entail employee development, cross-training, or new work organizations, such as high performance work teams.

Internal partnerships also might involve creating network relationships among work units to improve flexibility, responsiveness, and knowledge sharing.

External partnerships might be with customers, suppliers, and education organizations for a variety of purposes, including education and training. An increasingly important kind of external partnership is the strategic partnership or alliance. Such partnerships might offer entry into new markets or a basis for new products or services. Partnerships also might permit the blending of an organization's core competencies or leadership capabilities with the complementary strengths and capabilities of partners, thereby enhancing overall capability, including speed and flexibility.

Internal and external partners should develop longer-term objectives, thereby creating a basis for mutual investments. Partners should address the key requirements for success, means of regular communication, approaches to evaluating progress, and means for adapting to changing conditions. In some cases, joint education and training could offer a cost-effective method of developing employees.

Every high performing organization practices good **public responsibility and citizenship.**

- Organizations must determine and anticipate any adverse effects to the public of their products, services, and operations. Failure to do so can undermine public trust and distract workers, and also adversely affect the bottom line. This is true of both private and public organizations.
- Safety and legal requirements need to be met beyond mere compliance.

Public Responsibility and Citizenship

An organization's leadership needs to stress its responsibilities to the public and needs to practice good citizenship. These responsibilities refer to basic expectations of the organization—business ethics and protection of public health, safety, and the environment. Health, safety, and the environment include the organization's operations as well as the life cycles of its products and services. Organizations also need to emphasize resource conservation and waste reduction at the source. Planning should anticipate adverse impacts from production, distribution, transportation, use, and disposal of products. Plans should seek to prevent problems, to provide a forthright response if problems occur, and to make available information and support needed to maintain public awareness, safety, and confidence. Organizations should not only meet all local, state, and federal laws and regulatory requirements, they should treat these and related requirements as opportunities for continuous improvement "beyond mere compliance." This requires the use of appropriate measures in managing performance.

Practicing good citizenship refers to leadership and support—within the limits of an organization's resources—of publicly important purposes. Such purposes might include improving education, health care in the community, environmental excellence, resource conservation, community service, industry and business practices, and sharing non-proprietary information. Leadership as a corporate citizen also entails influencing other organizations, private and public, to partner for these purposes. For example, individual companies could lead efforts to help define the obligations of their industry to its communities.

A **results focus** helps organizations communicate requirements, monitor actual performance, make adjustments in priorities, and reallocate resources. Without a results focus, organizations can become fixated on processes and lose sight of the important factors for success.

Results Focus

An organization's performance measurements need to focus on key results. Results should be focused on creating and balancing value for all stakeholders—customers, employees, stockholders, suppliers and partners, the public, and the community. To meet the sometimes conflicting and changing aims that balance implies, organizational strategy needs to explicitly include all stakeholder requirements. This will help to ensure that actions and plans meet differing stakeholder needs and avoid adverse impact on any stakeholders. The use of a balanced composite of performance measures offers an effective means to communicate short- and longer-term priorities, to monitor actual performance, and to marshal support for improving results.

Every system, strategy, and method for achieving excellence must be guided by effective **leadership.**

- Effective leaders convey a strong sense of urgency to counter the natural resistance to change that can prevent the organization from taking the steps that these core values for success demand.
- Such leaders serve as enthusiastic role models, reinforcing and communicating the core values by their words and actions. Words alone are not enough.

Leadership

An organization's senior leaders need to set directions and create a customer orientation, clear and visible values, and high expectations. The directions, values, and expectations need to address all stakeholders. The leaders need to ensure the creation of strategies, systems, and methods for achieving excellence, stimulating innovation, and building knowledge and capabilities. The strategies and values should help guide all activities and decisions of the organization. The senior leaders need to commit to the development of the entire workforce and should encourage participation, learning, innovation, and creativity by all employees.

Through their ethical behavior and personal roles in planning, communications, review of organizational performance, and employee recognition, the senior leaders serve as role models, reinforcing values and expectations and building leadership and initiative throughout the organization.

There are always better ways to do things. Our challenge is to find them, but we are not likely to find them alone. We must create an environment—a work climate where better ways will be sought out, recognized, and put in place by everyone.

Practical Insights

Connections and Linkages

A popular children's activity, connect the dots, helps them understand that, when properly connected, apparently random dots create a meaningful picture. In many ways, the 7 categories, 19 items, and 27 areas to address in the Baldrige Criteria are like the dots that must be connected to reveal a meaningful picture. With no paths to make the web, or join the dots, human resource development and use are not related to strategic planning; information and analysis are isolated from process management; and overall improvement efforts are disjointed, fragmented, and do not yield robust results. This book describes the linkages for and between each item. The exciting part about having them identified is you can look for these linkages in your own organization and, if they don't exist, start building them.

Transition Strategies

Putting high performance management systems in place is a major commitment that will not happen quickly. At the beginning, you will need a transition strategy to get you across the bridge from management by opinion or intuition to more data-driven management. The next part of this section describes one approach that has worked for many organizations in various sectors: creating a performance improvement council.

Performance Improvement Council

Identify a top-level executive leadership group of 6 to 10 members. Each member over that number will seem to double the complexity of issues and make decision making much more cumbersome. The executive leadership group could send a message to the entire organization by naming the group the performance improvement council—reinforcing the importance of continuous performance improvement to the future success of the organization.

The performance improvement council should be the primary policy-making body for the organization. It should spawn other performance improvement councils at lower levels to share practices and policies with every employee in the organization as well as to involve customers and suppliers. The structure permeates the organization as members of the performance improvement council become area leaders for major improvement efforts and sponsors for several process or continuous improvement task teams throughout the organization. The council structure, networked and cascaded fully, can effectively align the work and optimize performance at all levels and across all functions.

Council Membership

Selecting members for the performance improvement council should be done carefully. Each member should be essential for the success of the operation, and together they must be sufficient for success. The most important member is the senior leader of the organization or work unit. This person must participate actively, demonstrating the kind of leadership that all should emulate. Of particular importance is a commitment to consensus building as the modus operandi for the council. This tool, a core of performance improvement programs, is often overlooked by leadership. Other council members selected should have leadership responsibility for broad areas of the organization such as human resources, operations planning, customers, and data systems.

Performance Improvement Council Learning and Planning

The performance improvement council should be extremely knowledgeable about high performance management systems. If not, as is often the case, performance improvement council members should be among the first in the organization to learn about continuous improvement tools and processes.

To be effective, every member of the council (and every member in the organization) must understand the Baldrige Criteria because the Criteria describe the components of the entire management system. Participation in examiner training has proved to be the very best way to understand the complexities of the system needed to achieve performance excellence. Any additional training beyond this should be carried out in the context of planning—that is, learn tools and use them to plan the performance improvement implementation, practices, and policies.

The performance improvement council should:

- Develop an integrated, continuous improvement strategic performance improvement and business plan.
- Create the web (communication plan and infrastructure) to transmit performance improvement policies throughout the organization.
- Define the roles of employees, including new recognition and reward structures to cause needed behavioral changes.
- Develop a master training and development plan. Involve team representatives in planning so they can learn skills close to when they are needed. Define what is provided to whom, and when and how success will be measured.
- Launch improvement projects that will produce both short- and long-term successes. Improvement projects should be clearly defined by the performance improvement council and driven by the strategic plan. Typical improvement projects include important human resource processes such as career development, performance measurement, and diversity, as well as improving operational products and services in the line areas.

- Develop a plan to communicate the progress and successes of the organization. Through this approach, the need for performance improvement processes is consistently communicated to all employees. Barriers to optimum performance are weakened and eliminated.
- Create champions to promote performance excellence through the Categories of the Baldrige Criteria.

Category Champions

This section describes the responsibilities of category champions. The people in the administrative or leadership cabinet should each be the champion of a category.

Organizational Leadership Champion

The Organizational Leadership Champion is a senior executive who, in addition to other executive duties, works to coordinate and enhance leadership effectiveness and alignment throughout the organization. It is both a strategic and an operational activity.

From the strategic side, the champion should focus on ensuring that all senior leaders:

- Understand what is expected of them as leaders of organizational change;
- Agree to achieve consensus, and subsequently act consistently and speak with one voice, as a senior leadership team;
- Serve as role models of performance excellence for managers and employees at all levels of the organization;
- Set clear strategy and directions to enhance future opportunities for the organization; and
- Create measurable performance expectations and monitor performance to achieve the key improvements and strategic objectives of the organization. This means that necessary data and analyses must be coordinated to ensure appropriate information is available for the champion and the entire senior leadership team.

From the operational side, the champion should work to identify and eliminate both individual and system deficiencies, territorial conflicts, and knowledge shortfalls that limit a leader's ability to meet expectations and goals consistently.

The champion should be the focal point in the organization to ensure all parts of the organization have systematic processes in place so they fully understand leadership and management requirements.

A process should exist to monitor ongoing initiatives to ensure leaders effectively set and communicate organizational values to employees.

- They must demonstrate that they focus on delivering value to customers and other stakeholders.
- They must aggressively reinforce an environment that promotes empowerment and innovation throughout the workforce. This may involve reviewing policies, systems, work processes, and the use of resources—ensuring sufficient data are available to assist in manager and employee decision making.

The champion should coordinate the activities involving the review of organizational performance and capabilities.

- Key performance measures should be defined.
- Systems to review organizational health, performance, and progress relative to goals should be in place.
- Performance review findings should be communicated widely throughout the organization and, as appropriate, to key suppliers and customers to help ensure organizational alignment.
- Performance review findings should be translated into priorities for improvement and innovation at different levels throughout the organization.
- Performance review findings, together with employee feedback, should be used systematically to assess and improve senior leadership effectiveness and the effectiveness of managers throughout the organization.

Finally the champion must work as part of the senior leadership team to help coordinate all facets of the management system to drive high performance. This involves teaching the team about the requirements of effective and consistent leadership at all levels and its impact on organizational performance. The senior leader of the organization usually serves as the Organizational Leadership Champion and leads this council.

Strategic Planning Champion

The Strategic Planning Champion is a senior executive who, in addition to other executive duties, works to coordinate and enhance strategic planning and action plan alignment throughout the organization. It is both a strategic and an operational activity.

From the strategic side, the champion should ensure that the focus of strategy development is on sustained competitive leadership, which usually depends on achieving revenue growth, as well as consistently improving operational effectiveness. The Strategic Planning Champion should help the senior leadership team acquire a view of the future and provide clear strategic guidance to the organization through goals, objectives, action plans, and measures.

From the operational side, the champion should work to ensure sufficient data are available about:

- The organization's operational and human resource capabilities;
- Internal and external risks; and
- The competitive environment and other challenges that might affect future direction.

The champion should be the focal point in the organization to ensure all parts of the organization have systematic processes in place so they fully understand the implications of strategy on their daily work.

The champion should ensure that strategy is customer and market focused and is actually used to guide ongoing decision making and resource allocation at all levels of the organization.

- A process should exist to convert strategy into actions at each level of the organization which are aligned to achieve goals necessary for business success.
- Every employee should understand his or her role in carrying out actions to achieve the organization's goals.

The champion should coordinate the activities involving strategy development and deployment to:

- Acquire and use various types of forecasts, projections, scenarios, or other techniques to understand the plausible range of future options;
- Determine how the projected performance of competitors is likely to compare with the projected performance of the organization in the same time frame in order to set goals to insure competitive advantage;
- Determine what capabilities must be developed within the organization to achieve strategic goals and coordinate with other members of the senior leadership team and category champions to ensure those capabilities are in place;
- Determine what changes in services or products might be needed as a part of strategic positioning and direction;
- Ensure a system is in place to develop action plans that address strategic goals and objectives. Ensure those action plans are understood throughout the organization, as appropriate;
- Ensure a system is in place to identify the human resource requirements necessary to achieve strategic goals and objectives. This may include training, support services for employees, reorganization, and new recruitment, to name a few;

- Ensure a system is in place to allocate resources throughout the organization sufficient to accomplish the action plans;
- Coordinate with the leadership system of performance review to help ensure priorities for improvement and innovation at different levels throughout the organization are aligned with strategy and action plans; and
- Ensure the process for strategic planning, plan deployment, the development of action plans, and the alignment of resources to support actions is systematically evaluated and improved each cycle. Also evaluate and improve the effectiveness of determining the projected performance of competitors for use in goal setting.

Finally the champion must work as contributing member of the senior leadership team to help coordinate all facets of the management system to drive high performance. This involves teaching the team about the requirements of strategic planning and its impact on organizational performance.

Customer Value Champion

The Customer Value Champion is a senior executive who, in addition to other executive duties, will coordinate and enhance customer satisfaction, relations, and loyalty throughout the organization. It is both a strategic and an operational activity.

From the strategic side, the champion should focus on ensuring that the drivers of customer satisfaction, customer retention, and related market share (which are key factors in competitiveness, profitability, and business success) are considered fully in the strategic planning process. This means that necessary data and analyses must be coordinated to ensure appropriate information is available for the executive planning councils.

From the operational side, the champion should work to identify and eliminate system deficiencies, territorial conflicts, and knowledge shortfalls that limit the organization's ability to meet customer satisfaction, retention, and loyalty goals consistently.

The champion should be the focal point in the organization to ensure all parts of the organization have systematic processes in place so they fully understand key customer, market, and operational requirements as input to customer satisfaction and market goals.

A process should exist to monitor ongoing initiatives to ensure they are aligned with the customer aspects of the strategic direction. This may involve:

- Reviewing policies, systems, work processes, the use of resources, and the availability of employees who are knowledgeable and focus on customer relations and loyalty;
- Ensuring sufficient data are available to assist in decision making about customer issues; and
- Ensuring that strategies and actions relating to customer issues are aligned at all levels of reorganization from the executives to the work unit or individual job level.

The champion should coordinate the activities involving understanding customer requirements as well as managing the interaction with customers, including how the organization determines customer satisfaction and satisfaction relative to competitors. (Satisfaction relative to competitors and the factors that lead to customer preference are of increasing importance to managing in a competitive environment.)

- The champion should also examine the means by which customers have access to seek information, assistance, or comment and complain.
- The champion should coordinate the definition of customer contact requirements and the deployment of those requirements to all points in the organization that have contact with customers.
- The champion should ensure that systems exist to respond quickly and resolve complaints promptly to recover customer confidence that might be otherwise lost.
- The champion should ensure that employees responsible for the design and delivery of products and services receive information about customer complaints so they may eliminate the causes of these complaints.
- The champion should work with appropriate line managers to help set priorities for improvement projects based on the potential impact of the cost of complaints and the impact of customer dissatisfaction and attrition on the organization.
- The champion should be charged with coordinating activities to build loyalty and positive referral as well as evaluating and improving customer relationship building processes throughout the organization.

Finally the champion must work as contributing member of the senior leadership team to help coordinate all facets of the management system to drive high performance. This involves teaching the team about the requirements of customer and market focus and its impact on organizational performance.

Information and Analysis Champion

The Information and Analysis Champion is an executive level person who, in addition to other executive duties, will coordinate and enhance information and analysis systems throughout the organization to ensure they meet the decision-making needs of managers, employees, customers, and suppliers. It is both a strategic and an operational activity.

From the strategic side, information and data can provide a competitive advantage. The champion should focus on ensuring, to the extent possible, that timely and accurate information and data are available to enhance the delivery of new and existing products and services to meet emerging market needs.

From the operational side, the champion should work to ensure that information and data are available throughout the organization to aid in decision making at all levels. This means coordinating with all other champions to ensure data are available for day-to-day review and decision making at all levels for their areas of responsibility.

The Information and Analysis Champion has responsibility for both information infrastructure as well as ensuring the appropriate use of data for decision making. The champion should coordinate activities throughout the organization involving data collection, accuracy, analysis, retrieval, and use for decision making. The Champion should ensure:

- Complete data are available and aligned to strategic goals, objectives, and action plans to ensure performance against these goals, objectives, and action plans can be effectively monitored;
- Systems are in place to collect and use comparative data and information to support strategy development, goal setting, and performance improvement;
- Data and information throughout the organization are accurate and reliable to enhance fact-based decision making;
- Data and information are used to support a better understanding of the cost and financial impact of various improvement options;
- Appropriate correlations and performance projections are available to support planning;
- The performance measurement system is evaluated and improved to ensure it meets business needs;
- Data analysis supports the senior executives' organizational performance review and organizational planning;
- Data analysis addresses the overall health of the organization;

- The results of organization-level analysis are available to workgroup and functional-level operations to support decision making at those levels; and
- Data analysis supports daily decisions regarding operations throughout the organization to ensure actions align with plans.

Finally the champion must work as part of an organization-wide council to help coordinate all facets of the management system to drive high performance.

Human Resource Focus Champion

The Human Resource Focus Champion is an executive level person who, in addition to other executive duties, will coordinate and enhance systems to enable employees to develop and utilize their full potential, consistent with the organization's strategic objectives. This includes building and maintaining a work environment conducive to full employee participation and growth. It is both a strategic and an operational activity.

From the strategic side, the human resource constraints of the organization must be considered in the development of strategy and subsequently eliminated to ensure the workforce is capable of achieving the strategies necessary for business success.

From the operational side, the champion should ensure that the work climate enhances employee satisfaction and well-being and that work is organized and jobs are designed to enable employees to achieve higher levels of performance.

The Human Resource Focus Champion has responsibility for ensuring that employees (including managers and supervisors at all levels; permanent, temporary, and part-time personnel; and contract employees supervised by the organization) receive the same kind of focus and attention as customers, so that their needs are met to enable them to contribute fully to the organization's goals and objectives. The champion should ensure:

- Work and jobs are structured to promote cooperation, collaboration, individual initiative, innovation, and flexibility;
- Managers and supervisors encourage and motivate employees to develop and use their full potential;
- An effective system exists to provide accurate feedback about employee performance and enhance their performance. This includes systems to identify skill gaps and recruit or reassign employees to

close those gaps; as well as ensuring that fair work practices are followed within the organization. This may also include evaluating managers and enhancing their ability to provide accurate feedback and effective coaching to improve employee performance;

- Compensation, recognition, and rewards are aligned to support high performance objectives of the organization (contained in strategic plans and reported in the balanced scorecard or business results report card);
- Education and training support business objectives and build employee knowledge, skills, and capabilities to enhance employee performance. This includes ensuring employees understand tools and techniques of performance measurement, performance improvement, quality control methods, and benchmarking. This also includes ensuring that managers and supervisors reinforce knowledge and skills on the job;
- The work environment is safe, with measurable performance measures and targets for each key factor affecting employee safety; and
- Factors that affect employee well-being, satisfaction, and motivation are routinely measured and actions are taken promptly to improve conditions that adversely affect morale, motivation, productivity, and other key business results.

Finally the champion must work as part of an organization-wide council to help coordinate all facets of the management system to drive high performance.

Process Management Champion

The Process Management Champion is an executive level person who, in addition to other executive duties, will coordinate and enhance all aspects of the organization's systems to manage and improve work processes to meet the organization's strategic objectives. This includes customer focused design, product and service delivery, internal support services, and supplier and partner systems. It is both a strategic and operational activity.

From the strategic side, rapid and accurate design, development, and delivery of products and services creates a competitive advantage in the marketplace.

From the operational side, the champion should work to ensure all key work processes are examined and optimized to achieve higher levels of performance, reduce cycle time and costs, and subsequently add to organizational profitability.

The Process Management Champion has responsibility for creating a process management orientation within the organization. Since all work is a process, the Process Management Champion must ensure that the process owners (including processes owned by other champions) systematically examine, improve, and execute their processes consistently. The champion should ensure:

- Systematic continuous improvement activities are embedded in all processes, which lead to ongoing refinements;
- Initial and ongoing customer requirements are incorporated into all product and service designs, production and delivery systems, and processes. This includes core production processes as well as internal support processes (such as finance and accounting, facilities management, research and development, administration, procurement, personnel, and sales and marketing);
- Design, production, and delivery processes are structured and analyzed to reduce cycle time; increase the use of learning from past projects or other parts of the organization; reduce costs; increase the use of new technology and other effectiveness or efficiency factors; and ensure all products and services meet performance requirements; and
- Supplier and partner performance requirements are met and capabilities are improved. This includes minimizing costs associated with inspections, tests, or performance audits; providing timely and actionable feedback to suppliers/partners so they can take quick corrective action as needed; and providing assistance or incentives to help them improve their overall performance and abilities. These actions will, in turn, enhance your organization's performance.

Finally the champion must work as part of an organization-wide council to help coordinate all facets of the management system to drive high performance.

Business Results Champion

The Business Results Champion is an executive level person who, in addition to other executive duties, will coordinate the display of the organization's business results. This champion has substantially different work than the champions for Categories 1 through 6. No actions leading to or resulting from the performance outcome data are championed by the Business Results Champion. Those actions are driven by the category one through six champions because they have responsibility for taking action to implement and deploy procedures necessary to produce the business results. For example, the Information and Analysis Champion (Category 4), is responsible for collecting data that reflect all areas of strategic importance leading to business results. The Category 4 champion is also responsible for ensuring data accuracy and reliability.

The Business Results Champion is responsible, however, for ensuring that the organization is able to display all business results required by Category 7 to provide evidence of the organization's performance and improvement in key business areas and facilitate monitoring by leaders. These include customer satisfaction, product and service performance, financial and marketplace performance, human resource results, supplier and partner results, and operational performance.

Results must be displayed by appropriate segment and group, such as different customer groups, market segments, employee groups, or supplier groups.

Appropriate comparison data must be included in the business results display to judge the relative "goodness" or "strength" of the results achieved.

Finally the champion must work as part of an organization-wide council to help coordinate all facets of the management system to drive high performance. For example, if the organization is not collecting data necessary for inclusion in the business results report card, the Business Results Champion coordinates work with the other champions on the council to ensure those data are available.

The Critical Skills

A uniform message, set of skills or core competencies, and constancy of purpose are critical to success. Core training should provide all employees with the knowledge and skills on which to build a learning organization that continually gets better. Such training typically includes team building, leadership skills, consensus building, communications, and effective meeting management. These are necessary for effective teams to become involved in solving critical problems.

Another important core skill involves using a common process to define customer requirements accurately, determining the ability to meet those requirements, measure success, and determine the extent to which customers—internal and external—are satisfied. When a problem arises, employees must be able to define the problem correctly, isolate the root causes, generate and select the best solution to eliminate the root causes, and implement the best solution.

It is also important to be able to understand data and make decisions based on facts, not merely intuition or feelings. Therefore, familiarity with tools to analyze work processes and performance data is important. With these tools, work processes can be analyzed and vastly improved. Reducing unnecessary steps in work processes, increasing process consistency, reducing variability, and reducing cycle time are powerful ways to improve quality and reduce cost simultaneously.

Courses in techniques to acquire comparison and benchmarking data, work process improvement and reengineering, supplier partnerships and certification, role modeling for leaders' strategic planning, and customer satisfaction and loyalty will help managers and employees expand their optimization and high performance thrust across the entire organization.

Lessons Learned

Twenty years ago the fierce global competition that inspired the quality movement in the United States was felt primarily by major manufacturers. Today, all sectors are under intense pressure to "be the best or be history." The demand for performance excellence reaches all corners of the economy, from manufacturing and service industries to professional services, education, health care, public utilities, and government. All of these segments have contributed valuable lessons to the quality movement and have played an important part in our recovery from the economic slump caused by poor service and products of the 1970s. Relying on the Baldrige model, we will share some of the insights and lessons learned from leaders of high performing organizations.

A Tale of Two Leaders

It was a time of turbulence; it was a time of peace. It was a time of growth and streamlining. It was the happiest of times; it was also the most painful of times. Most of all it was a time that demanded change—although it was more comfortable to consider it a time for the status quo.

The following tales are of two leaders. One who is consistent and persistent in communicating the direction and message that will bring about excellent results and high performance. Another is uncertain and vague. He does not wish to push his people into anything, let alone the difficult commitment related to using the Baldrige Criteria as the way to run the business. After all, they are still profitable and healthy. Why rock the boat? You may know these people or someone who reminds you of them. If so, you will understand the reason for this section.

There is no lonelier, more challenging, yet critical and rewarding job than that of the leader. I work with many, many leaders who listen to advice carefully. They really want to know the best approaches to use for their organizations. Yet what they do with the advice and counsel is always interesting and unpredictable. This section is intended to help those leaders go resolutely down the right path.

Neither leader exists in real life, but both leader profiles are based on actual events and observations of many different people in leadership positions.

The Tale

Background Tale One:

John was the CEO of a Fortune 500 manufacturing company that was slowly but surely losing market share. Shareholders and employees were happy because profits and growth, although slower, were still hearty. However, their business that once enjoyed a near monopoly position was rapidly becoming more and more competitive. Customers that had to beg and plead for limited products and service over the years were happily turning to competitors who were trying in earnest to meet their needs and even delight them. In such an environment, aggressive, customer focused companies were winning the hearts, minds, and pocketbooks of John's customers. John decided after working with a consulting firm or two and studying the work of Deming, that Performance Excellence was urgently needed to keep the company in business more than five years.

The first message to the leadership team

John called an urgent meeting of his senior team. Many members of this team had been there since the company began its growth spurt and had been good soldiers in times of runaway growth and profit. John was wondering how many of the senior staff would receive the message he was about to send. The meeting was scheduled the next week for five days at the corporate headquarters. Short of an emergency illness, attendance was required.

During the next few days, John received twenty phone calls from secretaries that informed John their bosses could not attend because of other priority commitments. Priorities were quickly realigned when they were informed that all top leaders *would* be in attendance.

The week-long meeting at corporate headquarters began with training. The kind of training where the group was required to participate, listen, and discuss the content. The training was presented by an outside firm with frequent discussions of company-wide application and emphasis presented by John. At the end of three days, John took over the meeting and asked for input on how best to apply these principles to the organization at all levels. The leadership group voiced resistance to change, some more than others. They basically voiced concern that "this performance excellence stuff with all of its requirements for empowerment and data" would get in the way of their doing business and was not needed.

John clarified the objectives of the group by walking to the white board and writing: "This new program, performance excellence, will be in the way of doing business effectively." The senior staff pretty much agreed.

John responded by placing a large "X" through the word "in." The statement now read, "Performance excellence, will be the way of doing business effectively." John notified the attendees, "I will negotiate an exit package with anyone who does not understand the implications of this message, and who does not want to be part of this new way of doing business."

The Next Steps

John focused on two next steps: (1) making sure his top team role modeled behavior that would facilitate the needed changes; and (2) planning and implementing a company-wide training requirement to communicate the new skills and performance expectations. John started to change his behavior and the behavior of his top staff, feeling that "walking the talk" would signal the importance of new behaviors more than any speech or videotaped presentation. The next top staff meeting was called within a week to plan the design and rollout of training corporate-wide, including all foreign and domestic sites. The top staff had very little interest in training, feeling largely that this was a human resource function and should be delegated to that department. Based on the advice of external advisors, John informed the staff that it was now their job to plan, design, and execute this training. A "core design team" was formed with senior leaders and expert content and course design specialists to design the training within one month and present it to the senior corporate leaders.

In spite of prior agreements to manage their meetings effectively, to be on time, not interrupt, and follow the agenda, most continued to ignore the rules. Behaviors of the top leadership group at this meeting included the usual set of interruptions, "I told you so's," and everyone talking at the same time. John, whose goal was to create a listening and learning environment, challenged the group to "ante up." He asked that all top leaders bring fifty $20 bills to the meeting. John introduced new meeting ground rules. They were simple. Interruptions, put downs, blocking behaviors, talking while someone else was, were violations of meeting ground rules. On the other hand, building on ideas, clarifying ideas, supporting, and disagreeing respectfully were good meeting behaviors. Every violation was worth a $20 dollar bill. Good meeting behaviors were rewarded, although they did not materialize until several meetings up the road. At first, it seemed that the pot would win big time—no one took John seriously. After about the third meeting, with penalties piling up, their behavior actually changed. Other meeting management skills were slowly introduced, such as time frame limits and action planning. Then John was able to ask his team to role model this behavior to others. He ordered that, "This is the way we treat each other at all meetings including staff meetings, communication forums, and all company business meetings." A core value and new behavior or courtesy and professionalism became deployed company-wide through the senior management team.

Training and the Change Process

Each five-day high performance management course was identical, ensuring a uniform message and set of skills was communicated. Each course was eventually taught by two instructors, a shop supervisor and a manager, so that management and the workforce would both be involved. John personally taught the top leadership team the entire five-day course, assisted by a member of the design team, and this tale spread across the organization like wildfire. It was the thing to be invited to take part in this instruction because their leader had done it. The core skills became part of the fabric of the organization—the way to conduct business. They included fact-based decisions, a focus on customers, and using and improving processes. Also included was a way to solve problems continually with a well-defined process at the level the problem was occurring.

The focus had shifted from status quo to a thirst for improvement. Improvement began to bring rewards whereas the status quo was disdained. A comprehensive business evaluation was conducted and improvement targets were identified. Clear assignments with reasonable goals were cascaded to all levels of the organization. Performance planning, goals, compensation, and recognition were aligned to support the overall business strategy. Managers who did not work to meet these new goals, who did not role model the behaviors necessary to achieve high performance, were reassigned to jobs that did not require their management skills. New role models emerged to lead the organization at all levels. Within three years the company regained market share, improved profitability, expanded its employee base, and became, once again, one of the world's most admired companies.

Background Tale Two

Jerry was the CEO of a West coast manufacturing company that also was a proud member of the Fortune 500. Company performance had been uneven over the past few years. Profits were low this year relative to previous years but the company still met financial targets. Product demands were high and the outlook was fairly good for the next quarter. The industry as a whole was fairly evenly matched as far as management problems. Trends for return on investment were also uneven, and other indicators such as sales volume and net profit were up and down. Investors were not happy, especially when other companies consistently outperformed them. Jerry thought that it was time to do something different. Jerry consulted several valuable and trusted advisors and then decided that High Performance Excellence might be worth considering.

The first message to the leadership team

Jerry scheduled a series of weekly dinner meetings over the next month (January) and engaged several different top consultants to talk to the group about the business case for using high performance management. He invited 50 top-level managers from across the country to attend. Most top leaders attended the meetings, enjoyed the dinners, and Jerry attended most but not all of them. The sessions were interesting—the top leaders found the meetings were a great forum for politicking, posturing, wining and dining, and trying to sharpshoot the consultant. Jerry asked his top leaders to come together for a half day in the spring to discuss the content and direction of the high performance initiative, being convinced intellectually by the dinner discussions that this was the right direction for the company. At the half-day meeting, it was obvious that about half of the group agreed with the CEO and about half were uncertain or downright resistant, particularly one very senior vice president. Jerry left the team with this message, "Let me take your comments under advisement and think about them as we go forward." Later, at the consultant's suggestion, he conducted an organizational assessment to identify problems that might be contributory to the uneven, up-and-down performance. The assessment uncovered several serious problems that required change, yet the senior leaders continued to resist.

The Next Steps

Jerry finally hired one of the external advisors who withstood the test of several dinner meetings and the challenges of his threatened senior management team. The advisor was asked to speak to the top leaders of Jerry's entire U.S.-based company about what a great group they were and how important the performance excellence initiative was going to be for the company. The advisor closed by telling them that only the best go after high performance; if they did not, their competitors would. During the following discussion sessions, Jerry's chief operating officer announced to the group that he was far from convinced and stated he was not going to change the way he did business. That comment went unchallenged by Jerry or anyone else in the company. Frustration continued to build.

In an effort to regain momentum, Jerry wanted to create a change team. He asked each division to send a person to "facilitate" the initiative and be trained by the external team. The people selected were far from the best each division could offer since no selection criteria were provided. They supplied people that were expendable. The people who formed the facilitator group, for their part, were very enthusiastic but not particularly respected or credible. They were given absolutely no relief from any regular duties so they were stretched very thin. Also, the division heads were not supportive in any way of their participation so they were almost punished for participating on this team. As the facilitators worked to please the demands of the CEO, there was no clear charter or mission as to what they were actually supposed to accomplish—no way to assess their performance or their accomplishment of their mission.

The power struggle intensified between the COO (who thought this was not the way to go and would have none of it), and the CEO. The CEO and the top management team arranged to travel to a leadership conference where they could hear presentations from high performance organizations that had used the performance excellence techniques successfully. The CEO made it a priority to plan to attend only morning presentations so everyone could play tennis together each afternoon. Tennis, not high performance, was the main topic of discussion at the evening dinners. A good time was had by all, but no consensus around change developed or was even discussed.

Training and the Change Process

Still, Jerry wanted the facilitators to continue their work to assist change. The internal facilitators were placed in charge of conducting training for the entire organization. After the initial training was designed, a date was set to present a half-day version to the senior staff. Although the entire training was a four-day course, the senior staff did not feel they needed the same skills as the workforce. However, Jerry made it a high priority for his direct reports to attend. At the last minute, Jerry had to attend a function related to the Board of Directors and did not attend.

The training was, to put it mildly, a disaster. The executives, prompted by the snide comments of the COO, never gave it a chance. They concluded that the training was not effective and should not be rolled out to the employees. In the face of compelling opposition, Jerry quietly diverted his attention elsewhere.

Summary

It is probably obvious what the current state is of John's high performance "way to run the business" versus the high performance "initiative" at Jerry's company. Perhaps you could spot some of the problems each type of leader addressed and solutions they supported.

Using symbols and language to manage the change to high performance is tricky and usually demands that some external person is involved who can provide good sound advice, based on experience and expertise, to the CEO. Using power constructively is absolutely critical since failure of the top leader to use all forms of power and influence available will intensify conflict and power struggles that act as a *de facto* barrier to change.

Motivating people to act constructively, and not feel threatened is another challenge. Providing a clear focus on the future state while rewarding behavior that facilitates the transition will work to ensure the change actually happens. Jerry's vision was unclear. He did not act as a leader. He ensured his facilitators would never succeed by never championing their work in any way. The next time Jerry gets a new idea, these people (if they are still employees) will take a nosedive rather than be at the forefront of the initiative.

John never lost his vision, control, or influence as CEO. He ensured his management team would also retain control by first insisting they climb on board and then giving them the skills and support to spread the approaches throughout the company. He used many points of contact for the seeds to take root.

Leadership

Based on the CEO research cited earlier, coupled with the relentless pace of change in all sectors and increasingly global competition, there are several strong messages leaders need to understand. ***Then they must be willing to take the necessary steps to change.*** This will require an assessment of current management systems ***and*** a willingness to drive the necessary adjustment. Once the assessment is complete and priorities are agreed upon, line up plans and resources and support the change wholeheartedly. ***Focus on the marketplace for your cues to change.*** Ask for example:

- Is your competition growing weaker?
- Is the economy more stable and secure?
- Are the demands of all of your customers declining?
- Do you have all of the resources you need to meet your future goals?
- Do you believe your employees will be willing or able to continue working at the pace you have set for them? Will they do more?

If answer is NO to any of these questions, read on.

Assess management systems and launch improvements. This will require your organization to assess their management against the Baldrige Criteria. After the assessment is complete, identify the vital few next steps, assign responsibility, make improvements, and re-evaluate.

Great Leaders Are Great Communicators Who Lead by Example

One characteristic of a high performance organization is outstanding performance results. How does an organization achieve such results? How does it become world-class? We have found unanimous agreement on the critical and fundamental role of leadership. There is not one example of an organization or unit within an organization that achieves superior levels of performance without the personal and active involvement of its top leadership. Top leaders in these organizations create a powerful vision that focuses and energizes the workforce. Everyone is pulling together toward the same goals. Frequently, an inspired vision, combined with appropriately aligned recognition and reward, is the catalyst that builds trust and launches initiatives to overcome the organizational status quo.

Great leaders are great communicators. They identify clear objectives and a game plan so the organization succeeds in its mission. They assign accountability, ensure that employees have the tools and skills required, and create a work climate where individual initiative and the transfer of learning thrives. They reward teamwork and data-driven improvement. While practicing what they preach they serve as role models for continuous improvement, consensus building, and fact-based decision making; they push authority and accountability to the lowest possible levels.

One lesson from great leaders is to refrain from the use of the word "quality." Too often, when skilled, hard-working, dedicated employees are told by leaders, "We are going to start a quality effort," they conclude that their leaders believe they have not been working hard enough. The workforce hears an unintended message, "We have to do this because we are not good." They frequently retort with, "We already do quality work!" Registered professionals (engineers, chemists, psychologists, physicians, teachers) often exacerbate the communication problem by arguing that they, not customers, are the best ones in a position to know and define "quality." These messages confuse the workforce. Unfortunately, the use of the word *quality* can create an unintended barrier of mistrust and negativism that leaders must overcome before even starting on the road to performance excellence.

As an alternative, we advise leaders to create a work climate that enables employees to develop and use their full potential, to improve continually the way they work—to seek higher performance levels and reduce activities that do not add value or optimize performance. Most employees readily agree that there is always room for improvement—all are exposed to work that does not add value.

The use of the word quality can also open leadership to challenges as to what definition of quality the organization should use. This leads to our second lesson learned.

Leaders will have to overcome two organizational tendencies—to reject any management model or approach "not invented here" and to think that there are many equally valid models. Quality differs from a decision tree or problem-solving model where there are many acceptable alternatives. The Baldrige model—and the many national, state, and organization assessment systems based on it—is accepted as the standard for defining performance excellence in organizations worldwide. Its criteria provide validated, leading-edge practices for managing an organization to achieve peak performance. A decade of extraordinary business results shown by Baldrige Award winners and numerous state-level, Baldrige Award-based winners have helped convince those willing to learn and listen.

To be effective, leaders must understand the Baldrige model and communicate to the workforce and leadership system their intention to use that model for assessment and improvement. Without clear leadership commitment to achieving the requirements of the comprehensive Baldrige model, resources may be spent chasing facts, narrow focuses, and isolated strategies such as activity-based costing, management by objective, reengineering, project management, quality circles, and ISO 9000 certification, to name a few. Without clear leadership there will be many "hikers" walking around but no marked trails for them to follow. Once leaders understand the system and realize that it is their responsibility to share the knowledge and mark the trails clearly, performance optimization is attainable. This brings us to our third leadership lesson learned.

A significant portion of senior leaders' time—as much as 60 percent to 80 percent—should be spent in visible Baldrige-related leadership activities such as goal setting, planning, reviewing performance, recognizing and rewarding high performance, and spending time understanding and communicating with customers and suppliers, ***not*** micro-managing subordinates' work. The senior leaders' perspective in goal setting, planning, and reviewing performance must look at the inside from the outside. Looking at the organization through the critical eyes of external customers, suppliers, and other stakeholders is a vital perspective.

The primary role of the effective senior leader is to focus the organization on satisfying customers through an effective leadership system. Leaders must role model the tools of consensus building and decision making as the organization focuses on its vision, mission, and strategic direction to keep customers loyal.

Falling back on command-and-control behavior will be self-defeating. The leadership system will suffer from crossed wires and mixed messages. Commandments such as "I want this mission rolled out by the end of the second quarter" fall into the self-defeating, major mistake category. However, leaders must be clear and resolute.

Using the consensus approach to focus the organization on its mission and vision will take longer, of course. This is similar to taking more time during the product design phase to ensure that problems are prevented later. The additional time is necessary for organizational learning, support, and buy-in, particularly around two areas—integrating global marketplace realities and better understanding the competitive environment. The resulting vision will have more depth and focus. The leadership system will be stronger. Finally, the deployment of the vision and focus will take a shorter time because of the buy-in and support created during the process.

L Is for Listen

Successful leaders know the power in listening to their people—those they rely on to achieve their goals. One vital link to the pulse of the organization is employee feedback. To determine whether what you have said has been understood, ask for feedback and then listen carefully. To know whether what you have outlined as a plan makes sense or has gaping faults, ask for feedback and then listen. Your leadership system cannot improve without your listening and acting on employee feedback, and your goals and action plans cannot be improved without it. In fact, the 1999 Baldrige Criteria [Item 1.1b(4)] specifically examines the extent to which leaders use employee feedback in assessing and improving their leadership effectiveness and the effectiveness of managers at all levels.

Manage and Drive Change

Business leaders can count on relentless, rapid change being part of the business world. The rate of change confronting business today is far faster than that driven by the Industrial Revolution. Skills driven by the Industrial Revolution carried our parents through a 40-year work life. Human knowledge now doubles every 5 to 7 years, instead of the 40 years it took in the 1930s. Today, our children are told to expect five career (not job) changes during their work life.

There are several lessons for leaders today. Change may not occur on the schedule they set for it. It is often faster or too uneven to predict at all. Also, change driven by leaders is often resisted by those most successful—they have difficulty seeing the need to change. Take, for example, a school district that scheduled a quality improvement workshop for its middle school faculty. The day before the training, the district leadership received a letter protesting the workshop on the grounds it was not needed. The letter was signed by the 20 best teachers in the school. To the credit of the school district leadership, they held the workshop anyway, and the truly outstanding teachers saw the value in continuous improvement once they began to listen.

Leaders who hold the values of high performance will need to drive change to make the necessary improvements. Change will not happen naturally. It is rarely driven by those at the bottom (except for revolutionaries). Embracing the concepts of organizational learning (not just individual) will facilitate change in the organization. Leaders will need organizational learning as an ally as they manage change and drive it through the organization.

Strategic Planning

Deploy Through People Not Paper

Strategic Planning is Performance Improvement Planning, Deployment, and Implementation. The organization's strategic plan is also its quality—business, human resources—performance improvement plan. Easily enough said, but trying to get agreement on exactly what strategic planning is will result in an interesting variety of ideas. Therefore, the planning process should begin by ensuring that all contributors agree on terminology. Otherwise the strategic plan may in fact be incomplete—a marketing plan, a budget plan, or a financial business plan, depending on who is leading the team.

Developing separate plans for each aspect of business success is counterproductive. It guarantees a nonintegrated and short-lived systematic performance improvement effort. Therefore, leaders should concentrate on the few critical improvement goals in the strategic plan necessary for organizational success, such as improving customer loyalty and reducing errors or cycle time. The well-developed strategic plan also:

- Documents the financial impact of achieving these few goals;
- Details actions to support the goals; and
- Discusses the competitive environment that drives the goals.

One highly successful organization simplified this document to a single electronic page, to which senior leaders referred each month by computer during performance results reviews. Everyone at all levels used their own one-page document to deploy the plan and define actions needed.

The most critical lesson learned when it comes to strategic plans is that there can be no rest until it is certain every person in the organization understands his or her role in the plan and how their contribution will be measured.

Customer and Market Focus

Customers Expect Solutions to Problems They Don't Know They Have

The high-performing organization systematically determines its customers' short-term and long-term service and product requirements. It does this based on information from former as well as current and potential customers. It builds relationships with customers and continuously obtains information, using it to improve its service and products and understand better customer preferences. The smart organization prioritizes the drivers of satisfaction and loyalty of its customers, compares itself to its competitors, and continuously strives to improve its satisfaction and loyalty levels.

As the organization becomes more and more systematic and effective in determining customer needs, it learns that there is high variation in customer needs. The more sophisticated the measurement system, the more variation will become apparent. It is particularly important that organizations focus on this vital process and make it a top priority that their customers have access to people to make known their requirements and their preferences. How else can modern organizations ensure they are building relationships with their customers? After all, few of us have store front windows on Main Street where our customers come and chat regularly.

One specific lesson learned comes from voice mail—a big step forward in convenience and efficiency can be a big step backward in customer relationship building if used poorly. For example, a major international financial institution put their highest priority customers on a new voice mail system. Customers were never informed about the system and one day called their special line to find rock music and a three-tiered voice mail system instead of their personal financial account manager. This is a good example of a step in the wrong direction—customers were never asked about their requirements and preferences and the organization heard about it quickly in the form of lost accounts and angry, frustrated customers.

Another important first lesson is to segment customers according to their needs and preferences and do what is necessary to build strong, positive relationships with them. More and more customers are looking for service providers to define their unique needs for them and respond to those unique needs. In short, customers are expecting solutions to problems that they, the customers, have not yet realized.

Organizations that make it easy for customers to complain are in a good position to hear about problems early so that they can fix them and plan ahead to prevent them. If organizations handle customer complaints effectively at the first point of contact, customer loyalty and satisfaction will increase. When organizations do not make it easy for customers to complain, when finally given the chance to provide feedback, they will not bother to complain; they simply will no longer do business with these organizations.

As the customer focused organization matures, it will likely evolve around customer types. This evolution leads to restructuring that is guided by shared organizational values. The speed with which this restructuring occurs varies according to marketplace conditions and the organization's ability to change. Today we see more restructuring that eliminates parochial, regional centers in favor of creating customer service groups that meet customer requirements around the world using up-to-date technologies.

The next lesson has to do with educating the organization's leadership in the fundamentals of customer loyalty and customer satisfaction research models before beginning to collect customer satisfaction data. Failure to do this may affect the usefulness of the data as a strategic tool. At the very least, it will make the development of data collection instruments a long, misunderstood effort, creating rework and unnecessary cost.

Do not expect everyone to welcome customer feedback—many fear accountability. Time and time again, the organizations most resistant to surveying customers, conducting focus groups, and making it easy for customers to complain are the same organizations that do not have everyday contact handling systems, response time standards, or trained and empowered frontline employees to serve customers and deal with their concerns promptly. Frontline employees who are not ready to acknowledge customer concerns are not capable of assuming responsibility to solve customer problems.

No single feedback tool is intended to stand alone. A mail-based survey does not take the place of personal interviews. Focus groups do not replace surveys. The high performance organization uses multiple listening posts and trains frontline employees to collect customer feedback and improve those listening posts. In the high performance organization, for example, even an accounts receivable system is viewed as a listening post.

Do not lose sight of the fact that the best customer feedback method, whether it be a survey, focus group, or one-on-one interview, is only a tool.

- Make sure the data gathered are actionable.
- Aggregate the data from all sources to permit complete analyses.
- Use the data to improve strategic planning and operating processes.

Finally, be aware that customers are not interested in your problems. They merely want products or services delivered as promised. They become loyal when consistent value is provided that sets you above all others. Merely meeting their basic expectations brands you as marginal. To be valued you must consistently delight and exceed the customers' expectations.

Information and Analysis

Data-Driven Management and Avoiding Contephobia

The high performance organization collects, manages, and analyzes data and information to drive excellence and improve its overall performance. Said another way, information is used to drive actions. Using data and information as strategic weapons, effective leaders compare their organization constantly to competitors, similar service providers, and world-class organizations.

While people tend to think of data and measurement as objective and hard, there is often a softer by-product of measurement. That by-product is the basic human emotion of fear. This perspective on data and measurement leads to the first lesson learned about information and analysis. Human fear must be recognized and managed in order to practice data-driven management.

This fear can be found in two types of people. The first are those who have a simple fear of numbers—those who hated mathematics in school and probably stretch their quantitative capabilities to balance their checkbook. These individuals are lost in numerical data discussions. When asked to measure or when presented with data, they can become fearful, angry, and resistant. Their reactions can actually undermine improvement efforts.

The second type of individual, who understands numbers, realizes that numbers can impose higher levels of accountability. The fear of accountability, *contephobia* (from fourteenth-century Latin *to count*, modified by the French *to account*), is based on the fear of real performance failure that numbers might reveal or, more often, an overall fear of the unknown that will drive important decisions. Power structures can and do shift when decisions are data-driven.

Fearful individuals can undermine effective data-driven management systems. In managing this fear, leaders must believe and communicate through their behavior that a number is not inherently right or wrong. It is important for leaders at all levels to demonstrate that system and process improvement, not individuals, are the focus of performance improvement.

A mature, high performance organization will collect data on competitors and similar providers and benchmark itself against world-class leaders. Some individuals may not be capable of seeing the benefit of using this process performance information. This type of data is known as benchmarking data. The focus is on identifying, learning from, and adopting best practices or methods from similar processes, regardless of industry or product similarity. Adopting the best practices of other organizations has driven quantum leap improvements and provided great opportunities for breakthrough improvements.

Lesson number two, therefore, is that an organization that has difficulty comparing itself with dissimilar organizations is not ready to benchmark and is not likely to be able to optimize its own performance as a result.

The third lesson in this area relates to not being a DRIP. This refers to a tendency to collect so much data (which contributes to contephobia) that the organization becomes data rich and information poor. This is wrong. Avoid wasting capital resources and stretch the resources available for managing improvement by asking this question: "Will these data help make improvements for our customers, key financials, employees, or top result areas?" If the answer is no, do not waste time collecting, analyzing, and trying to use the data.

Human Resource Focus

Human Resource (Not the Department)

Personnel departments have been renamed in many organizations, often to "human resources." This name change is intended to draw attention to the fact that people are valuable resources of the organization, not just commodities to be hired and fired and filed. Now, however, the leap made by successful organizations is that human resources need to be part of every strategic and operational decision of the organization. This focus goes far beyond the department of human resources. In high performing organizations, employees are treated like any valuable asset of the organization—investment and development are critical to optimize the asset. People should be perceived as internal customers, and a vital part of the chain that eventually serves an external customer.

One of the valuable lessons learned in this regard is not to let an out-of-date or territorial "personnel or human resources department" use archaic rules to stop your performance improvement program. Although many human resources professionals are among the brave pioneers in high performance organizations, others have tried to keep compensation and promotions tied to "seat time" and tenure rather than performance. This outdated approach will definitely stop progress in its tracks or slow it significantly.

The Big Challenge Is Trust

The high performing organization values its employees and demonstrates this by enabling people to develop and realize their full potential while providing them incentives to do so. The organization that is focused on human resource excellence maintains a climate that builds trust. Trust is essential for employee participation, engagement, personal and professional growth, and high organizational performance.

The first human resource lesson is perhaps the most critical one. That is, revise—overhaul, if necessary—recognition, compensation, promotion, and feedback systems to support high performance work systems. If leaders personally demonstrate all the correct leadership behaviors, yet continue to recognize and reward "fire fighting" performance, offer pay and bonuses tied only to traditional bottom-line results, and promote individuals who do not represent high performance role models—those leaders will find their improvement effort is short-lived. The leadership system with all its webs and intricate circuits will short out due to mixed signals.

Promotion, compensation, recognition, and reward must be tied to the achievement of key business results, including customer satisfaction, innovation, and performance improvement. The promotion/compensation/recognition tool is a powerful tool in aligning, or misaligning, the work of the organization.

A second human resource lesson learned relates to training and development. Training is not a panacea or a goal in itself. The organization's direction and goals must support training, and training must support organization priorities.

Its human resources are the competitive edge of a high performing organization. Training must be part of an overall business strategy. If not, money and resources are probably better spent on a memorable holiday party.

Timing is critical. Broad-based workforce skill training should not come first. Many organizations rush out and train their entire workforce only to find themselves having to retrain months or years later. Key participants should be involved in planning skill training so that important skills are delivered just in time for them to use in their assignments.

Continuous skill development requires management support to reinforce and strengthen skills on the job. Leadership development at all levels of the organization needs to be built into employee development. New technology has increased training flexibility so that all knowledge does not have to be transferred in a classroom setting. Consider many options when planning how best to update skills. After initial skill building occurs, high performing organizations emphasize organizational learning where employees take charge of their own learning, using training courses as only one avenue for skill upgrading. Transferring learning to other parts of the organization or projects is a valuable organizational learning strategy and reinforcement technique. Training must be offered when an application exists to use and reinforce the skill. Otherwise, most of what is learned will be forgotten. The effectiveness of training must be assessed based on the impact on the job, not merely the likability of the instructor or the clarity of course materials.

Employee surveys are often used to measure employee satisfaction and improve employee satisfaction. Surveys are especially useful to identify key issues that should be discussed in open employee forums. Such forums are truly useful if they clarify perceptions, provide more in-depth understanding of employee concerns, and open the communication channels with leaders. Organizations have success in improving employee satisfaction by conducting routine employee satisfaction surveys, meeting with employees to plan improvements, and tying improvements in satisfaction ratings to managers' compensation.

Two final human resource excellence lessons have to do with engaging and involving employees in decisions about their work. Involving employees in decision making without the right skills or a sense of direction produces chaos, not high performance.

- First, leaders who empower employees before communicating and testing that a sense of direction has been fully understood will find that they are managing chaos.
- Second, not everyone wants to be empowered, and to do so represents

a barrier to high performance. While there may be individuals who truly seek to avoid responsibility for making improvements, claiming "that's management's job," these individuals do not last long in a high performing organization. They begin to stick out like a lone bird in the winter. Team members who want the organization to thrive and survive do not permit such people to influence (or even remain on) their team.

The bigger reason for individuals failing to "take the empowerment and run with it" is management's mixed messages. In short, management must convince employees that they (managers) really believe that employees know their own processes best and can improve them. Consistent leadership is required to help employees overcome legitimate, long-standing fear of traditional management practices used so often in the past to control and punish.

Remember, aligning compensation and reward systems to reinforce performance plans and core values is one of the most critical things to enhance organizational performance; however, getting employees to believe their leaders really trust them to improve their own processes is difficult.

Process Management

Listen to Process Owners and Keep Them Involved

Process management involves the continuous improvement of processes required to meet customer requirements and deliver quality products and services. Virtually every high performance organization identifies key processes and manages them to ensure that customer requirements are met consistently and performance is continuously improved.

The first lesson learned has to do with the visibility of processes. Many processes are highly visible such as serving a meal or purchasing. However, when a process is hard to observe, such as course design or customer response, as so many are in the service sector, it cannot be assumed that everyone will see the organization as a collection of processes. The simple exercise of drawing a process flow diagram with people involved in an invisible process can be a struggle, but also a valuable revelation. With no vantage point from which to see work as a process, many people never think of themselves as engaged in a process. Some even deny it. The fact that all work—visible and invisible—is part of a process must be understood throughout the organization before employees can begin to manage and improve key processes.

Once this is understood, a second process management lesson comes to light. Process owners are the best ones, but not the only ones, to improve their processes. They must be part of process improvement teams. These teams are often made up of carefully selected cross-discipline, cross-functional, multilevel people who bring fresh insight to the examination of a process. Do not lose sight of the process owner—the person with expert knowledge of the process who should be accountable for long-term improvement to it. To try to ensure that all of its process improvement teams were cross-functional and multilevel, one organization enlisted volunteers to join process improvement teams. Using this democratic but misguided process, a marketing process improvement team ended up with no marketing expertise among its members. Instead, a group of frustrated support and technical staff members, who knew nothing about marketing, wasted time and money mapping and redesigning a process doomed to fail.

The third process management lesson learned involves an issue mentioned earlier. When focusing too closely on internal process data, there is a tendency to lose sight of external requirements. Organizations often succeed at making their processes better, faster, and (maybe) cheaper for them, but not necessarily to the benefit of their customers. When analyzing internal process data, someone must stubbornly play the role of advocate for the external customers' perspective. Ensure that the data will help make improvements for customers, key financials, employees, or top result areas. Avoid wasting resources on process improvements that do not benefit customers, employees, or the key performance of your organization.

A fourth lesson involves design processes, an important but often neglected part of process management. The best organizations have learned that improvements made early in the process, beginning with design, save more time and money than those made farther "downstream." To identify how design processes can be improved it is necessary to include ongoing evaluation and improvement cycles.

Business Results

Encourage Activities That Lead to Desired Business Results

Results fall into five broad categories.

- Customer focused, such as customer satisfaction and product and service quality
- Financial and market
- Human resource
- Supplier and partner
- Organizational effectiveness, such as key design, production, delivery and support performance and regulatory/legal compliance.

Customer focused is a critical and ongoing result that every successful organization or work unit within an organization must achieve. Systems must exist to make sure that the data from customer satisfaction and dissatisfaction are used at all levels to plan and make improvements. Remember that when customers are asked their opinion, an expectation is created in their minds that the information will be used to make improvements that benefit them.

Some organizations have found it beneficial to have their customers analyze some of their business results with the idea of learning from them as well as building and strengthening relationships. This may or may not be appropriate for your organization, but many successful ones have shared results with key customer groups at a level appropriate for their specific organization.

Product and service quality results provide useful information on key measures of the product or service itself. This information allows an organization to predict whether customers are likely to be satisfied—usually without asking them. For example, one of the nation's most successful and fastest-growing coffee shops knows from its customers that a good cup of coffee is hot, has a good taste, not too bitter, and has a rich aroma. The measures for these product characteristics are temperature, pH (acidity), and the time lapsed between brewing and serving. With these measures, they can predict whether their customers are likely to be satisfied with the coffee before they serve it. One important lesson in this area is to select measures that correlate with, and predict, customer preference, satisfaction, and loyalty.

Financial and market performance is a key to survival. Organizations that make improvements that do not ultimately improve financial performance are wasting resources and growing weaker financially. This is true for both private sector (for profit) and public sector (not-for-profit, education, government) organizations. It is important to avoid over-reliance on financial results. Financial results are the lagging indicators of organization performance. Leaders who focus primarily on financials often overlook or cannot respond quickly to changing business needs. Focusing on finances to run the business—to the exclusion of leading indicators such as operational performance and employee satisfaction—is like driving your car by looking only in the rear view mirror. You cannot avoid pot holes and turns in the road.

Human resource performance results provide early alert to problems that may threaten success. Absenteeism, turnover, accidents, low morale, grievances, and poor skills or ineffective training suboptimize organizational effectiveness. By monitoring performance in these areas, leaders can adjust quickly and prevent little problems from overwhelming the organization.

Supplier quality performance can significantly affect organizational operating effectiveness and customer satisfaction. To the extent an organization depends on suppliers, it must ensure that supplier performance improves—otherwise it must absorb (or pass on to customers) supplier waste, errors, inefficiency, and rework. An organization that tolerates poor supplier performance places its own business at risk.

Organizational effectiveness operational and service results pertain to measures of internal effectiveness that may not be of immediate interest to customers, such as cycle time (how long it takes to brew a pot of coffee), waste (how many pots you have to pour out because the coffee sat too long), and payroll accuracy (which may upset the affected workers). Ultimately, improving internal work process efficiency can result in reduced cost, rework, waste, scrap, and other factors that affect the bottom line, whether profit-driven or budget-driven. As a result, customers are indirectly affected. To stay in business, to remain competitive, or to meet increased performance demands with fewer resources, the organization will be required to improve processes that enhance operational and support service results. The results also need to address the organization performance regarding regulatory, legal compliance and citizenship. Results relating to accomplishment of organizational strategy are also to be addressed.

Award Criteria Framework

The Baldrige performance excellence criteria contain three basic elements.

- Strategy and action plans—the context for aligning work and achieving performance excellence
- System—consisting of the driver triad and work core, producing business results
- Information and analysis—the brain center of high performing organizations

Figure 1 depicts the entire system. Figures 2, 3, and 4 break out the major components of the system.

Strategy and Action Plans

Strategy and action plans are the set of organization-level requirements, derived from short- and long-term strategic planning, that must be done well for the organization's strategy to succeed. Strategy and action plans set the context for action in high performing organizations and provide the vehicle through which leaders drive the organization to achieve success. Strategy and action plans guide overall resource decisions and drive the alignment of measures for all work units to ensure customer satisfaction and market success.

Strategy and action plans are represented in the framework as an umbrella that covers the organization's entire work system.

Criteria for Performance Excellence—Systems Framework

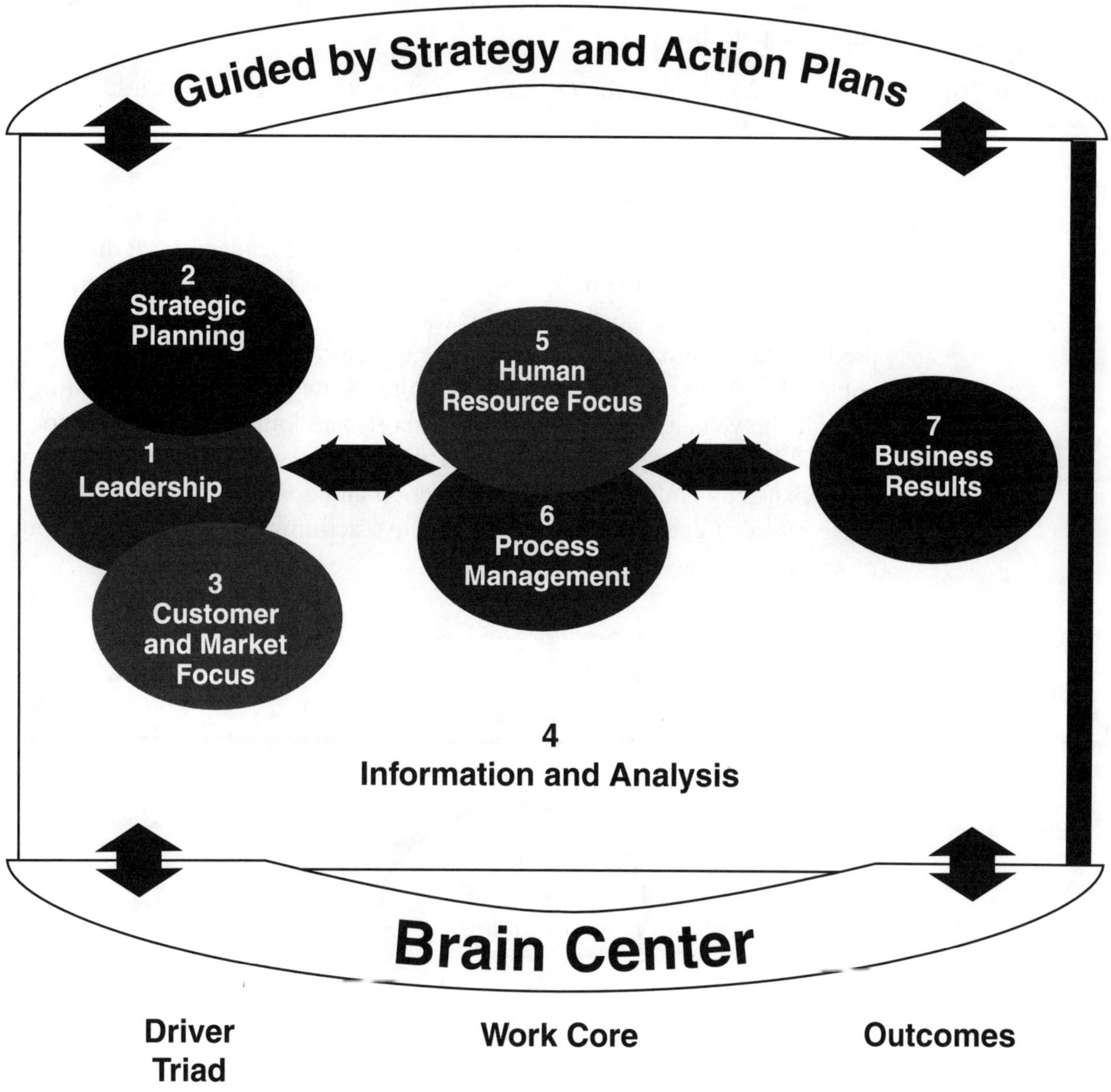

Figure 1

System The system is comprised of the six Baldrige Categories in the center of the figure that define the organization, its operations, and its results. The *system* is further shown to be comprised of two core activities that produce key business results.

- The driver triad
- The work core

The business outcomes are a composite of customer, financial, and nonfinancial performance results, including human resource development and public responsibility.

The Driver Triad

As Figure 2 indicates, the *Driver Triad* consists of three categories.

- Leadership
- Strategic Planning
- Customer and Market Focus

The processes that make up these categories require leaders to set direction and expectations for the organization to meet customer and market requirements (Category 1). Customer and market focus (Category 3) processes produce the information that leaders use to determine what current and potential customers want. Strategic planning (Category 2) and goal setting provide the vehicle for determining the short- and long-term strategies for success as well as communicating and aligning the work of the organization. Leaders use this information to set direction and goals, monitor progress, make resource decisions, and take corrective action when progress does not proceed according to plan.

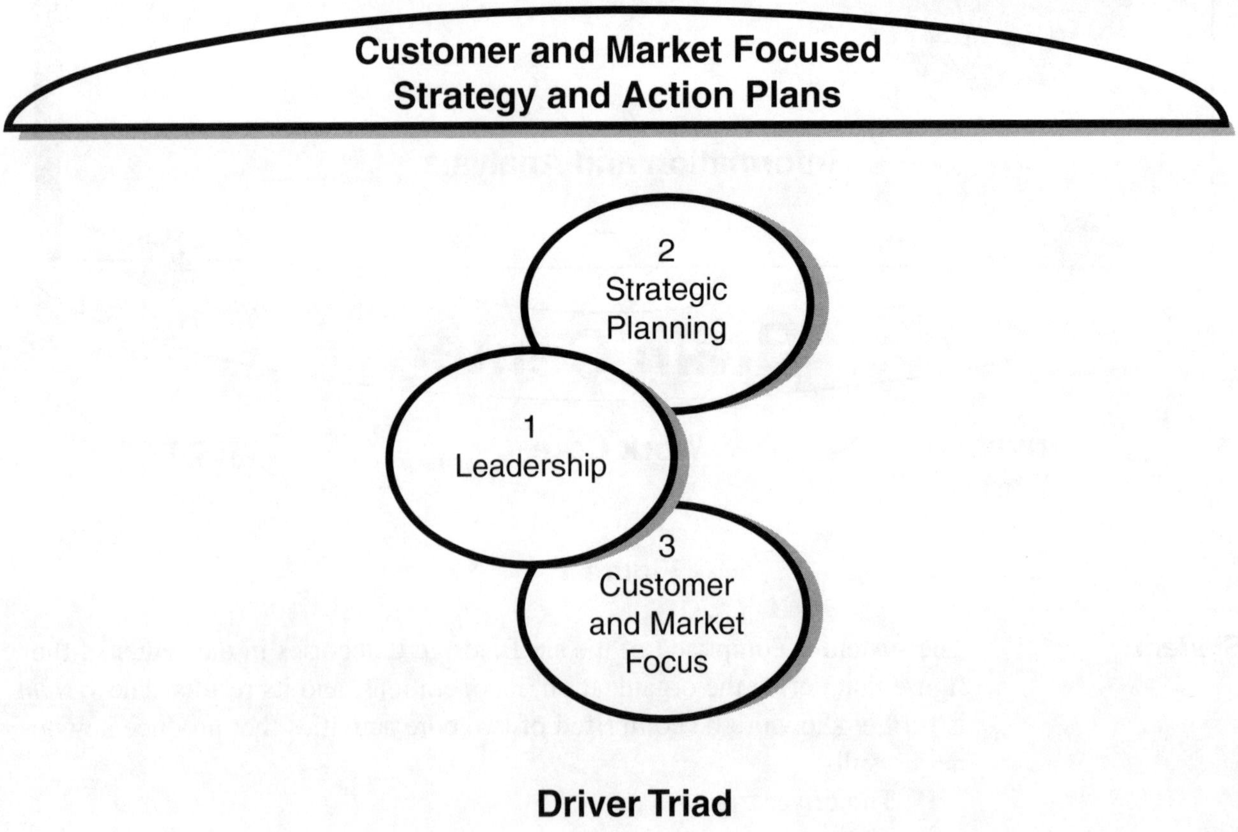

Figure 2

The Work Core

The work core, as the name suggests, describes the processes through which the core work of the organization takes place. As Figure 3 indicates, the work core consists of human resource focus (Category 5) and process management (Category 6), which produce the business results (Category 7).

These categories recognize that the people of an organization are responsible for doing the work. To achieve performance excellence, these people must possess the right skills and must be allowed to work in an environment that promotes initiative and self-direction. The work processes provide the structure for continuous learning and improvement to optimize performance.

Business results reflect the organization's actual performance in terms critical for success. These include customer satisfaction, financial and market performance, human resource performance, supplier performance, and internal operating effectiveness.

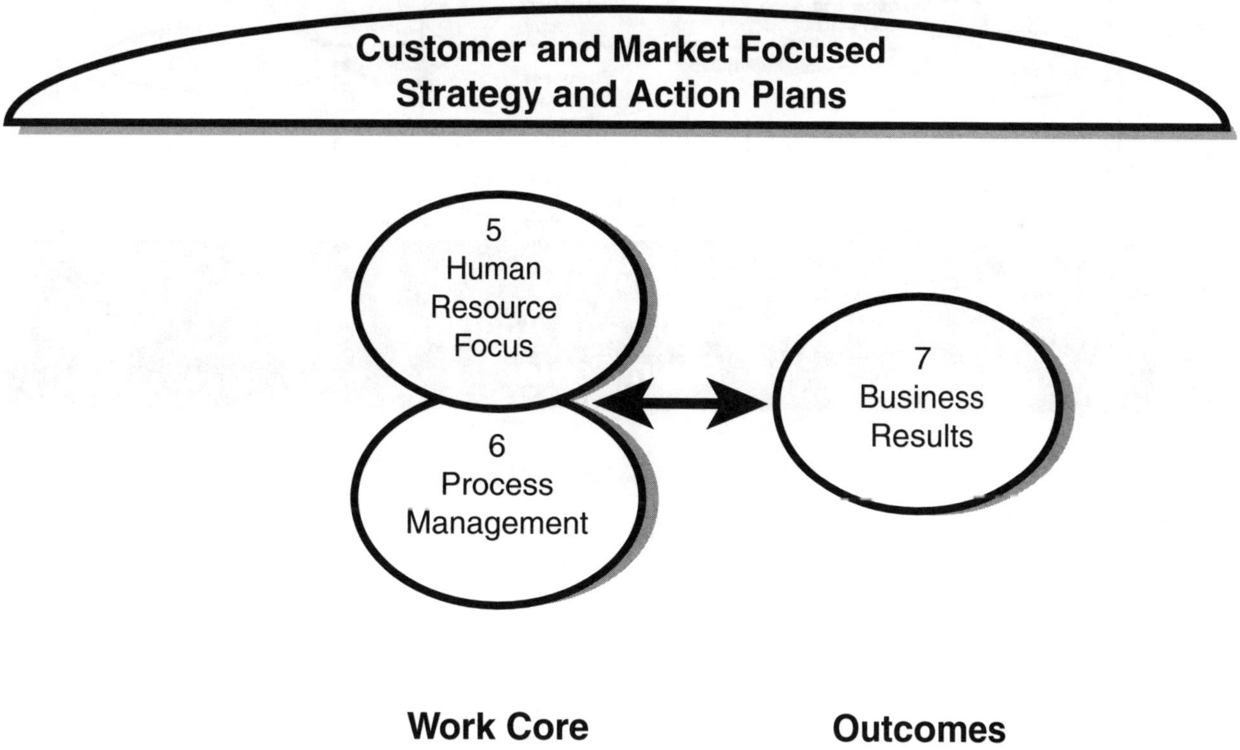

Figure 3

Information and Analysis

Figure 4 depicts how information and analysis (Category 4) is the foundation for the entire management system. Information and analysis is the "brain center" of the management system. It is the platform on which the entire system operates. Information and analysis processes are critical to the effective management of the organization and to a fact-based system for improving organizational performance and competitiveness.

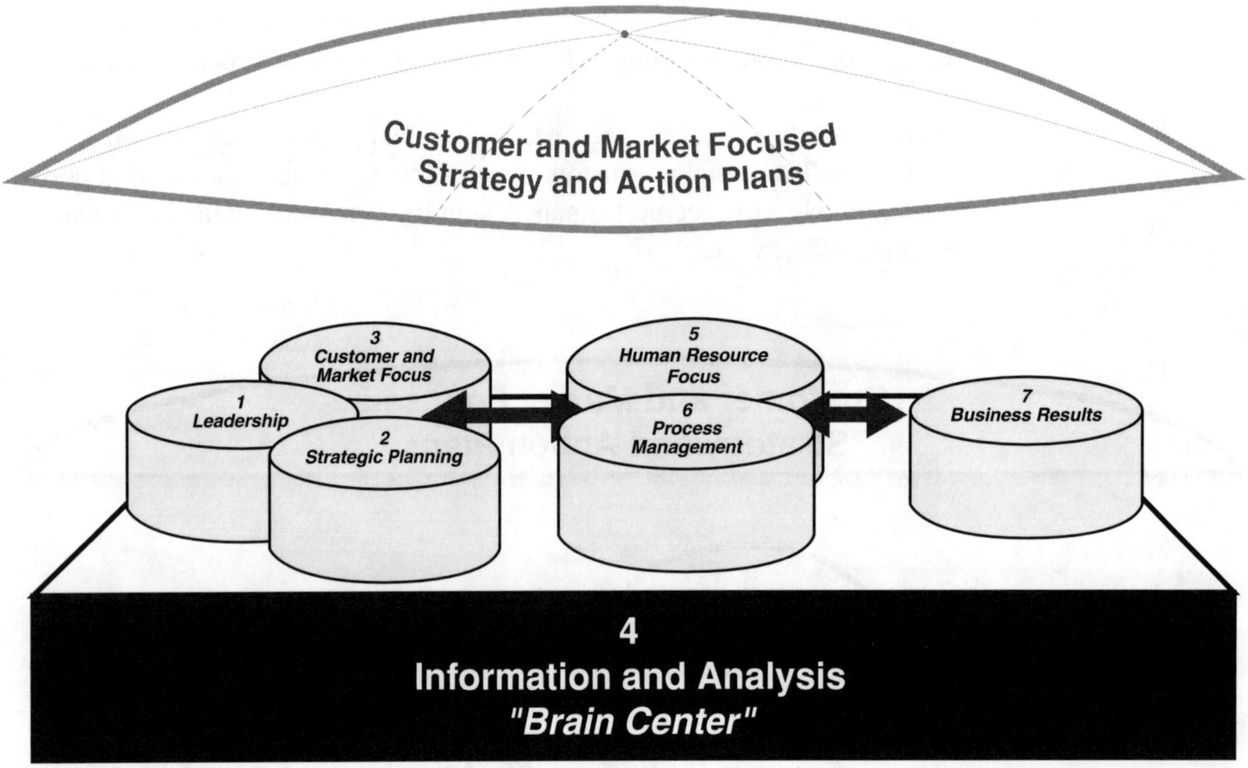

Figure 4

Award Criteria Organization

The seven criteria categories are subdivided into items and areas to address. Figure 5 demonstrates the organization of Category 1.

Items

There are 19 items, each focusing on a major requirement. Item titles and point values are on page 60.

Areas to Address

Items consist of one or more areas to address (areas). Information is submitted by applicants in response to the specific requirements of these areas. There are 27 Areas to address.

Subparts

There are 85 subparts in the 1999 Criteria, compared to 63 in the 1998 Criteria. Areas consist of one or more subparts, where numbers are shown in parentheses. A response should be made to each subpart.

Notes

In 1999 the notes have been decreased to 46 from the 1998 total of 51. **Notes do not add requirements.** Examiners may not use the explanations in the notes as if they were Criteria requirements.

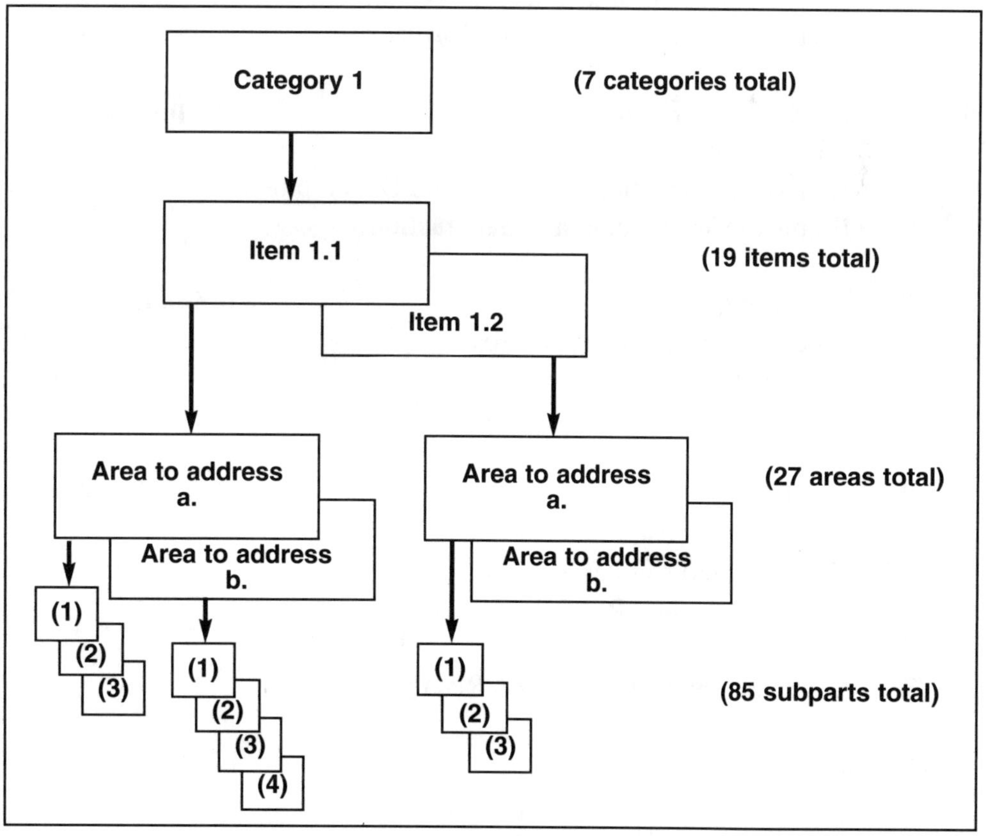

Figure 5

Baldrige Award Categories and Point Values

	Examination Categories/Items		Maximum Points
1	**Leadership**	**(125 points)**	
	1.1 Organizational Leadership		85
	1.2 Public Responsibility and Citizenship		40
2	**Strategic Planning**	**(85 points)**	
	2.1 Strategy Development		40
	2.2 Strategy Deployment		45
3	**Customer and Market Focus**	**(85 points)**	
	3.1 Customer and Market Knowledge		40
	3.2 Customer Satisfaction and Relationships		45
4	**Information and Analysis**	**(85 points)**	
	4.1 Measurement of Organizational Performance		40
	4.2 Analysis of Organizational Performance		45
5	**Human Resource Focus**	**(85 points)**	
	5.1 Work Systems		35
	5.2 Employee Education, Training, and Development		25
	5.3 Employee Well-Being and Satisfaction		25
6	**Process Management**	**(85 points)**	
	6.1 Product and Service Processes		55
	6.2 Support Processes		15
	6.3 Supplier and Partnering Processes		15
7	**Business Results**	**(450 points)**	
	7.1 Customer Focused Results		115
	7.2 Financial and Market Results		115
	7.3 Human Resource Results		80
	7.4 Supplier and Partner Results		25
	7.5 Organizational Effectiveness Results		115
Total Points			**1000**

Key Characteristics—1999 Performance Excellence Criteria

The Criteria focus on business results and the processes required to achieve them. Business results are a composite of the following:

- Customer satisfaction and retention;
- Financial and marketplace performance;
- Product and service performance;
- Productivity, operational effectiveness, and responsiveness;
- Human resource performance and development;
- Supplier performance and development; and
- Public responsibility and good citizenship.

These results areas cover overall organization performance, including financial performance. The results areas also recognize the importance of suppliers and of community and national well-being. The use of a composite of indicators helps to ensure that strategies are balanced—that they do not inappropriately trade off among important stakeholders or objectives or between short- and long-term goals.

The Criteria allow wide latitude in how requirements are met. Accordingly, the Criteria do not prescribe:

- Specific tools, techniques, technologies, systems, measures, or starting points; that organizations should or should not have departments for quality, planning, or other functions; and
- How the organization or business units within the organization should be organized.

Processes to achieve performance excellence are very likely to change as needs and strategies evolve. Hence, the Criteria themselves are regularly evaluated as part of annual performance reviews to ensure that they continue to distinguish high performing organizations from all others.

The Criteria do not prescribe specific approaches or methods, because:

- The focus is on results, not on procedures, tools, or organizational structure. Organizations are encouraged to develop and demonstrate creative, adaptive, and flexible approaches for meeting basic requirements. Nonprescriptive requirements are intended to foster incremental and major (breakthrough) improvement as well as basic change;
- Selection of tools, techniques, systems, and organizations usually depends on many factors such as business size, business type, the

organization's stage of development, and employee capabilities and responsibilities; and
- Focusing on common requirements within an organization, rather than on common procedures, fosters better understanding, communication, sharing, and alignment, while supporting creativity and diversity in approaches.

The Criteria support a systems approach to organization-wide goal alignment. The systems approach to goal alignment is embedded in the integrated structure of the Criteria and the results-oriented, cause-effect linkages among the Criteria parts.

The measures in the Criteria tie directly to customer value and to overall performance that relate to key internal and external requirements of the organization. Measures serve both as a communications tool and a basis for deploying consistent overall performance requirements. Such alignment ensures consistency of purpose while at the same time supporting speed, innovation, and decentralized decision making.

Learning Cycles and Continuous Improvement

In high performing organizations, action-oriented learning takes place through feedback between processes and results facilitated by learning or continuous improvement cycles. The learning cycles have four, clearly defined and well-established stages.

1. Plan—planning, including design of processes, selection of measures, and deployment of requirements
2. Do—execute plans
3. Study/check—assess progress, taking into account internal and external results
4. Act—revise plans based on assessment findings, learning, new inputs, and new requirements

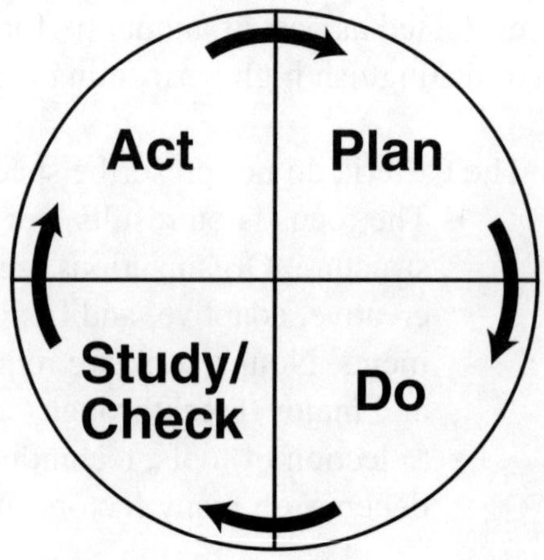

Goal-Based Diagnosis

The Criteria and the scoring guidelines make up the diagnostic assessment system. The Criteria, as discussed previously, are a set of 19 items. The scoring guidelines spell out the assessment dimensions—approach, deployment, and results—and the key factors used to assess against each dimension. An assessment provides a profile of strengths and areas for improvement to help organizations identify areas that, if addressed, will move the organization ahead. As a result, this diagnostic assessment is a useful management tool that goes beyond traditional performance reviews.

Changes from the 1998 Award Criteria

The Criteria continue to evolve toward comprehensive coverage of strategy-driven performance, addressing the needs of all stakeholders—customers, employees, stockholders, suppliers, partners, and the public. The 1999 Criteria place a greater emphasis on the alignment of organization strategy, customer and market knowledge, a high performance workforce, key organization processes, and business results through a focus on aligning action plans throughout the organization. Increased emphasis has also been given to organizational and employee learning.

- The number of Items was reduced from 20 to 19 with the essential requirements for benchmarking and comparative information (formerly 4.2) now included in Item 4.1.
- The number of Areas to Address was reduced from 29 to 27 with the elimination of Area 3.2c (much of which was moved to 3.2a); and the elimination of 5.1b (which was consolidated in 5.1a). Except for some of the details of the benchmarking processes, no substantial requirements from 1998 were eliminated as a result of these changes.
- The word "company" was replaced with "organization" whenever possible.
- The Scoring Guidelines were revised, providing scoring bands of 20 percentage points instead of 30.

Specific Changes by Category

Leadership

Item 1.1 was renamed Organizational Leadership to emphasize the role of senior leaders in setting direction and guiding the entire organization. Senior leaders must create an environment that supports employee empowerment and innovation, review organizational performance systematically, and set priorities using this information. In addition, senior leaders must systematically improve their own personal effectiveness and the effectiveness of management throughout the organization.

Item 1.2 was renamed Public Responsibility and Citizenship to emphasize the organization's responsibilities to the public and its key communities. In addition, Area 1.2a(3) was added to ensure ethical business practices in all stakeholder interactions.

Strategic Planning

Item 2.1 was renamed Strategy Development and contains two Areas: 2.1a examines the process of strategy development (like the 1998 version), and a new 2.1b examines the strategic objectives, the timetable for accomplishing them, and how well the organization evaluates strategic options (from area 2.1a(2)) that are most important to performance.

Item 2.2 was renamed Strategy Deployment to emphasize the process of ensuring that all employees understand strategy, related action plans, and performance measures to track progress.

Customer and Market Focus

In Item 3.1, organizations must determine key requirements and drivers of purchase decisions for current, former, and potential customers.

Item 3.2 has two Areas to Address, reduced from three in 1998. Area 3.2c, Relationship Building, was substantially moved to Area 3.2a. Now Area 3.2a examines issues that deal with accessibility, complaint management, and relationship building. Area 3.2a(3) makes it clear that complaint data must be used to drive improvements organization-wide.

Requirements to ensure approaches are current with business needs (evaluate and refine) are still in place but distributed across Areas 3.2a and 3.2b.

Information and Analysis

Category 4 now contains two Items, reduced from three in 1998. The essential requirements of Item 4.2 in 1998 (which related to collecting and using comparative information) have been added to Item 4.1 in 1999. Combining the Items recognized the need for organizations to continue to collect and use benchmarking and comparative data and information. However, specific processes or techniques for prioritizing, collecting, deploying, or using this type of information and data are not required.

Item 4.1 was renamed Measurement of Organizational Performance to emphasize the main purposes for data and information gathering—the need for an effective system to measure performance and ensure the alignment of measures at all levels of the organization. In addition, the measurement system must be able to increase the cost/financial understanding of improvement options and provide correlations/projections of data to support planning.

Item 4.2 was renamed Analysis of Organizational Performance (instead of Analysis and Review of Company Performance), because the "review" processes contained in 1998 Item 4.3b were moved to Area 1.1b.

The requirements of new Item 4.2 refocus on the need for analyses that support senior executives' review of organizational performance, organizational health, organizational planning, and daily operational decision making. These analyses also help ensure that measures align with action plans.

Human Resource Focus

Item 5.1, Work Systems, was expanded in scope to ensure managers and supervisors effectively encourage and motivate employees to develop and use their full potential. The employee performance management system, including feedback to employees, must support high performance.

Area 5.1a(4) requires compensation, recognition and related reward/incentive practices to reinforce high performance. This replaces Area 5.1b in 1998, which required compensation and recognition approaches to reinforce "customer satisfaction, performance improvement, and employee and company learning." The intent of the change was to broaden, not narrow the requirement to ensure the focus of incentives included those factors important to organization success. If, for example, high performance objectives include customer satisfaction, then compensation, recognition, and reward/incentives should address customer satisfaction.

Area 5.1a(6) sets forth new requirements that examine the organization's systems for recruiting and hiring employees and for determining the skills needed by potential employees, after considering the organization's key performance requirements, community diversity, and fair workforce practices.

Item 5.2 was expanded to stipulate that education and training must prepare employees to use performance measures, performance standards, skill standards, performance improvement, quality control methods, and benchmarking, as appropriate. This provides more detail than the 1998 requirement that organizations provide for the "leadership development of employees."

Item 5.3 was modified to include consideration of a diverse workforce when assessing employee satisfaction or providing a suitable work climate.

Process Management

Area 6.1a has been expanded to make it clear that design processes for both products/services and related production/delivery are examined.

Area 6.1a(4) moves the focus of improvements to cycle time and transfer of learning from the post design evaluation to initial inclusion in the design process. It also examines how the design process addresses cost control, productivity, and other effectiveness and efficiency factors.

Item 6.3 was expanded to make it clear that business assistance and or incentives should be provided by the organization to increase supplier performance.

Business Results

Item 7.1 was renamed Customer Focused Results and expanded to include all results that indicate an organization's success in all aspects of the customer experience. These results include both direct measures of customer satisfaction as well as indirect measures such as loyalty, positive referrals, and product/service performance (formerly Item 7.5).

Human Resource Results point values, Item 7.3, were increased by 30 points to reflect the importance of employees as internal customers. Points in Items 7.1, 7.2, and 7.5 were each reduced by 10 points, keeping the Category 7 total the same at 450 points.

Item 7.5 was renamed Organizational Effectiveness Results to focus attention on those operational performance results that reflect achievement of organizational effectiveness.

Scoring Guidelines

The Scoring Guidelines provide a better description of the performance attributes that reflect higher scores and system maturity.

Scores are presented in 20 percent ranges to provide better definitions and more differentiation of performance.

Specific approach/deployment descriptors have been added to emphasize the maturity (and greater score) that results from cycles of evaluation, improvement, and organizational learning. As in the past, to score 50 percent or higher, a fact-based, systematic evaluation and improvement process must be in place. Scores go higher as more cycles of evaluation, improvement, and integration are evident.

1 Leadership—125 Points

The **Leadership** Category examines how your organization's senior leaders address values and performance expectations, as well as a focus on customers and other stakeholders, empowerment, innovation, learning, and organizational directions. Also examined is how your organization addresses its responsibilities to the public and supports its key communities.

Leadership addresses how the senior leaders guide the organization in setting directions and seeking future opportunities. Primary attention is given to how the senior leaders set and deploy clear values and high performance expectations that address the needs of all stakeholders. The Category also includes the organization's responsibilities to the public and how the organization practices good citizenship.

The leadership system addresses values, sets high performance expectations, and focuses on customers, learning, and innovation.

Organizational Leadership

- Communicating and reinforcing clear values, performance expectations, and a focus on creating value for customers and other stakeholders.
- Reinforcing environment for empowerment and innovation and employee and organizational learning.
- Reviewing organizational performance and capabilities, competitiveness, and progress relative to goals, and setting priorities for improvement.
- Evaluating and improving the effectiveness of senior leadership and management throughout the organization, including employee input in the process.

Public Responsibility and Citizenship

- For regulatory and other legal requirements in areas such as safety, environmental protection, and waste management; anticipating public concerns and addressing risks to the public; ensuring ethical business practices.
- For strengthening and supporting key communities.

1.1 Organizational Leadership (85 Points) Approach/Deployment Scoring

Describe how senior leaders guide your organization and review organizational performance.

Within your response, include answers to the following questions:

a. Senior Leadership Direction

(1) How do senior leaders set, communicate, and deploy organizational values, performance expectations, and a focus on creating and balancing value for customers and other stakeholders? Include communication and deployment through your leadership structure and to all employees.

(2) How do senior leaders establish and reinforce an environment for empowerment and innovation, and encourage and support organizational and employee learning?

(3) How do senior leaders set directions and seek future opportunities for your organization?

b. Organizational Performance Review

(1) How do senior leaders review organizational performance and capabilities to assess organizational health, competitive performance, and progress relative to performance goals and changing organizational needs? Include the key performance measures regularly reviewed by your senior leaders.

(2) How do you translate organizational performance review findings into priorities for improvement and opportunities for innovation?

(3) What are your key recent performance review findings, priorities for improvement, and opportunities for innovation? How are they deployed throughout your organization and, as appropriate, to your suppliers/partners and key customers to ensure organizational alignment?

(4) How do senior leaders use organizational performance review findings and employee feedback to improve their leadership effectiveness and the effectiveness of management throughout the organization?

Note:

Organizational performance results should be reported in Items 7.1, 7.2, 7.3, 7.4, and 7.5.

This Item addresses how senior leaders set directions and build and sustain an organization conducive to high performance, individual and organizational learning, empowerment, and innovation. Leadership must take into account all key stakeholders—customers, employees, suppliers, partners, stockholders, the public, and the community. Senior leaders must systematically review overall organizational performance and capabilities and use this information to set priorities for action and improvement.

Area 1.1a calls for information on the major aspects of leadership—creating values and expectations; setting directions; projecting a strong customer focus; encouraging innovation; developing and maintaining an effective leadership structure; and effectively demonstrating, communicating, and deploying values, directions, expectations, and a strong customer focus. Setting directions includes creating future opportunities for the organization and its stakeholders. An effective leader promotes continuous learning, not only to improve overall performance, but also to involve all employees in the ongoing challenge to enhance customer value. To be successful, leadership must ensure that the organization captures and shares learning. Communication by leadership is critical to organizational success. Communications need to include performance objectives and measures that help provide focus as well as alignment of work units and work processes.

Area 1.1b addresses the senior leaders' role in reviewing overall organizational performance, including using employee feedback to improve leadership effectiveness. This aspect of leadership is crucial, because reviews help to build consistency behind goals and allocation of resources. A major aim is to create organizations that are flexible and responsive—changing easily to adapt to new needs and opportunities. Through their roles in developing strategy and reviewing overall performance, senior leaders develop leadership and create an organization capable of adapting to changing opportunities and requirements.

An important part of organizational reviews for all levels of the organization is the translation of review findings into an action agenda—sufficiently specific so that deployment throughout the organization and to suppliers/partners and key customers is possible. The action agenda could include opportunities for innovation to gain a performance leadership position relative to competitors and/or other organizations with similar processes, products, or services. Another important piece of organization review is the setting of priorities and an assurance that the review findings are deployed throughout the organization. This deployment includes key suppliers/partners and customers.

1.1 Organizational Leadership

How senior leaders guide the organization in setting direction and developing and sustaining an effective leadership throughout the organization

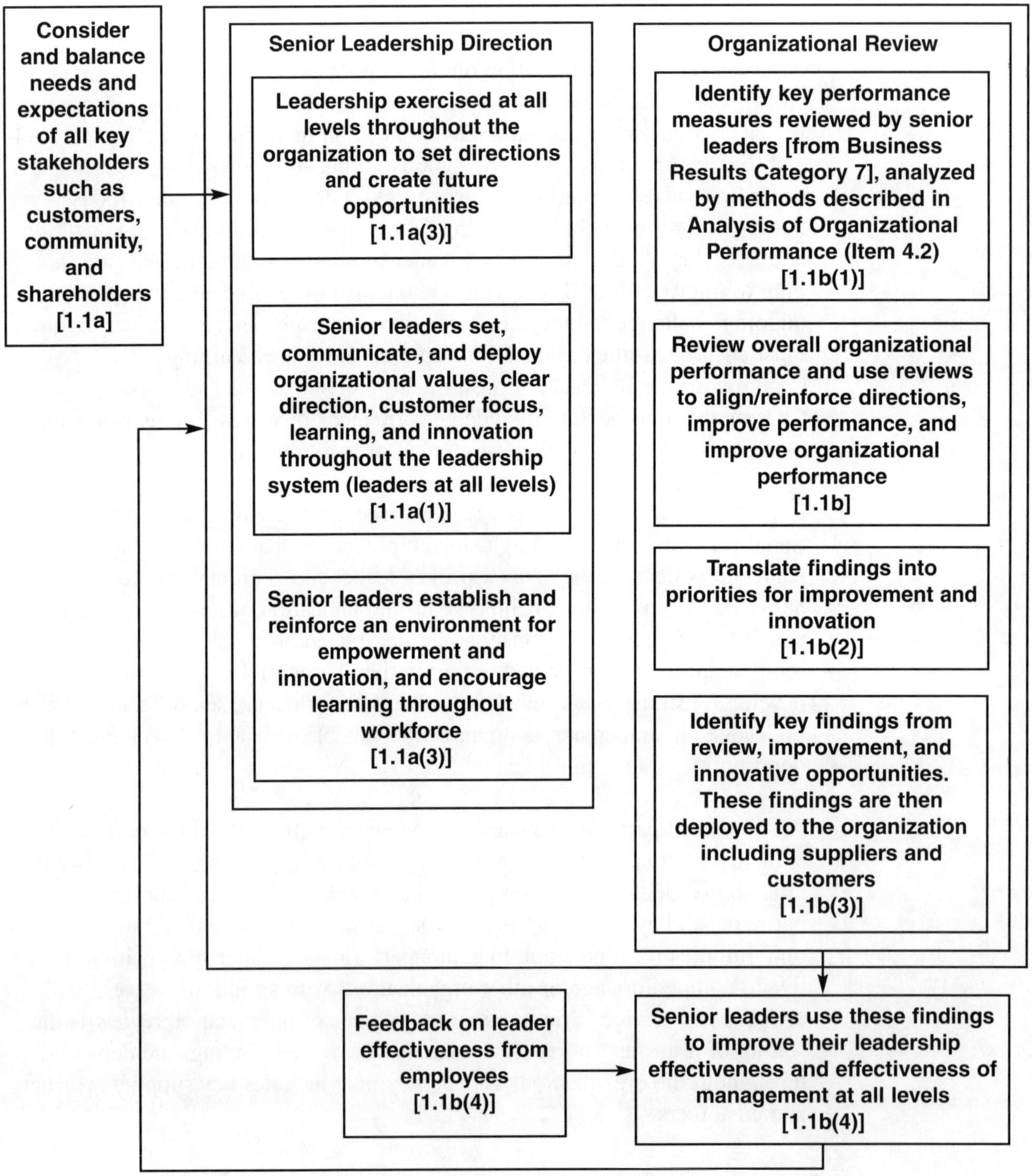

1.1 Organizational Leadership Item Linkages

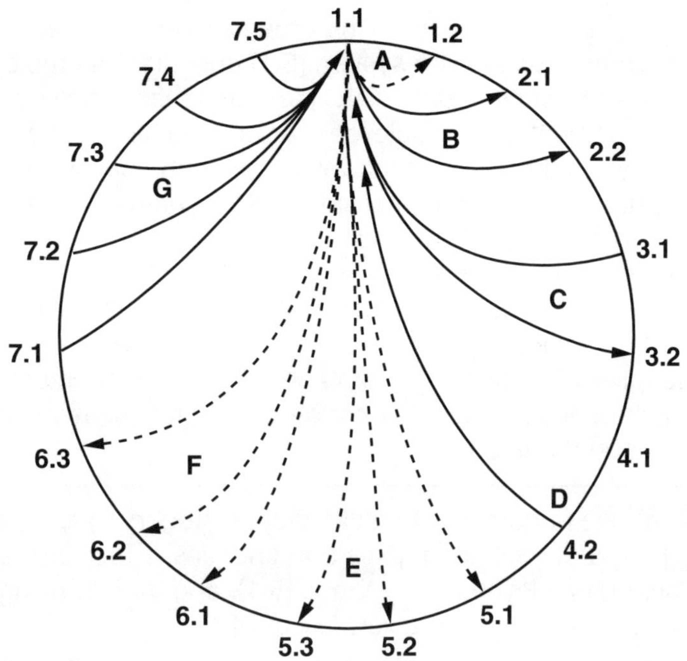

	Nature of Relationship
A	Leaders at all levels [1.1] must role model and support corporate responsibility and practice good citizenship [1.2].
B	Leaders [1.1] participate in the strategic planning process [2.1] and ensure that plans are deployed at all levels throughout the organization and used to align work [2.2a]. Leaders [1.1] also approve the goals and measurements set forth in the plan [2.2b]. They are responsible for using comparative data to set stretch goals.
C	Leaders [1.1] use information from customers [3.1 and 3.2] to set direction and create opportunity for the organization. Leaders [1.1] also have a responsibility for personally building relationships with key customers [3.2a] (creating a bidirectional relationship).
D	Leaders [1.1] use analyses of data [4.2] to monitor organizational performance and understand relationships among performance, employee satisfaction, customers, markets, and financial success. These analyses are also used for decision making at all levels to set priorities for action and allocate resources for maximum advantage.

Continued on next page

	Nature of Relationship (continued)
E	Leaders [1.1] at all levels work to improve the organization's work and job design and ensure that the compensation and recognition system [5.1] encourages employees at all levels to achieve performance excellence. Leaders [1.1] are also responsible for supporting appropriate skill development of all employees through training and development systems and the use of learning on the job [5.2] as well as creating effective systems to enhance employee satisfaction, well-being, and motivation [5.3]. Leaders are also responsible for evaluating and refining all of these processes.
F	Leaders [1.1] at all levels are responsible for creating an environment that supports high performance, including monitoring processes for design and delivery [6.1], support services [6.2], and better supplier and partner performance [6.3]. Leaders must ensure that design, production/delivery, support, and supplier performance processes are aligned and consistently evaluated and refined.
G	Senior leaders [1.1b] use performance results data [Category 7] for many activities including strategic planning [2.1] and for setting goals and priorities, allocating resources [2.2], reinforcing or rewarding employee performance [5.1], and for improving their effectiveness and the effectiveness of leaders at all levels [1.1b(4)].

1.1 Organizational Leadership—Sample Effective Practices

A. Senior Leadership Direction

- All senior leaders are personally involved in performance improvement.
- Senior leaders spend a significant portion of their time on performance improvement activities.
- Senior leaders carry out many visible activities (for example, goal setting, planning, and recognition and reward of performance and process improvement).
- Senior leaders regularly communicate performance excellence values to managers and ensure that managers demonstrate those values in their work.
- Senior leaders participate on performance improvement teams and use quality tools and practices.
- Senior leaders spend time with suppliers, partners, and customers.
- Senior leaders mentor managers and ensure that promotion criteria reflect organizational values.
- Senior leaders study and learn about the improvement practices of other organizations.
- Senior leaders clearly and consistently articulate values (customer focus, customer satisfaction, role model leadership, continuous improvement, workforce involvement, and performance optimization) throughout the organization.
- Senior leaders ensure that organizational values are used to provide direction to all employees in the organization to help achieve the mission, vision, and performance goals.
- Senior leaders use effective and innovative approaches to reach out to all employees to spread the organization's values and align its work to support organizational goals.
- Senior leaders effectively surface problems and encourage employee risk taking.
- Roles and responsibilities of managers are clearly defined, understood by them, and used to judge their performance.
- Managers walk the talk (serve as role models) in leading quality and systematic performance improvement.
- Job definitions with quality indices are clearly delineated for each level of the organization, objectively measured, and presented in a logical and organized structure.
- Many different communication strategies are used to reinforce quality values.
- Leader behavior (not merely words) clearly communicates what is expected of the organization and its employees.

- Systems and procedures are deployed that encourage cooperation and a cross-functional approach to management, team activities, and problem solving.
- Leaders monitor employee acceptance and adoption of vision and values using annual surveys, employee focus groups, and e-mail questions.
- A systematic process is in place for evaluating and improving the integration or alignment of quality values throughout the organization.

B. Organizational Performance Review

- Reviews against measurable performance standards are held frequently.
- Actions are taken to assist units that are not meeting goals or performing to plan.
- Senior leaders systematically and routinely check the effectiveness of their leadership activities (for example, seeking annual feedback from employees and peers (upward evaluation)), and take steps to improve.
- Leaders at all levels determine how well they carried out their activities (what went right or wrong and how they could be done better).
- There is evidence of adopting changes to improve leader effectiveness.
- Priorities for organizational improvement and innovation are driven by customer, performance, and financial data.
- Senior leaders base their business decisions on reliable data and facts pertaining to customers, operational processes, and employee performance and satisfaction.
- Senior leaders hold regular meetings to review performance data and communicate problems, successes, and effective approaches to improve work.
- Senior leaders conduct monthly reviews of organizational and key supplier performance. This requires that subordinates conduct biweekly reviews and that workers and work teams provide daily performance updates. Corrective actions are developed to improve performance that deviates from planned performance.

1.2 Public Responsibility and Citizenship (40 Points) Approach/Deployment Scoring

Describe how your organization addresses its responsibilities to the public and how your organization practices good citizenship.

Within your response, include answers to the following questions:

a. Responsibilities to the Public

(1) How do you address the impacts on society of your products, services, and operations? Include your key practices, measures, and targets for regulatory and legal requirements and for risks associated with your products, services, and operations.

(2) How do you anticipate public concerns with current and future products, services, and operations? How do you prepare for these concerns in a proactive manner?

(3) How do you ensure ethical business practices in all stakeholder transactions and interactions?

b. Support of Key Communities

How do your organization, your senior leaders, and your employees actively support and strengthen your key communities? Include how you identify key communities and determine areas of emphasis for organizational involvement and support.

Notes:

N1 Public responsibilities in areas critical to your business also should be addressed in Strategy Development (Item 2.1) and in Process Management (Category 6). Key results, such as results of regulatory/ legal compliance or environmental improvements through use of "green" technology or other means, should be reported as Organizational Effectiveness Results (Item 7.5).

N2 Areas of community support appropriate for inclusion in 1.2b might include efforts to strengthen local community services, education, the environment, and practices of trade, business, or professional associations.

N3 Health and safety of employees are not addressed in Item 1.2; these are addressed in Item 5.3.

This Item addresses how the organization integrates its values and expectations regarding its public responsibilities and citizenship into its performance management practices.

Area 1.2a calls for information on how the organization addresses three basic aspects of public responsibility in planning products, services, and operations:

- Making legal and regulatory requirements and risk factors an integral part of performance management and improvement;
- Being sensitive to issues of public concern, whether or not these issues are currently embodied in law; and
- Ensuring ethical behavior in all stakeholder interactions.

Fulfilling public responsibilities means not only meeting all local, state, and federal laws and regulatory requirements, but also treating these and related requirements as opportunities for improvement "beyond mere compliance." By analyzing and addressing concerns of the public before serious problems occur, organizations not only build goodwill and public confidence, they often prevent costly corrective actions and litigation. This means that the organization should maintain constant awareness of potential public concerns related to its products, services, and operations.

Area 1.2b calls for information on how the organization practices good citizenship in support of its key communities, as a contributing member and as a positive influence upon other organizations. Opportunities for involvement and leadership include efforts by the organization, senior leaders, and employees to strengthen community services, education, health care, the environment, and practices of trade, business, and professional associations. Levels of involvement and leadership are dependent upon organization size and available resources.

Good citizenship activities include community service by employees, which is encouraged and supported by the organization. For example, organizations, their leaders, and employees could help to influence the adoption of higher standards in education by communicating employability requirements to schools. Organizations could partner with other businesses and health care providers to improve health in the local community by providing education and volunteer services to address public health issues. Also, organizations could partner to influence trade and business associations to engage in beneficial cooperative activities, such as sharing best practices to improve overall U.S. global competitiveness.

1.2 Public Responsibility and Citizenship

How the organization addresses public responsibilities and practices good citizenship

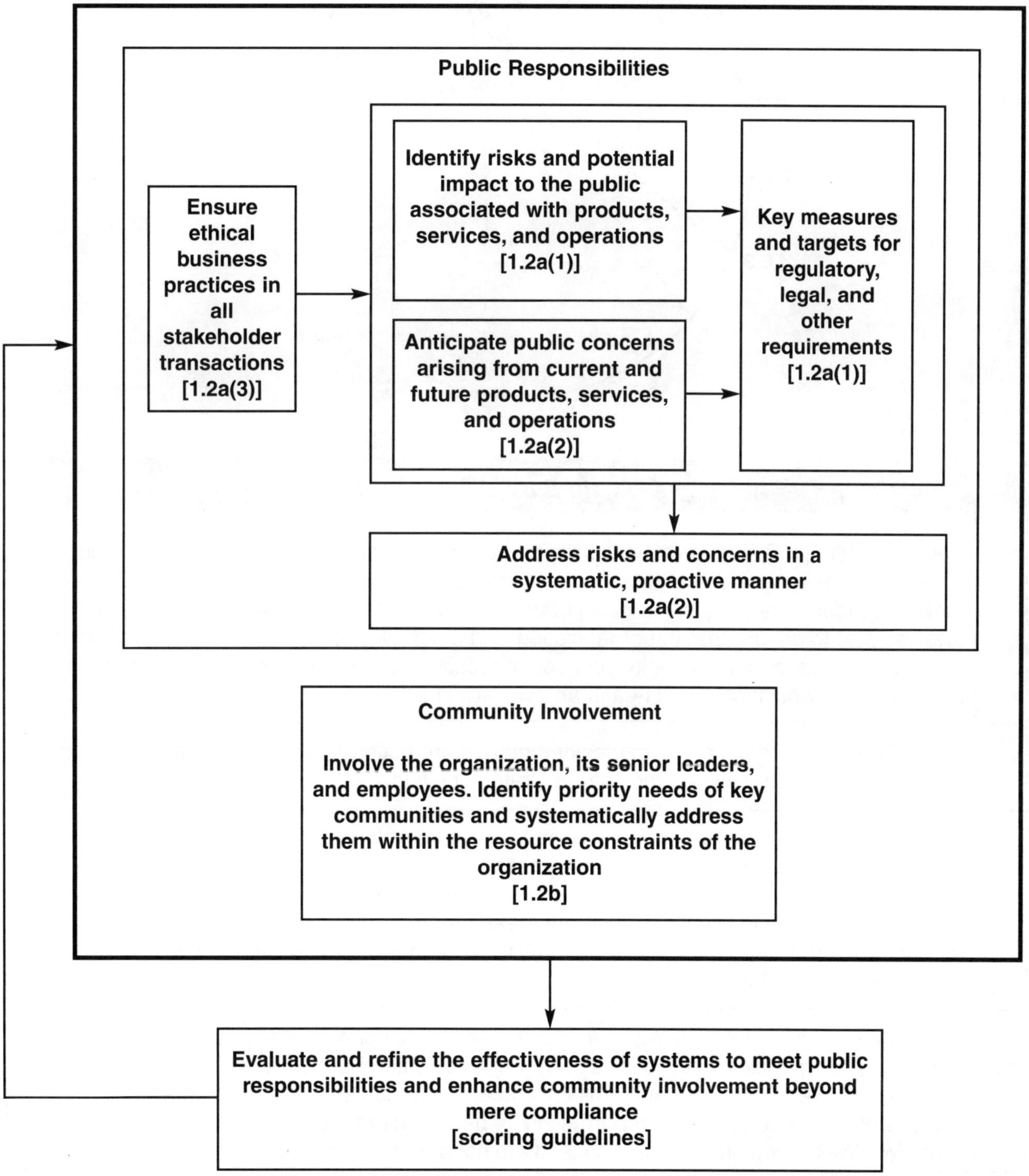

1.2 Public Responsibility and Citizenship Item Linkages

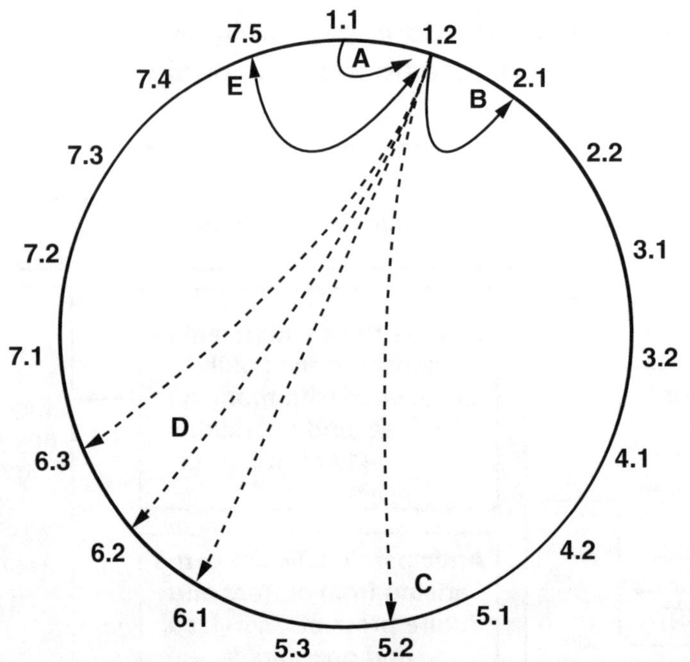

Nature of Relationship	
A	Senior leaders [1.1] have a responsibility for setting policies and ensuring that practices and products of the organization and its employees do not adversely impact society or violate ethical standards, regulations, or law [1.2a]. They are also responsible to be personally involved and to ensure that the organization and its employees strengthen key communities in areas such as local community services, education, the environment, business and professional associations, and health and welfare [1.2b].
B	Public health and safety concerns, environmental protection, and waste management issues [1.2] are important factors to consider in strategy development [2.1].
C	Training [5.2] is provided to ensure all employees understand organization ethical and business practices as well as the importance of strengthening key communities [1.2].
D	Managers at all levels have responsibility for ensuring that work practices of the organization [6.1 and 6.2] and its suppliers [6.3] are consistent with the organization's standards of ethics and public responsibility [1.2].
E	Key results, such as results of regulatory compliance, environmental improvements, and support to key communities, are reported in Organization-Effectiveness Results [7.5]. In addition, these results are monitored to determine if process changes are needed. (Compliance results in areas of employee safety are reported in 7.3, based on processes described in Item 5.3, Employee Well-Being and Satisfaction, and are not a part of the requirements in 1.2.)

1.2 Public Responsibility and Citizenship—Sample Effective Practices

A. Public Responsibilities

- The organization's principal business activities include systems to analyze, anticipate, and minimize public hazards or risk.
- Indicators for risk areas are identified and monitored.
- Continuous improvement strategies are used consistently, and progress is reviewed regularly.
- The organization considers the impact its operations, products, and services might have on society and considers those impacts in planning.
- The effectiveness of systems to meet or exceed regulatory or legal requirements is systematically evaluated and improved.

B. Support of Key Communities

- Senior leaders and employees at various levels in the organization are involved in professional organizations, committees, task forces, or other community activities.
- Organizational resources are allocated to support involvement in community activities outside the organization.
- Employees participate in local, state, or national quality award programs and receive recognition from the organization.
- Employees participate in a variety of professional quality and business improvement associations.
- The effectiveness of processes to support and strengthen key communities is systematically evaluated and improved.

2 Strategic Planning—85 Points

The **Strategic Planning** Category examines your organization's strategy development process, including how your organization develops strategic objectives, action plans, and related human resource plans. Also examined are how plans are deployed and how performance is tracked.

Strategic Planning addresses strategic and action planning and deployment of plans.

The Category stresses that customer-driven quality and operational performance excellence are key strategic issues that need to be integral parts of overall planning. Specifically:

- Customer-driven quality is a strategic view of quality. The focus is on the drivers of customer satisfaction, customer retention, new markets, and market share—key factors in competitiveness, profitability, and business success; and
- Operational performance improvement contributes to short-term and longer-term productivity growth and cost/price competitiveness. Building operational capability—including speed, responsiveness, and flexibility—represents an investment in strengthening competitive fitness.

The Criteria emphasize that improvement and learning need to be embedded in work processes. The special role of strategic planning is to align work processes with the organization's strategic directions, thereby ensuring that improvement and learning reinforce organizational priorities.

The Strategic Planning Category examines how organizations:

- Understand the key customer, market, and operational requirements as input to setting strategic directions. This helps ensure that ongoing process improvements are aligned with the organization's strategic directions.
- Optimize the use of resources, ensure the availability of trained employees, and ensure bridging between short-term and longer-term requirements that may entail capital expenditures, supplier development, etc.

- Ensure that deployment will be effective—that there are mechanisms to transmit requirements and achieve alignment on three basic levels:
  - the organization/ executive level;
  - the key process level; and
  - the work-unit/individual-job level.

The requirements for the Strategic Planning Category are intended to encourage strategic thinking and acting—to develop a basis for a distinct competitive position in the marketplace. These requirements do not imply formalized plans, planning systems, departments, or specific planning cycles. Also, the Category does not imply that all improvements could or should be planned in advance. An effective improvement system combines improvements of many types and degrees of involvement. This requires clear strategic guidance, particularly when improvement alternatives compete for limited resources. In most cases, setting priorities depends heavily upon a cost rationale. However, there also might be critical requirements such as societal responsibilities that are not driven by cost considerations alone.

Strategic planning consists of the planning process, the identification of goals and actions necessary to achieve success, and the deployment of those actions to align the work of the organization.

Strategy Development

- Customers: market requirements and evolving expectations
- Competitive environment: industry, market, and technology
- Financial and societal risks
- Human resource capabilities and needs
- Operational capabilities and needs including resource availability
- Supplier capabilities and needs
- Develop clear strategic objectives with timetables

Strategy Deployment

- Translate strategy into action plans and related human resource plans
- Align and deploy action plan requirements, performance measures, and resources throughout the organization
- Project expected performance results including assumptions of competitor performance increases

2.1 *Strategy Development (40 points) Approach/Deployment Scoring*

Describe your organization's strategy development process to strengthen organizational performance and competitive position. Summarize your key strategic objectives.

Within your response, include answers to the following questions:

a. ***Strategy Development Process***

(1) What is your strategic planning process? Include key steps and key participants in the process.

(2) How do you consider the following key factors in your process? Include how relevant data and information are gathered and analyzed.

The factors are:

- Customer and market needs/expectations, including new product/service opportunities
- Your competitive environment and capabilities, including use of new technology
- Financial, societal, and other potential risks
- Your human resource capabilities and needs
- Your operational capabilities and needs, including resource availability
- Your supplier and/or partner capabilities and needs

b. ***Strategic Objectives***

What are your key strategic objectives and your timetable for accomplishing them? In setting objectives, how do you evaluate options to assess how well they respond to the factors in 2.1a(2) most important to your performance?

Notes:

N1. Strategy development refers to your organization's approach (formal or informal) to a future-oriented basis for business decisions, resource allocations, and management. Such development might utilize various types of forecasts, projections, options, scenarios, and/or other approaches to addressing the future. Strategy might depend upon or require you to develop different kinds of capabilities, such as rapid response, customization, market understanding, lean or virtual manufacturing, relationships, rapid innovation, technology management, leveraging assets, business process excellence, and information management.

Continued on next page

N2. The word *strategy* should be interpreted broadly. It might be built around or lead to any or all of the following: new products, services, and markets; revenue growth; cost reduction; business acquisitions; and new partnerships and alliances. Strategy might be directed toward becoming a preferred supplier, a low-cost producer, a market innovator, and/or a high-end or customized service provider.

Strategy might depend upon or require you to develop different kinds of capabilities, such as rapid response, customization, market understanding, lean or virtual manufacturing, relationships, rapid innovation, technology management, leveraging assets, business process excellence, and information management. Responses to Item 2.1 should address the key factors from your point of view.

N3. Item 2.1 addresses overall organizational directions and strategy, that might include changes in services, products, and/or product lines. However, the Item does not address product and service design; these are addressed in Item 6.1.

This Item addresses how the organization develops its view of the future and sets strategic directions.

The focus of the Item is on competitive leadership, which usually depends upon revenue growth as well as operational effectiveness. This requires a view of the future that includes not only the markets or segments in which the organization competes, but also how it competes. "How it competes" presents many options and requires understanding of the organization's and competitors' strengths and weaknesses. Although no specific time horizon is included, the thrust of the Item is sustained competitive leadership.

Area 2.1a calls for basic information on the planning process and for information on all the key influences, risks, challenges, and other requirements that might affect the organization's future opportunities and directions—taking as long a view as possible. The main purpose of the Item is to provide a thorough and realistic context for the development of a customer and market focused strategy to guide ongoing decision making, resource allocation, and overall management. An increasingly important part of strategic planning is projecting the competitive environment. The purposes of such projections are to detect and reduce competitive threats, to shorten reaction time, and to identify opportunities. Depending on the size and type of business, organizations might use a variety of modeling, scenario, or other techniques and judgments to project the competitive environment.

Area 2.1b addresses the organization's strategic objectives—those that are to serve as the basis for strategy deployment. The Area requires the identification of the strategic objectives and when they will be accomplished. The Area also calls for information on how the strategic objectives are evaluated against the key factors spelled out in Area 2.1a.

2.1 Strategy Development

How the organization sets strategic direction to define and strengthen competitive position

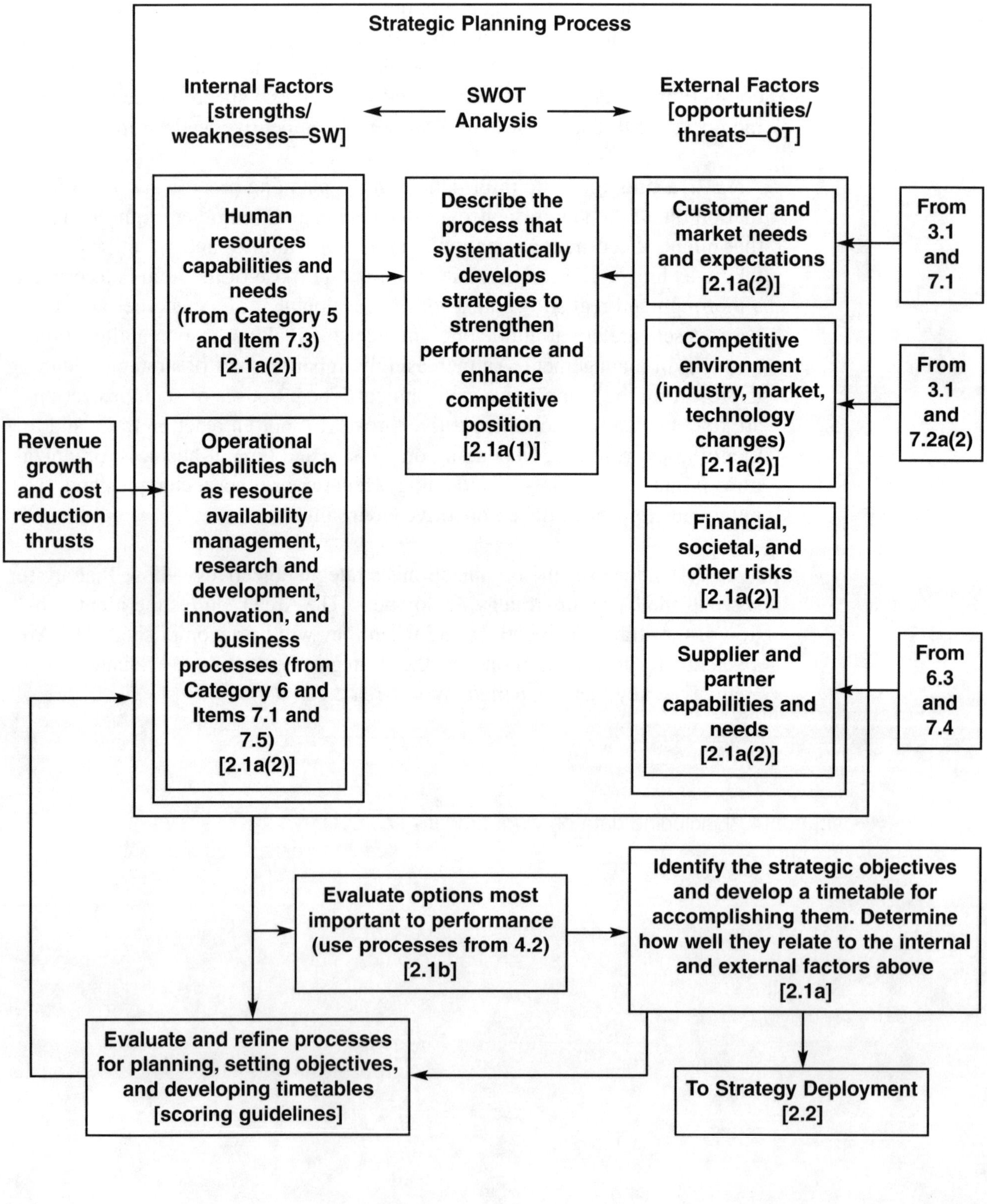

2.1 Strategy Development Item Linkages

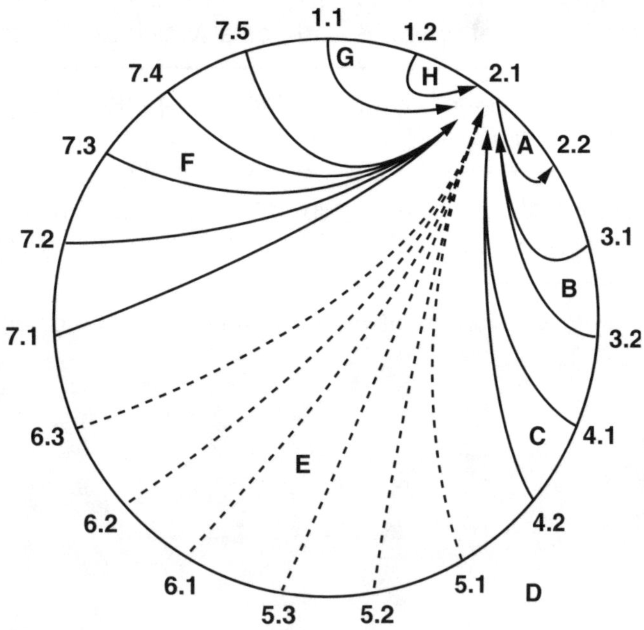

	Nature of Relationship
A	The planning process [2.1] produces a set of actionable plans that are deployed to the workforce [2.2].
B	The business planning process [2.1] includes information on current and potential customer requirements and the projected competitive environment [3.1] as well as intelligence obtained from customer-contact people (complaints and comments) [3.2a].
C	Key organizational [4.1] and competitive comparison data [4.2] are used for planning [2.1].
D	Analytical data [4.2] including data on work process improvement strategies, realigning work processes, improving operational performance, and reducing waste are used in the planning process [2.1].
E	Information on human resource capabilities [Category 5] and work process capabilities [Category 6] is considered in the strategic planning process as part of the determination of internal strengths and weaknesses. To avoid cluttering diagrams 5.1–6.3, these arrows will not be repeated there.

Continued on next page

Nature of Relationship (continued)	
F	Customer focused and financial and market results [7.1 and 7.2] and human resource, supplier and partner, and organization effectiveness results [7.3, 7.4, and 7.5] are used in the planning process [2.1] to set priorities and goals (which are reported in 2.2).
G	The planning process [2.1] includes senior leader participation and guidance as well as participation by leaders at all levels [1.1].
H	Public health, environmental, waste management, and related concerns [1.2a] are considered, as appropriate, in the strategy development process [2.1].

NOTE: The many inputs to strategy development will not all be repeated on other linkage diagrams to avoid clutter.

2.1 Strategy Development—Sample Effective Practices

A. Strategy Development Process

- Business goals, strategies, and issues are addressed and reported in measurable terms. Goals consider future requirements needed to achieve organizational leadership after considering the quality levels other organizations are likely to achieve.
- The planning and goal-setting process encourages input (but not necessarily decision making) from a variety of people at all levels throughout the organization.
- Data on customer requirements, key markets, benchmarks, supplier and partner, human resource, and organizational capabilities (internal and external factors) are used to develop business plans.
- Plans are evaluated each cycle for accuracy and completeness—more often if needed to keep pace with changing business requirements.
- Areas for improvement in the planning process are identified systematically and carried out each planning cycle.
- Refinements in the process of planning, plan deployment, and receiving input from work units have been made. Improvements in plan cycle time, plan resources, and planning accuracy are documented.

B. Strategic Objectives

- Strategic objectives are identified and a timetable for accomplishing the objectives are set.
- Options to obtain best performance for the strategic objectives are systematically evaluated against the internal and external factors used in the strategy development process.

2.2 Strategy Deployment (45 points) Approach/Deployment Scoring

Describe your organization's strategy deployment process. Summarize your organization's action plans and related performance measures. Project the performance of these key measures into the future.

Within your response, include answers to the following questions:

a. Action Plan Development and Deployment

(1) How do you develop action plans that address your key strategic objectives? What are your key short- and longer-term action plans? Include key changes, if any, in your products/services and/or your customers/markets.

(2) What are your key human resource requirements and plans, based on your strategic objectives and action plans?

(3) How do you allocate resources to ensure accomplishment of your overall action plan?

(4) What are your key performance measures and/or indicators for tracking progress relative to your action plans?

(5) How do you communicate and deploy your strategic objectives, action plans, and performance measures/indicators to achieve overall organizational alignment?

b. Performance Projection

(1) What are your two- to five-year projections for key performance measures and/or indicators? Include key performance targets and/or goals, as appropriate.

(2) How does your projected performance compare with competitors, key benchmarks, and past performance, as appropriate? What is the basis for these comparisons?

Continued on next page

Notes:

N1. Action plan development and deployment are closely linked to other Items in the Criteria and to the performance excellence framework on page 5. Examples of key linkages are:

- Item 1.1 for how senior leaders set and communicate directions;
- Category 3 for gathering customer and market knowledge as input to strategy and action plans, and for deploying action plans;
- Category 4 for information and analysis to support development of strategy, to provide a sound performance basis for performance measurements, and to track progress relative to strategic objectives and action plans;
- Category 5 for work system needs, employee education, training, and development needs, and related human resource factors resulting from action plans;
- Category 6 for process requirements resulting from action plans; and
- Item 7.5 for accomplishments relative to organizational strategy.

N2. Measures and/or indicators of projected performance (2.2b) might include changes resulting from new business ventures, business acquisitions, new value creation, market entry and/or shifts, and/or significant anticipated innovations in products, services, and/or technology.

This Item addresses how the organization's strategic objectives are translated into action plans and how they are deployed. The Item also calls for a projection of the organization's performance. The main intent of the Item is effective translation and implementation of the organization's directions, incorporating measures that permit clear communication and tracking of progress and performance.

Area 2.2a calls for information on how the action plans are developed and deployed. This includes spelling out key performance requirements and measures, as well as aligning work unit, supplier, and/or partner plans. Of central importance in this Area is how alignment and consistency are achieved—for example, via key processes and key measurements. Alignment and consistency are intended also to provide a basis for setting and communicating priorities for ongoing improvement activities—part of the daily work of all work units. Performance measures are also critical to performance tracking.

Without effective alignment, routine work and acts of improvement can be random and serve to suboptimize organizational performance. In Figure 2.2-1, the arrows represent the well-intended work carried out by employees of organizations who lack a clear set of expectations and direction. Each person, each manager, and each work unit works diligently to achieve goals they believe are important. Each is pulling hard—but not necessarily in ways that ensure performance excellence. This encourages the creation of "feifdoms" within organizations.

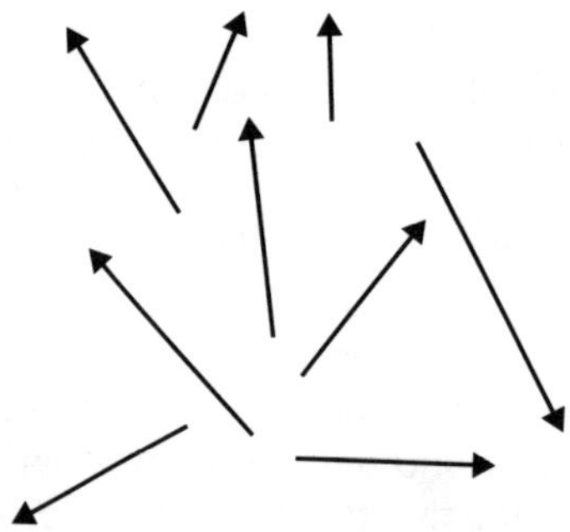

Figure 2.2-1—Nonaligned Work

With a clear, well-communicated strategic plan, it is easier to know when daily work is out of alignment. The large arrow in Figure 2.2-2 represents the strategic plan pointing the direction the organization must take to be successful and achieve its mission and vision. The strategic plan and accompanying measures make it possible to know when work is not aligned and help employees, including leaders, to know when adjustments are required.

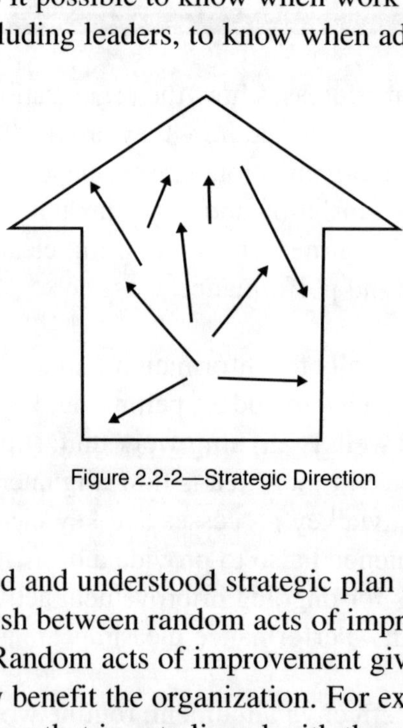

Figure 2.2-2—Strategic Direction

A well-deployed and understood strategic plan helps everyone in the organization distinguish between random acts of improvement and aligned improvement. Random acts of improvement give a false sense of accomplishment and rarely benefit the organization. For example, a decision to improve a business process that is not aligned with the strategic plan (as the small bold arrow in Figure 2.2-3 represents) usually results in a wasteful expenditure of time, money, and human resources—improvement without benefiting customers or enhancing operating effectiveness.

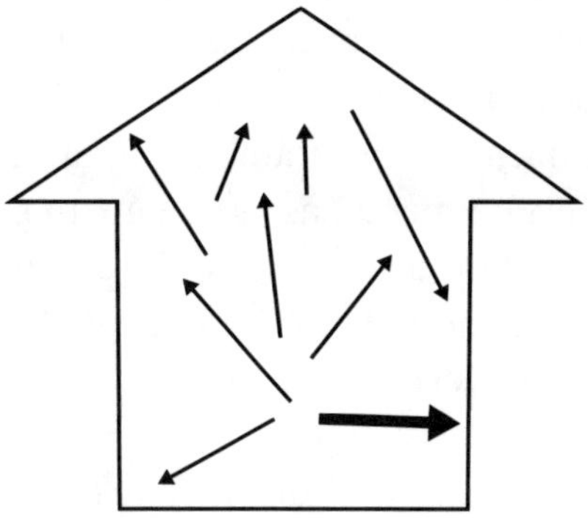

Figure 2.2-3—Random Improvement

On the other hand, by working systematically to strengthen processes that are aligned with the strategic plan, the organization moves closer to achieving success, as Figure 2.2-4 indicates. Ultimately, all processes and procedures of an organization should be aligned to maximize the achievement of strategic plans, as Figure 2.2-5 demonstrates.

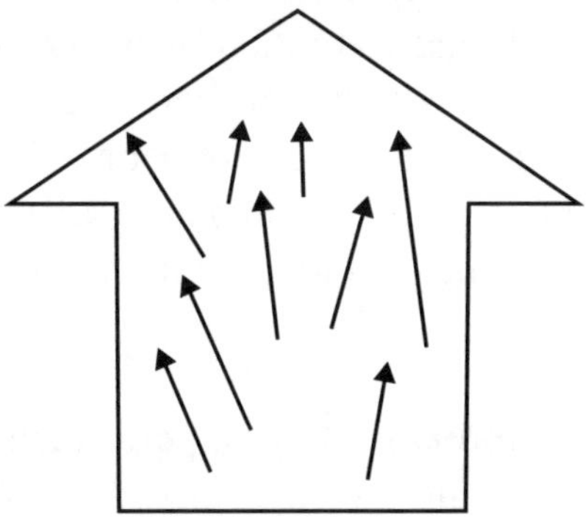

Figure 2.2-4—Moving Toward Alignment

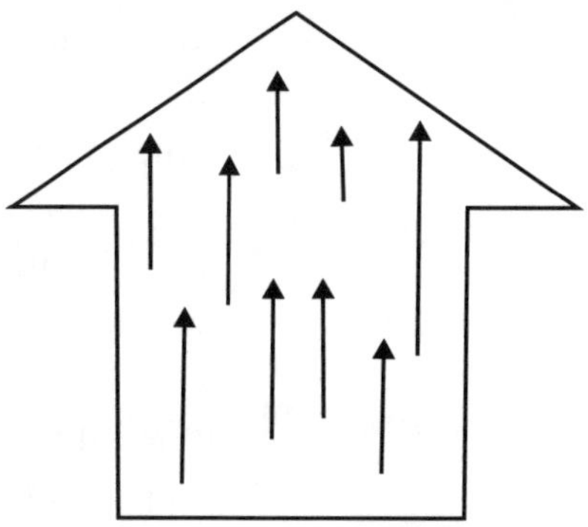

Figure 2.2-5—Systematic Alignment

Critical action plan requirements include human resource plans to support the overall strategy. Examples of possible human resource plan elements are:

- Redesign of work organizations and/or jobs to increase employee responsibility and decision making;
- Initiatives to promote labor-management cooperation, such as partnerships with unions;
- Initiatives to foster knowledge sharing and cross-functional interactions throughout the organization;
- Creation or modification of compensation and recognition systems based on building shareholder value and/or customer satisfaction;

- Creation of opportunities for employees to learn and use skills that go beyond current job assignments through redesign of processes or organizations;
- Education and training initiatives, including those that involve developmental assignments to prepare future managers/leaders;
- Creation of individual development and/or learning plans;
- Formation of partnerships with educational institutions to develop employees or to help ensure the future supply of well-prepared employees; and
- Introduction of distance learning or other technology-based learning approaches.

Area 2.2b calls for a two- to five-year projection of key measures and/or indicators of the organization's performance. It also calls for a comparison of projected performance versus targets and/or goals, as well as competitors and key benchmarks. This projection/comparison is intended to encourage organizations to improve their ability to understand and track dynamic, competitive performance factors. Through this tracking process, organizations should be better prepared to take into account their rates of improvement and change relative to competitors and relative to their own targets or stretch goals as a diagnostic management tool. Without this comparison information, it is possible to set goals that, even if attained, may not result in competitive advantage. More than one high performing company has been surprised by a competitor that set and achieved more aggressive goals. See example on next page.

In addition to improvement relative to past performance and to competitors, projected performance also might include changes resulting from new business ventures, entry into new markets, product/service innovations, or other strategic thrusts.

Consider the following example. Imagine that you are ahead of your competition and committed to a 10 percent increase in profit over your base year. After eight years you are twice as profitable. To your surprise, you find that your competitor has increased 20 percent each year. You have achieved your goal, but your competitor has beaten you, making slightly more. After ten years, the competitor has a significant lead. It is not enough to make your goals unless your goals place you in a competitive position.

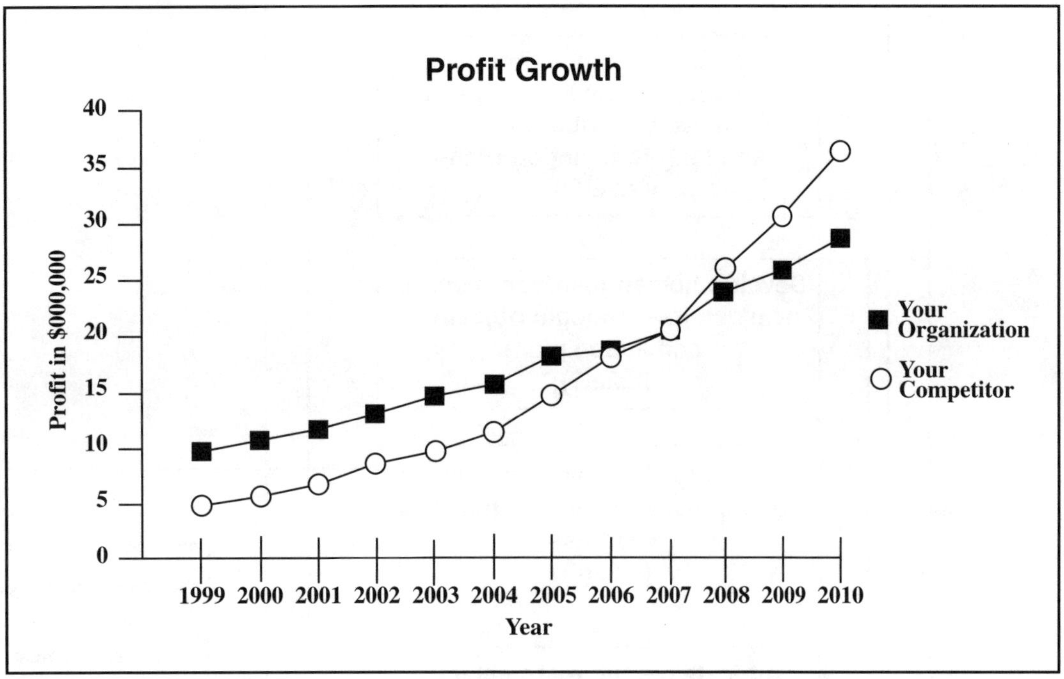

2.2 Strategy Deployment

Summary of strategy, action plans, and performance projections; how they are developed, communicated, and deployed.

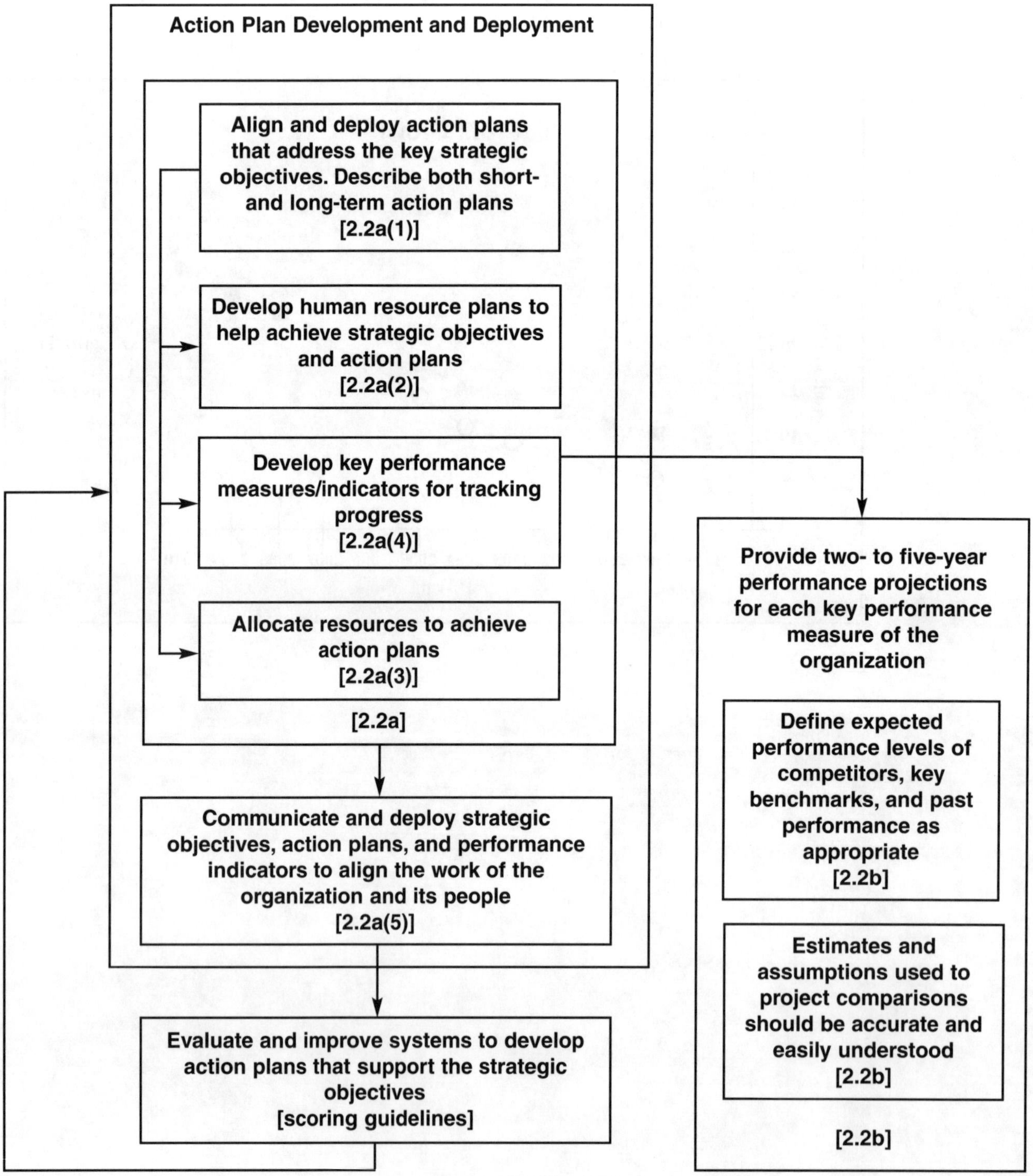

2.2 Strategy Deployment Item Linkages

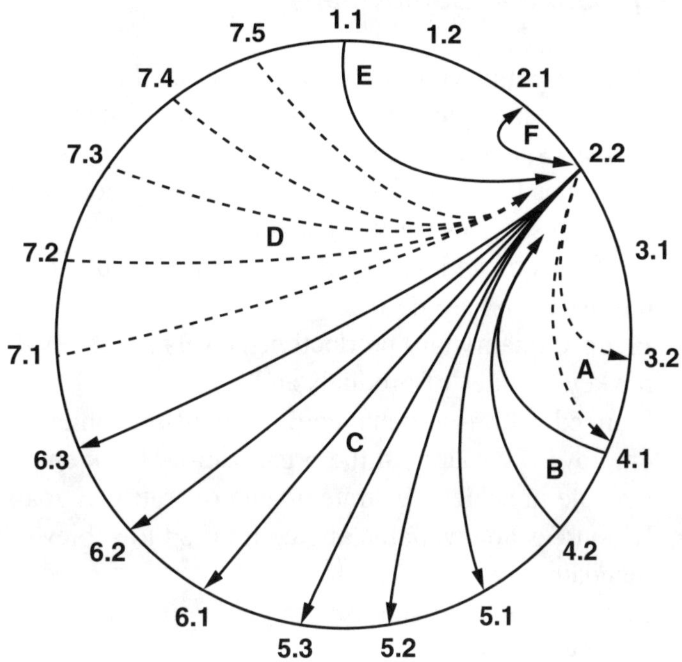

	Nature of Relationship
A	The goals and strategy [2.2] will influence the data and measures that need to be collected to monitor alignment [4.1], customer relations management, and customer satisfaction determination [3.2].
B	Benchmarking comparison data [4.1] and analytical processes [4.2] are used to set organizational measures and objectives [2.2].
C	Measures, objectives, and plans, deployed to the workforce [2.2], are used to drive and align actions to achieve improved performance [Category 6] and develop human resources [Category 5].
D	Results data [Category 7] are used to help set goals [2.2]. (To avoid clutter, these relationships will not be repeated on the Category 7 linkage diagrams.)
E	The leadership team [1.1] sets the organization's goals and objectives [2.2].
F	The planning process [2.1] develops the strategic objectives that produce action plans to support these objectives [2.2].

2.2 Strategy Deployment—Sample Effective Practices

A. Action Plan Development and Deployment

- Plans are in place to optimize operational performance and improve customer focus using tools such as reengineering, streamlining work processes, and reducing cycle time.
- Strategies to retain or establish leadership positions exist for major products and services for key customers or markets.
- Strategies to achieve key organizational results (operational performance requirements) are defined.
- Planned quality and productivity levels are defined in measurable terms for key features of products and services.
- Planned actions are challenging, realistic, achievable, and understood by employees throughout the organization. Each employee understands his or her role in achieving strategic and operational goals and objectives.
- Resources are available and committed to achieve the plans (no unfunded mandates).
- Plans are realistic and used to guide operational performance improvements.
- Incremental (short-term) strategies to achieve long-term plans are defined in measurable terms.
- Business plans, short- and long-term goals, and performance measures are understood and used to drive actions throughout the organization.
- Each individual in the organization, at all levels, understands how his or her work contributes to achieving organizational goals and plans.
- Plans are followed to ensure that resources are deployed and redeployed as needed to support goals.
- Capital projects are funded according to business improvement plans.
- Human resource plans support strategic plans and goals. Plans show how the workforce will be developed to enable the organization to achieve its strategic goals.
- Key issues of training and development, hiring, retention, employee participation, involvement, empowerment, and recognition and reward are addressed as a part of the human resource plan.
- Innovative strategies may involve one or more of the following:
  - Redesign of work to increase employee responsibility
  - Improved labor-management relations (That is, prior to contract negotiations, train both sides in effective negotiation skills so that people focus on the merits of issues, not on positions. The goal is to improve relations and shorten negotiation time by 50 percent.)

  - Forming partnerships with education institutions to develop employees and ensure a supply of well-prepared future employees
  - Developing gain-sharing or equity-building compensation systems for all employees to increase motivation and productivity
  - Broadening employee responsibilities; creating self-directed or high performance work teams
- Key performance measures (for example, employee satisfaction or work climate surveys) have been identified to gather data to manage progress. (Note: Improvement results associated with these measures should be reported in 7.3.)
- The effectiveness of human resource planning and alignment with strategic plans is evaluated systematically.
- Data are used to evaluate and improve performance and participation for all types of employees (for example, absenteeism, turnover, grievances, accidents, recognition and reward, and training participation).
- Routine, two-way communication about performance of employees occurs.
- The process to develop action plans to support strategic objectives is systematically evaluated.

B. Performance Projection

- Projections of two- to five-year changes in performance levels are developed and used to track progress.
- Data from competitors, key benchmarks, and/or past performance form a valid basis for comparison. The organization has strategies and goals in place to meet or exceed the planned levels of performance for these competitors and benchmarks.
- Plans include expected future levels of competitor or comparison performance and are used to set and validate the organization's own plans and goals.

3 Customer and Market Focus—85 Points

The **Customer and Market Focus** Category examines how your organization determines requirements, expectations, and preferences of customers and markets. Also examined is how your organization builds relationships with customers and determines their satisfaction.

Customer and Market Focus addresses how the organization seeks to understand the voices of customers and of the marketplace. The Category stresses relationships as an important part of an overall listening and learning strategy. Customer satisfaction results provide vital information for understanding customers and the marketplace. In many cases, such results and trends provide the most meaningful information, not only on customers' views but also on their marketplace behaviors—repeat business and positive referrals.

Customer and market focus contains two Items that focus on understanding customer and market requirements, and determining satisfaction.

Customer and Market Knowledge

- Determining market or customer segments
- Determining customer requirements through sound listening and learning approaches
- Determining important product or service features
- Using complaint information and data from potential and former customers

Customer Satisfaction and Relationships

- Making customer contact and feedback easy and useful
- Develop and deploy customer contact requirements
- Ensure complaint data are used to eliminate causes of complaints
- Build customer relationships and loyalty
- Systematically determine customer satisfaction and the satisfaction of competitor's customers
- Follow up with customers after every transaction

3.1 Customer and Market Knowledge (40 points) Approach/Deployment Scoring

Describe how your organization determines short- and longer-term requirements, expectations, and preferences of customers and markets to ensure the relevance of current products/services and to develop new opportunities.

Within your response, include answers to the following questions:

a. Customer and Market Knowledge

(1) How do you determine or target customers, customer groups, and/or market segments? How do you consider customers of competitors and other potential customers and/or markets in this determination?

(2) How do you listen and learn to determine key requirements and drivers of purchase decisions for current, former, and potential customers? If determination methods differ for different customers and/or customer groups, include the key differences.

(3) How do you determine and/or project key product/service features and their relative importance/value to customers for purposes of current and future marketing, product planning, and other business developments, as appropriate? How do you use relevant information from current and former customers, including marketing/sales information, customer retention, won/lost analysis, and complaints, in this determination?

(4) How do you keep your listening and learning methods current with business needs and directions?

Notes:

N1. If products and services are sold to end users via other businesses such as retail stores or dealers, customer groups [3.1a(1)] should include both the end users and these intermediate businesses.

N2. Product and service features [3.1a(3)] refer to all important characteristics and to the performance of products and services throughout their full life cycle and the full "consumption chain." The focus should be on features that bear upon customer preference and repurchase loyalty—for example, those features that differentiate products and services from competing offerings. Those features might include factors such as price, value, delivery, customer or technical support, and the sales relationship.

This Item examines how the organization determines current and emerging customer requirements and expectations. This information is intended to support marketing, business development, and planning. In a rapidly changing competitive environment, many factors may affect customer preference and loyalty, making it necessary to listen and learn on a continuous basis. To be effective, such listening and learning strategies need to have a close connection with the organization's overall business strategy. For example, if the organization customizes its products and services, the listening and learning strategy needs to be backed by a capable information system—one that rapidly accumulates information about customers and makes this information available where needed throughout the organization or elsewhere within the overall value chain.

A variety of listening and learning strategies are commonly used. Selection depends upon the type and size of the organization and other factors. Some examples are:

- Close integration with key customers;
- Rapid innovation and field trials of products and services to better link research and development (R&D) and design to the market;
- Close tracking of technological, competitive, and other factors that may bear upon customer requirements, expectations, preferences, or alternatives;
- Seeking to understand in detail customers' value chains and how they are likely to change;
- Focus groups with leading-edge customers;
- Training customer-contact employees in customer listening;
- Use of critical incidents, such as complaints, to understand key service attributes from the point of view of customers and customer-contact employees;
- Interviewing lost customers to determine the factors they use in their purchase decisions; and
- Won/lost analysis relative to competitors.

This item focuses on identifying the product and service features that influence customer preference and loyalty. Organizations must be able to determine which features of products and services customers value most.

This Item also seeks information on how organizations recognize market segments, customers of competitors, and other former and potential customers. Accordingly, the Item addresses how the organization tailors its listening and learning to different customer groups and market segments.

For example, a relationship strategy might be possible with some customers, but not with others. Other information sought relates to sensitivity to specific product and service requirements and their relative importance or value to customer groups. This determination should be supported by use of information and data, such as complaints and gains and losses of customers.

This Item also addresses how the organization keeps its listening and learning strategies current with changing business needs and directions.

3.1 Customer and Market Knowledge

How the organization determines longer-term requirements, expectations, and preferences of target or potential customers and markets to anticipate their needs and to develop business opportunities

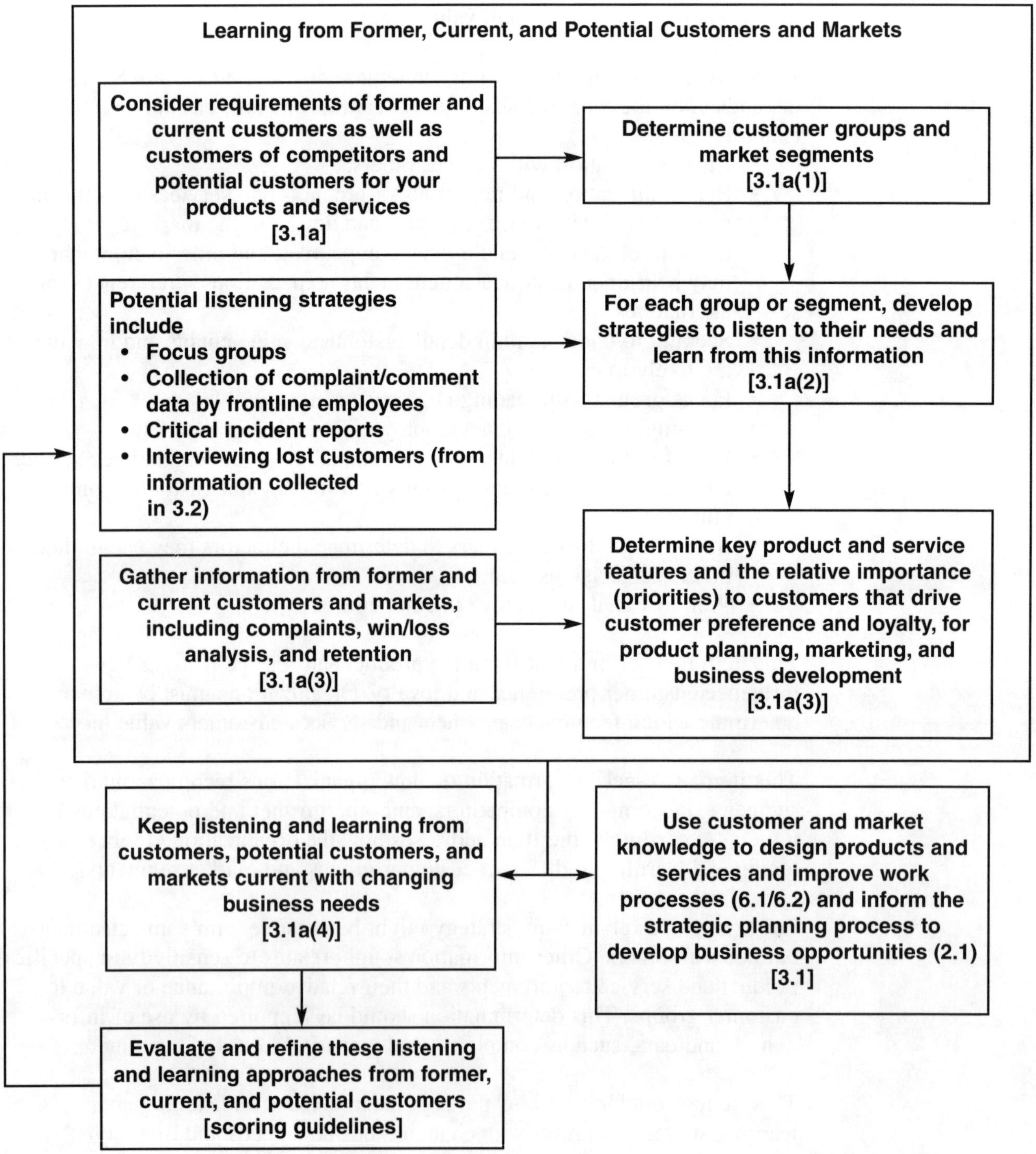

3.1 Customer and Market Knowledge Item Linkages

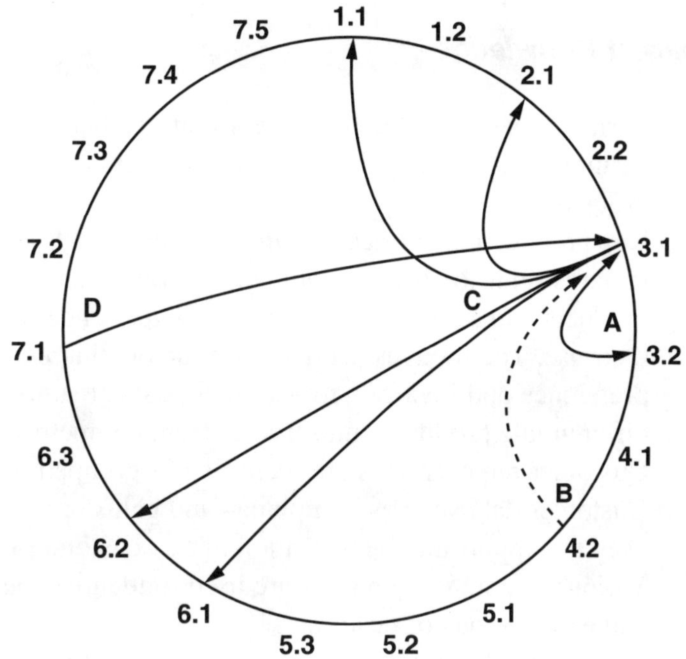

	Nature of Relationship
A	Customer complaints [3.2a] are used to help assess current customer expectations and refine requirements [3.1]. Information about customer requirements [3.1] is used to build instruments to assess customer satisfaction [3.2b].
B	Information from customer satisfaction data are analyzed [4.2] and used to help determine ways to assess current and potential customer requirements [3.1].
C	Information about current and future customer and market requirements [3.1] is used for strategic planning [2.1] to design products and services and revise work processes [6.1 and 6.2], and to help leaders set directions for the organization [1.1].
D	Customer satisfaction data and complaints [7.1] are used to assess customer expectations and refine requirements [3.1].

3.1 Customer and Market Knowledge—Sample Effective Practices

A. Customer and Market Knowledge

- Various systematic methods are used to gather data and identify current requirements and expectations of customers (for example, surveys, focus groups).
- Key product and service features are defined. Product and service features refer to all important characteristics and to the performance of products and services that customers experience or perceive throughout their use. The focus is primarily on factors that bear on customer preference and loyalty—for example, those features that enhance or differentiate products and services from competing offerings.
- Customer requirements are identified or grouped by customer segments.
- Customer data such as complaints and gains or losses of customers are used to support the identification of key customer requirements.
- Various systematic methods are used to identify the future requirements and expectations of customers.
- Customers of competitors are considered and processes are in place to gather expectation data from potential customers.
- Effective listening and learning strategies include:
    - Close monitoring of technological, competitive, societal, environmental, economic, and demographic factors that may bear on customer requirements, expectations, preferences, or alternatives;
    - Focus groups with demanding or leading-edge customers;
    - Training of frontline employees in customer listening;
    - Use of critical incidents in product or service performance or quality to understand key service attributes from the point of view of customers and frontline employees;
    - Interviewing lost customers;
    - Won/lost analysis relative to competitors; and
    - Analysis of major factors affecting key customers.
- Analytical tools such as forced choice or paired choice (where customers select between options A and B, A and C, B and C, and so forth). Using this technique, organizations quickly prioritize requirements and focus on delivering those that make the greatest impact on satisfaction, repeat business, and loyalty.

  Methods to listen and learn from customers are evaluated and improved through several cycles. Examples of factors that are evaluated include:
    - The adequacy and timeliness of customer-related information;
    - Improvement of survey design;

- Approaches for getting reliable and timely information—surveys, focus groups, customer-contact personnel; and
- Improved aggregation and analysis of information.

• Best practices for gathering customer requirements and forecasting are gathered and used to make improvements.

3.2 Customer Satisfaction and Relationships (45 points) Approach/Deployment Scoring

Describe how your organization determines the satisfaction of customers and builds relationships to retain current business and to develop new opportunities.

Within your response, include answers to the following questions:

a. Customer Relationships

(1) How do you determine key access mechanisms to facilitate the ability of customers to conduct business, seek assistance and information, and make complaints? Include a summary of your key mechanisms.

(2) How do you determine key customer contact requirements and deploy these requirements to all employees involved in the response chain?

(3) What is your complaint management process? Include how you ensure that complaints are resolved effectively and promptly, and that all complaints received are aggregated and analyzed for use in overall organizational improvement.

(4) How do you build relationships with customers for repeat business and/or positive referral?

(5) How do you keep your approaches to customer access and relationships current with business needs and directions?

b. Customer Satisfaction Determination

(1) What processes, measurement methods, and data do you use to determine customer satisfaction and dissatisfaction? Include how your measurements capture actionable information that reflects customers' future business and/or potential for positive referral. Also include any significant differences in processes or methods for different customer groups and/or market segments.

(2) How do you follow up with customers on products/services and recent transactions to receive prompt and actionable feedback?

(3) How do you obtain and use information on customer satisfaction relative to competitors and/or benchmarks, as appropriate?

(4) How do you keep your approaches to satisfaction determination current with business needs and directions?

Notes:

N1. Customer relationships (3.2a) might include the development of partnerships or alliances.

Continued on next page

N2. Customer satisfaction and dissatisfaction determination (3.2b) might include any or all of the following: surveys, formal and informal feedback from customers, use of customer account data, and complaints.

N3. Customer satisfaction measurements might include both a numerical rating scale and descriptors for each unit in the scale. Actionable customer satisfaction measurements provide reliable information about customer ratings of specific product, service, and relationship features, the linkage between these ratings, and the customer's likely future actions—repurchase and/or positive referral. Product and service features might include overall value and price.

N4. Customer satisfaction and dissatisfaction results and information on product/service measures that contribute to customer satisfaction or dissatisfaction should be reported in Item 7.1. These latter measures might include trends and levels in performance of customer-desired product features or customer complaint handling effectiveness (such as complaint response time, effective resolution, and percent of complaints resolved on first contact).

This Item addresses how the organization effectively manages its interaction and follow-up with customers. Relationships provide a potentially important means for organizations to understand and manage customer expectations and to develop new business. Also, customer-contact employees may provide vital information to build partnerships and other longer-term relationships with customers.

This Item also addresses how the organization determines customer satisfaction and satisfaction relative to competitors. Satisfaction relative to competitors and the factors that lead to preference are of critical importance to managing in a competitive environment.

Overall, Item 3.2 emphasizes the importance of obtaining actionable information, such as feedback and complaints from customers. To be actionable, the information gathered should meet two conditions:

- Responses should be tied directly to key business processes, so that opportunities for improvement are clear; and
- Responses should be translated into cost/revenue implications to support the setting of improvement priorities.

Area 3.2a focuses on relationship building—how the organization builds loyalty and positive referral. Increasingly, business success, business development, and product/service innovation depend upon maintaining close relationships with customers. Approaches to relationship building vary greatly, depending on products/services and types of customers. Relationships often change quickly. Accordingly, this Area addresses how the organization evaluates and improves its customer relationship building and ensures that approaches are kept current with changing business needs.

Area 3.2a also calls for information on how the organization provides easy access for customers seeking information or assistance and/or to comment and complain. Organizations should establish customer contact required to meet the needs of its customers for service—especially after the sale and delivery. These customer contact requirements, also called service standards, must be deployed to all employees who are in contact with customers. Such deployment needs to take account all key points in the response chain—all units or individuals in the organization that make effective interactions possible. These standards then become one source of information to evaluate the organization's performance in meeting customer contact requirements.

The principal issue in complaint management is prompt and effective resolution of complaints, including recovery of customer confidence. This is enhanced by resolution made by the first person the customer contacts. In addition, Area 3.2a addresses how the organization learns from complaints and ensures that design/production/delivery process employees receive information needed to eliminate the causes of complaints. Effective elimination of the causes of complaints involves aggregation of complaint information from all sources for evaluation and use in overall organizational improvement—both design and delivery stages (see Items 6.1 and 6.2).

The complaint management process might include analysis and priority setting for improvement projects based upon potential cost impact of complaints, taking into account customer retention related to resolution effectiveness.

Area 3.2b addresses how the organization determines customer satisfaction and dissatisfaction. Four types of requirements are considered:

- How the organization gathers information on customer satisfaction and dissatisfaction, including any important differences in approaches for different customer groups or market segments. This highlights the importance of the measurement scale in determining those factors that best reflect customers' market behaviors—repurchase, new business, and positive referral;
- How the organization follows up with customers regarding products, services, and recent transactions to determine satisfaction and to resolve problems quickly; and
- How satisfaction relative to competitors is determined. Such information might be derived from organization-based comparative studies or independent studies. The purpose of this comparison is to

develop information that can be used for improving performance relative to competitors and to better understand the factors that drive markets.
- How the organization keeps their approaches to determining customer satisfaction current with changing business needs and directions.

The customer satisfaction data gathered from the complaint management process in Area 3.2a ensure timely resolution and can help recover or build customer loyalty. Data collected by survey or similar means, as required by Area 3.2b, produce information at the convenience of the organization. However, data from the complaint processes in Area 3.2a are collected at the customer's convenience. Customers complain when they have a problem. They do not tend to hold their complaint until the organization finds it convenient to ask them. Although the complaint-type customer feedback (from Area 3.2a) is timely, it is often difficult to develop reliable trend data. The processes in Area 3.2b make it easier to track satisfaction over time. Both techniques are valuable in helping to understand the dynamics that build loyalty. To be effective, both must be used to drive improvement actions.

3.2 Customer Satisfaction and Relationships

How customer satisfaction is determined, relationships strengthened, and current products and services enhanced to support customer- and market-related planning

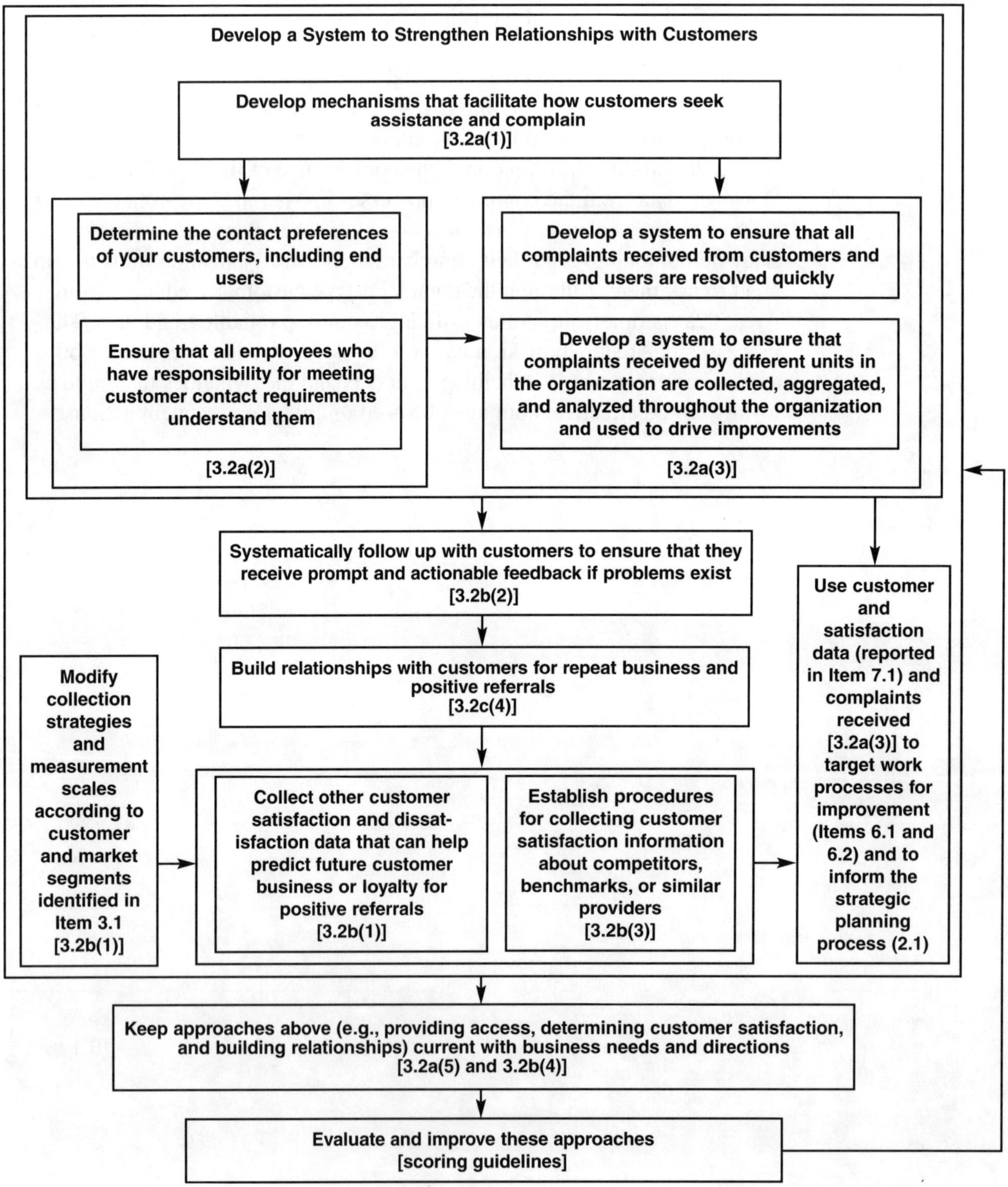

3.2 Customer Satisfaction and Relationships Item Linkages

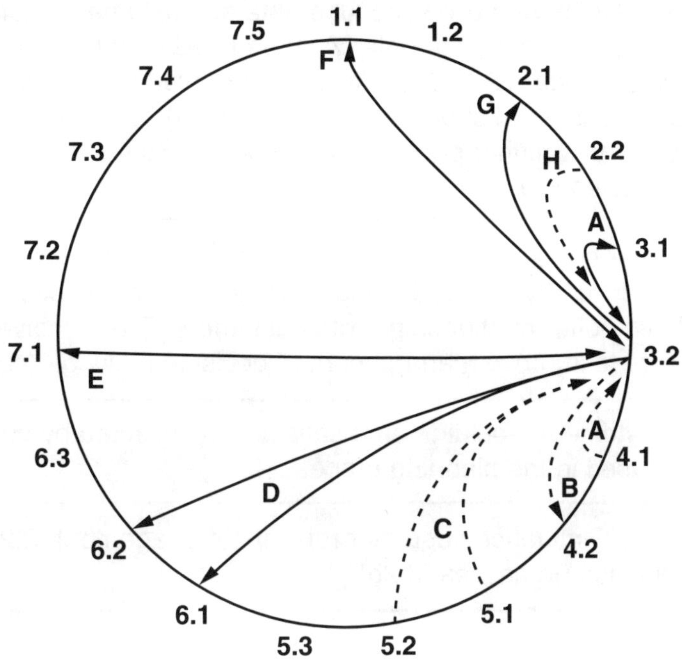

	Nature of Relationship
A	Information concerning customer requirements and expectations [3.1] and benchmark data [4.1] are used to set and deploy customer contact requirements (service standards) [3.2a]. Customer complaint data [3.2a] are used to help assess customer requirements and expectations [3.1].
B	Customer relations and satisfaction data [3.2] are analyzed and used to set priorities for action [4.2].
C	Training [5.2] and improved flexibility and self-direction [5.1] can enhance the development and effectiveness of customer-contact employees [3.2a].
D	Information collected through customer relations employees [3.2a] is used to enhance design of products and services and to improve operational and support processes [6.1 and 6.2].

Continued on next page

	Nature of Relationship (continued)
E	Information from customer relations processes [3.2a] can help in the design of customer satisfaction measures [3.2b] and even produce data on customer satisfaction [7.1]. In addition, customer satisfaction results data [7.1] are used to set customer contact requirements (service standards) [3.2a]. Efforts of improved accessibility and responsiveness in complaint management [3.2a] should result in improved complaint response time, effective complaint resolution, and a higher percentage of complaints resolved on first contact. These results should be reported in 7.1.
F	Priorities and customer-contact requirements (service standards) for customer service personnel [3.2a] are driven by top leadership [1.1]. Leaders at all levels [1.1] personally interact with and build better relationships with customers. They receive useful information from those customers to improve management of decision making.
G	Information about customer complaints and satisfaction collected by customer-contact employees [3.2a] is used in the planning process [2.1].
H	Goals and strategy [2.2] influence customer relations management [3.2a] and customer satisfaction determination processes [3.2b].

3.2 Customer Satisfaction and Relationships—Sample Effective Practices

A. Customer Relationships

- Several methods are used to ensure ease of customer contact, 24 hours a day if necessary (for example, toll-free numbers, pagers for contact personnel, web sites, e-mail, surveys, interviews, focus groups, electronic bulletin boards).
- Customer-contact employees are empowered to make decisions to address customer concerns.
- Adequate staff are available to maintain effective customer contact.
- Performance expectations are set for employees whose job brings them in regular contact with customers.
- The performance of employees against these expectations is measured and tracked.
- A system exists to ensure that customer complaints are resolved promptly and effectively.
- Complaints and customer concerns are resolved at first contact. This often means training customer-contact employees and giving them authority for resolving a broad range of problems.
- Complaint data are tracked and used to initiate prompt corrective action to prevent the problem from recurring.
- Procedures are in place and evaluated to ensure that customer contact is initiated to follow up on recent transactions to build relationships.
- Training and development plans and replacement procedures exist for customer-contact employees.
- Objective customer-contact requirements (service standards) have been derived from customer expectations (for example, timeliness, courtesy, efficiency, thoroughness, and completeness).
- Requirements for building relationships are identified and may include factors such as product knowledge, employee responsiveness, and various customer contact methods.
- A systematic approach exists to evaluate and improve service and customer relationships.

B. Customer Satisfaction Determination

- Several customer satisfaction indicators are used (for example, repeat business measures, praise letters, and direct measures using survey questions and interviews).

- Comprehensive satisfaction and dissatisfaction data are collected and segmented or grouped to enable the organization to predict customer behavior (likelihood of remaining a customer).
- Customer satisfaction and dissatisfaction measurements include both a numerical rating scale and descriptors assigned to each unit in the scale. An effective (actionable) customer satisfaction and dissatisfaction measurement system provides the organization with reliable information about customer ratings of specific product and service features and the relationship between these ratings and the customer's likely market behavior.
- Customer dissatisfaction indicators include complaints, claims, refunds, recalls, returns, repeat services, litigation, replacements, performance rating downgrades, repairs, warranty work, warranty costs, misshipments, and incomplete orders.
- Satisfaction data are collected from former customers.
- Competitors' customer satisfaction is determined using various means such as external or internal studies.
- Methods are in place to ensure objectivity of these data.
- Organization-based or independent organization comparative studies take into account one or more indicators of customer dissatisfaction as well as satisfaction. The extent and types of such studies depend on industry and organization size.
- The process of collecting complete, timely, and accurate customer satisfaction and dissatisfaction data is regularly evaluated and improved. Several improvement cycles are evident.

4 Information and Analysis—85 Points

The **Information and Analysis** Category examines your organization's performance measurement system and how your organization analyzes performance data and information.

Information and Analysis is the main point within the Criteria for all key information to effectively measure performance and manage the organization, and to drive improvement of performance and competitiveness. In simplest terms, Category 4 is the "brain center" for the alignment of an organization's operations with its strategic directions. However, since information and analysis might themselves be primary sources of competitive advantage and productivity growth, the Category also includes such strategic considerations.

Information and analysis evaluates the selection, management, and effectiveness of use of information and data to support processes, action plans, and the performance management system. The analysis and information of data are evaluated.

Measurement of Organizational Performance

- Data, information, and measures (including comparative data) for planning, decision making, improving performance, and supporting action plans and operations

Analysis of Organizational Performance

- Analyze data, deploy findings throughout the organization, to support organization-level review, decision making, planning and alignment of action plans.

4.1 Measurement of Organizational Performance (40 points) Approach/Deployment Scoring

Describe how your organization provides effective performance measurement systems for understanding, aligning, and improving performance at all levels and in all parts of your organization.

Within your response, include answers to the following questions:

a. Measurement of Organizational Performance

(1) How do you address the major components of an effective performance measurement system, including the following key factors?

- Selection of measures/indicators, and extent and effectiveness of their use in daily operations
- Selection and integration of measures/indicators and completeness of data to track your overall organizational performance
- Selection, and extent and effectiveness of use of key comparative data and information
- Data and information reliability
- A cost/financial understanding of improvement options
- Correlations/projections of data to support planning

(2) How do you keep your performance measurement system current with business needs and directions?

Notes:

N1. The term information and analysis refers to the key metrics used by your organization to measure and analyze performance. Performance measurement is used in fact-based decision making for setting and aligning organizational directions and resource use at the work unit, key process, departmental, and whole organization levels.

N2. Deployment of data and information might be via electronic or other means. Reliability [4.1a(1)] includes reliability of software and delivery systems.

N3. Comparative data and information include benchmarking and competitive comparisons. Benchmarking refers to processes and results that represent best practices and performance for similar activities, inside or outside the organization's industry. Competitive comparisons refer to performance relative to competitors in the organization's markets.

This Item addresses the organization's selection, management, and use of information and data for performance measurement in support of organizational planning and performance improvement. Overall, the Item represents a key foundation for a performance-oriented organization that effectively utilizes nonfinancial and financial information and data.

The Item examines the major components of an effective performance measurement system. It examines the selection and use of measures and indicators for tracking daily operations and those for tracking overall organizational performance. Alignment and integration of measures are viewed in terms of extent and effectiveness of use to meet organizational needs. Alignment and integration include how measures are aligned throughout the organization, how they are integrated to yield organization-wide measures, and how performance measurement requirements are deployed by the senior leaders to track work group and/or functional-level performance on key measures targeted for organization-wide improvement. Data and information reliability is an important component for monitoring operations and for data integration to assess overall performance.

Performance information and data could be especially advantageous in business networks, alliances, and supply chains. Responses to this Item should take into account such strategic use of performance information and data. Accordingly, "users" should then be interpreted as partners as well as organizational work units.

The Item also calls for information on how competitive comparisons and benchmarking information are selected and used to help drive performance improvements. Included in effective selection and use of competitive comparisons and benchmarking information and data are: determination of needs and priorities; criteria for seeking appropriate information—from within and outside the organization's industry and markets; and use of information and data to set stretch targets and to promote major improvements in areas most critical to the organization's competitive strategy.

The major premises underlying the use of comparative information are:

- Organizations facing tough competition need to know "where they stand" relative to competitors and to best practices;
- Comparative and benchmarking information often provides impetus for significant ("breakthrough") improvement or changes and might alert organizations to competitive threats and new practices; and
- Organizations need to understand their own processes and the processes of others before they compare performance levels. Benchmarking information may also support business analysis and decisions relating to core competencies, alliances, and outsourcing.

Finally, the Item examines how requirements are met to keep the organization's performance measurement system current with changing business needs and directions.

4.1 Measurement of Organizational Performance

How the organization selects, manages, and uses information and data to support decision making for key processes and to improve performance

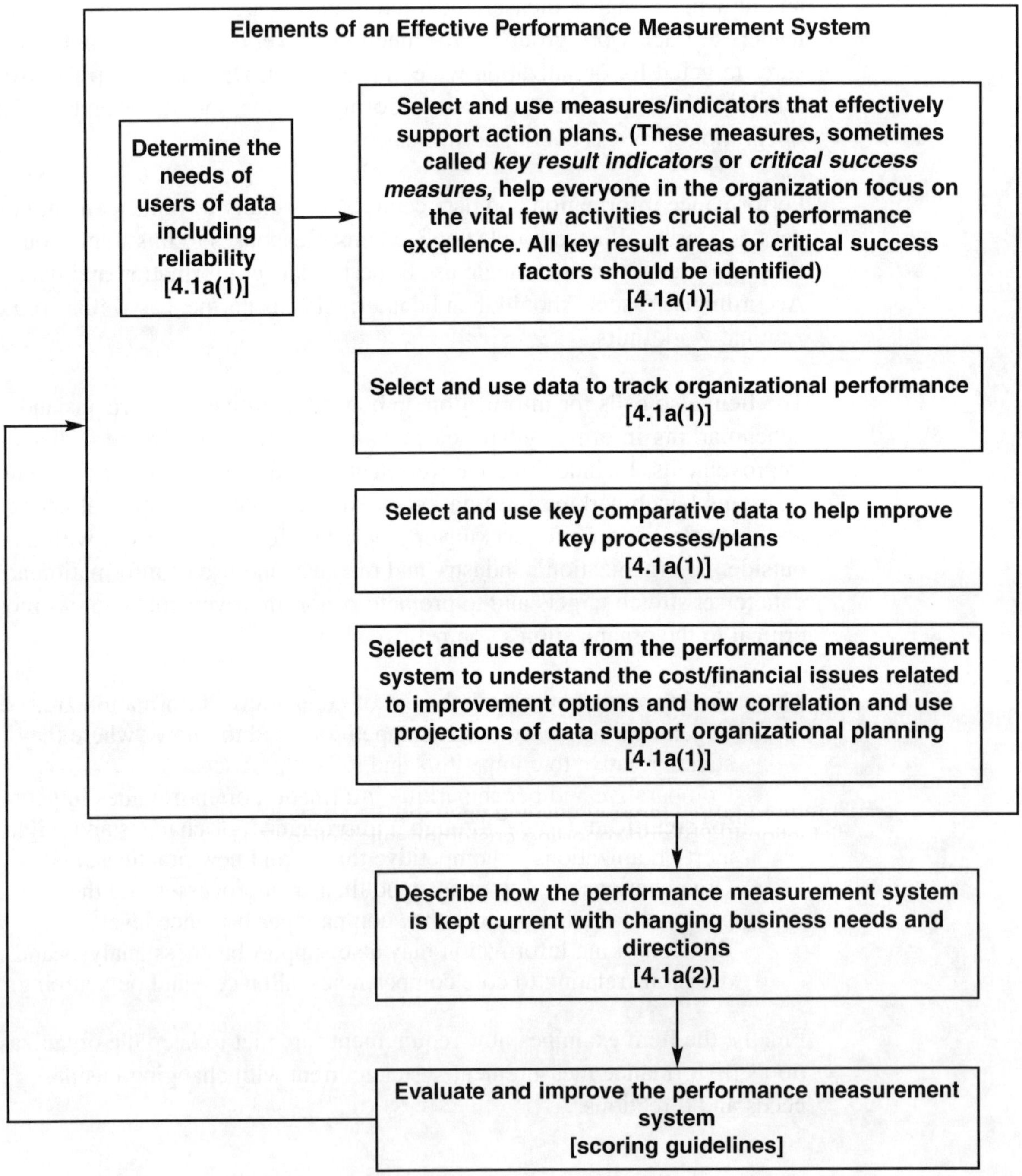

4.1 Measurement of Organizational Performance Item Linkages

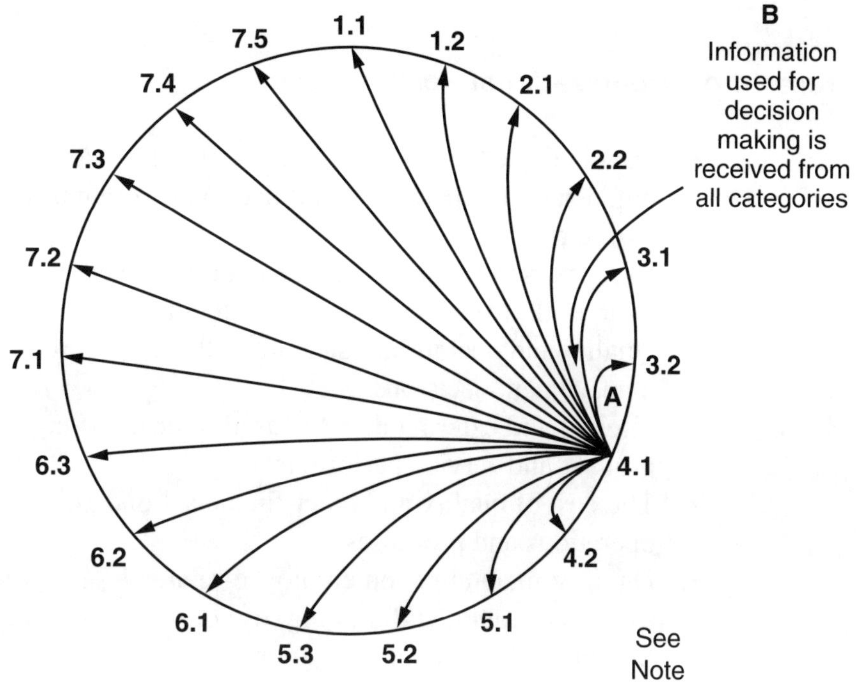

Nature of Relationship	
A	Information collected [4.1] is used for planning [2.1], goal setting [2.2], analysis [4.2], benchmarking priority setting [4.1], day-to-day leadership [1.1], setting public responsibility standards (regulatory, legal, ethical) for community involvement [1.2], monitoring of quality and operational performance results [7.2, 7.3, 7.4, 7.5], improving work processes [6.1, 6.2, 6.3] and human resource systems [5.1, 5.2, 5.3], determining customer requirements [3.1], managing customer complaints and building customer relations [3.2a], and determining customer satisfaction [3.2b] and reporting customer satisfaction [7.1].
B	Information used for decision making and continuous improvement [4.1] is collected from all categories.

NOTE: Because the information collected and used for decision-making links with all other items, the linkage arrows will not all be repeated on the other item maps. The more relevant connections will be identified.

4.1 Measurement of Organizational Performance—Sample Effective Practices

A. Measurement of Organizational Performance

- Data collected at the individual worker level are consistent across the organization to permit consolidation and organization-wide performance monitoring.
- Every person has access to the data they need to make decisions about their work, from top leaders to individual workers or teams of workers.
- Quality and operational data are collected and routinely used for management decisions.
- Internal and external data are used to describe customer satisfaction and product and service performance.
- The cost of quality and other financial concerns are measured for internal operations and processes.
- Data are maintained on employee-related issues of satisfaction, morale, safety, education and training, use of teams, and recognition and reward.
- Supplier performance data are maintained.
- The performance measurement system is systematically evaluated and refined.
- Improvements have been made to reduce cycle time for data collection and to increase data access, reliability, and use.
- Employees, customers, and suppliers are involved in validating data.
- A systematic process exists for data review and improvement, standardization, and easy employee access to data. Training on the use of data systems is provided as needed.
- Data used for management decisions' focus on critical success factors are integrated with work processes for the planning, design, and delivery of products and services.
- Users of data help determine what data systems are developed and how data are accessed.
- A systematic process is in place for identifying and prioritizing comparative information and benchmark targets.
- Research has been conducted to identify best-in-class organizations, which may be competitors or noncompetitors.
- Key processes or functions are the subject of benchmarking. Activities such as those that support the organization's goals and objectives, action plans, and opportunities for improvement and innovation are the subject of benchmarking.

- Benchmarking covers key products, services, customer satisfiers, suppliers, employees, and support operations.
- The organization reaches beyond its own business to conduct comparative studies.
- Benchmark or comparison data are used to improve the understanding of work processes and to discover the best levels of performance that have been achieved. Based on this knowledge, the organization sets goals or targets to stretch performance as well as drive innovations.
- A complete understanding of the cost and benefit of improvement options exists.
- Correlations and projections of data are used to support business planning at all levels.
- Any systematic process is in place to improve the use of benchmark or comparison data in the understanding of all work processes.

4.2 Analysis of Organizational Performance (55 points) Approach/Deployment Scoring

Describe how your organization analyzes performance data and information to assess and understand overall organizational performance.

Within your response, include answers to the following questions:

a. Analysis of Organizational Performance

(1) How do you perform analyses to support your senior executives' organizational performance review and your organizational planning? How do you ensure that the analyses address the overall health of your organization, including your key business results and strategic objectives?

(2) How do you ensure that the results of organizational-level analysis are linked to work group and/or functional-level operations to enable effective support for decision making?

(3) How does analysis support daily operations throughout your organization? Include how this analysis ensures that measures align with action plans.

Note:

N1. Analysis includes trends, projections, comparisons, and cause-effect correlations intended to support performance reviews and the setting of priorities for resource use. Accordingly, analysis draws upon all types of data: customer-related, financial and market, operational, and competitive.

N2. Performance results should be reported in Items 7.1, 7.2, 7.3, 7.4, and 7.5.

This Item addresses organizational analysis of performance—the principal basis for assessing an organization's overall health. Analysis guides an organization's process management toward key business results and toward attaining strategic objectives. Despite their importance, individual facts and data do not usually provide a sound basis for actions or priorities. Action depends upon understanding cause/effect connections among processes and between processes and business results. Process actions may have many resource implications; results may have many cost and revenue implications as well. There is a critical need to provide a sound analytical basis for decisions since resources for improvement are limited and cause/effect connections are often unclear.

A close connection between analysis and performance review and between analysis and organizational planning helps to ensure that analysis is relevant to decision making. This Item is the central analysis point in an integrated performance measurement system. This system is built around financial and nonfinancial information and data.

The Item examines how information and data from all parts of the organization are analyzed to assess overall organizational health and to support daily operations.

Analyses that organizations perform to gain understanding of performance vary widely. Selection depends upon many factors, including organization type, size, and competitive position. Examples include:

- How product and service quality improvement correlates with key customer indicators such as customer satisfaction, customer retention, and market share;
- Cost/revenue implications of customer-related problems and problem resolution effectiveness;
- Interpretation of market share changes in terms of customer gains and losses and changes in customer satisfaction;
- Improvement trends in key operational performance indicators such as productivity, cycle time, waste reduction, new product introduction, and defect levels;
- Relationships between employee/organizational learning and value added per employee;
- Financial benefits derived from improvements in employee safety, absenteeism, and turnover;
- Benefits and costs associated with education and training;
- Benefits and costs associated with improved organizational knowledge management and sharing;
- How the ability to identify and meet employee requirements correlates with employee retention, motivation, and productivity;
- Cost/revenue implications of employee-related problems and effective problem resolution;
- Trends in individual measures of productivity, such as workforce productivity;

- Individual or aggregate measures of productivity and quality relative to competitors;
- Cost trends relative to competitors;
- Relationships between product/service quality, operational performance indicators, and overall financial performance trends, as reflected in indicators such as operating costs, revenues, asset utilization, and value added per employee;
- Allocation of resources among alternative improvement projects based on cost/revenue implications and improvement potential;
- Net earnings derived from quality/operational/human resource performance improvements;
- Comparisons among business units showing how operational performance improvement affect financial performance;
- Contributions of improvement activities to cash flow, working capital use, and shareholder value;
- Profit impacts of customer retention;
- Cost/revenue implications of new market entry, including global market entry or expansion;
- Market share versus profits;
- Trends in aggregate measures such as total factor productivity; and
- Trends in economic, market, and shareholder indicators of value.

An important part of the senior leaders' organizational review is the translation of review findings into an action agenda—sufficiently specific so that deployment throughout the organization, and to suppliers/partners and key customers is possible. This can only be done with a clear understanding of cause and effect relationships among processes and between processes and business results.

4.2 Analysis of Organization Performance

How the organization analyzes performance to assess the overall health of the organization

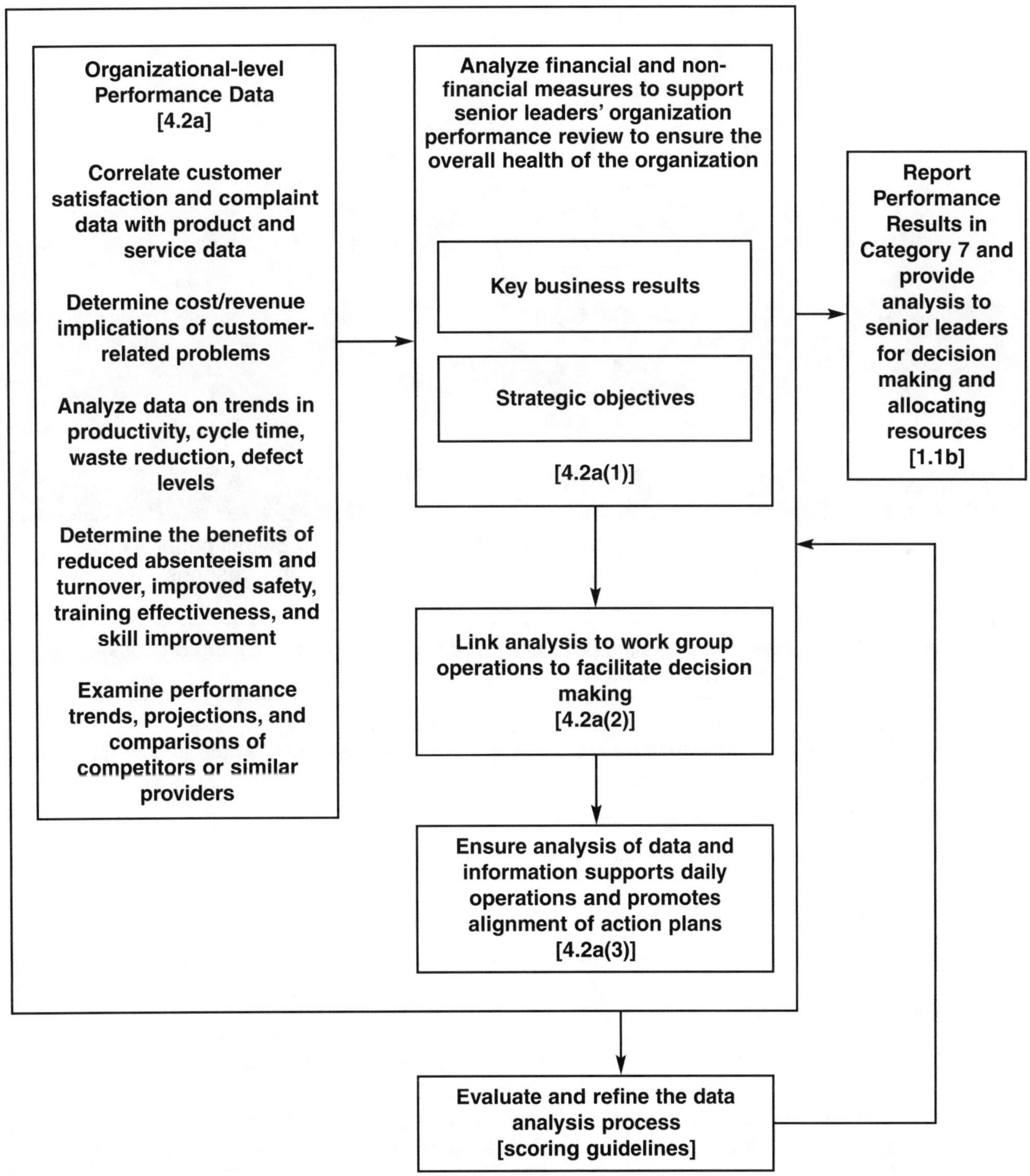

4.2 Analysis of Organization Performance Item Linkages

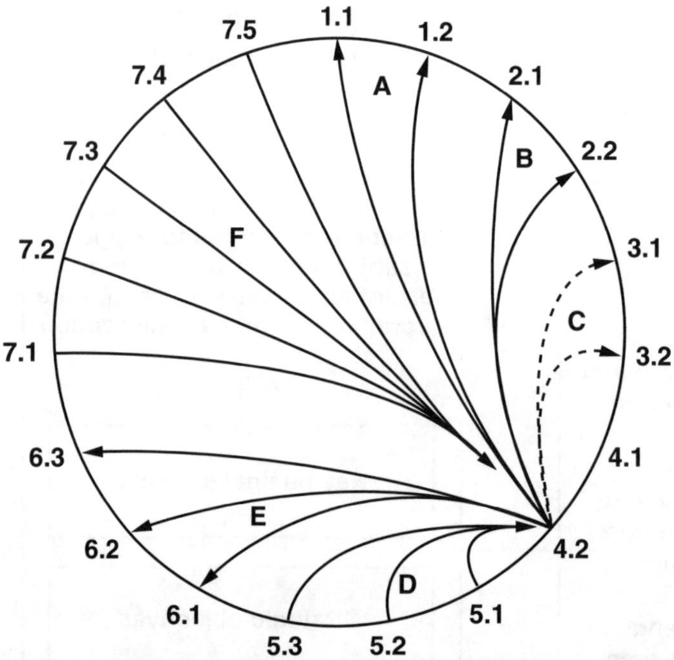

	Nature of Relationship
A	Leaders at all levels [1.1] use data and information [4.2] to review overall performance, assess progress relative to plans, ensure regulatory, legal, and public responsibilities are met or exceeded [1.2], and identify key areas for improvement.
B	Aggregated information is analyzed [4.2] and used in the strategic planning process [2.1] and to help set goals [2.2].
C	Information from customer satisfaction data [7.1] are analyzed [4.2] and used to help determine ways to assess customer requirements [3.1], to determine standards or required levels of customer service and relationship development [3.2a], and to design instruments to assess customer satisfaction [3.2b].
D	Information regarding human resources capabilities, including work system efficiency, initiative, and self-direction [5.1], training and development [5.2], and well-being and satisfaction [5.3] is analyzed [4.2] to improve safety, retention, absenteeism, and organizational effectiveness.
E	Data are aggregated and analyzed [4.2] to improve work processes [6.1, 6.2, 6.3] that will reduce cycle time, waste, and defect levels.
F	Performance data from all parts of the organization are integrated and analyzed [4.2] to assess performance in key areas such as customer-related performance [7.1], operational performance [7.5], financial and market performance [7.2], human resource performance [7.3], and supplier and partner performance [7.4], relative to competitive performance in all areas.

4.2 Analysis of Organization Performance—Sample Effective Practices

A. Analysis of Organizational Performance

- Systematic processes are in place for analyzing all types of data and to determine overall organizational health, including key business results, action plans, and strategic objectives. Part of the process is a method to evaluate the effectiveness of the analysis process and improve.
- Facts, rather than intuition, are used to support most decision making at all levels based on the analyses conducted to make sense out of the data collected.
- The analysis process itself is analyzed to make the results more timely and useful for decision making for quality improvement at all levels.
- Analysis processes and tools, and the value of analyses to decision making, are systematically evaluated and improved.
- Analysis is linked to work groups to facilitate the decision making (sometimes daily) throughout the organization.
- Analysis techniques enable meaningful interpretation of the cost and performance impact of organization processes. This analysis helps people at all levels of the organization make necessary trade-offs, set priorities, and reallocate resources to maximize overall organization performance.

5 Human Resource Focus—85 Points

The **Human Resource Focus** Category examines how your organization enables employees to develop and utilize their full potential, aligned with the organization's objectives. Also examined are your organization's efforts to build and maintain a work environment and an employee support climate conducive to performance excellence, full participation, and personal and organizational growth.

Human Resource Focus addresses key human resource practices—those directed toward creating a high performance workplace and toward developing employees to enable them and the organization to adapt to change. The Category covers human resource development and management requirements in an integrated way, aligned with the organization's strategic objectives. Included in the focus on human resources is a focus on the work environment and the employee support climate.

To ensure the basic alignment of human resource management with overall strategy, the Criteria also include human resource planning as part of organizational planning in the Strategic Planning Category.

Human resource focus evaluates how the organization enables employees to develop and use their full potential.

Work Systems

- Design, organize, and manage work and jobs to optimize employee performance and potential
- Recognition and reward practices support objectives for customer satisfaction, performance improvement, and employee and organization learning goals
- Identify skills needed by potential employees, recruit, and hire

Employee Education, Training, and Development

- Deliver, evaluate, and reinforce appropriate training to achieve action plans and address organization needs including building knowledge, skills, and abilities to improve employee development and performance

Employee Well-Being and Satisfaction

- Improve employee safety, well-being, development, and satisfaction and maintain a work environment free from distractions to high performance
- Leaders at all levels encourage and motivate employees to reach full potential
- Systematically evaluate employee well-being, satisfaction, and motivation and identify improvement priorities that promote key business results

5.1 Work Systems (35 Points) Approach/Deployment Scoring

Describe how your organization's work and job design, compensation, career progression, and related workforce practices enable employees to achieve high performance in your operations.

Within your response, include answers to the following questions:

a. Work Systems

(1) How do you design, organize, and manage work and jobs to promote cooperation and collaboration, individual initiative, innovation, and flexibility, and to keep current with business needs?

(2) How do your managers and supervisors encourage and motivate employees to develop and utilize their full potential? Include formal and/or informal mechanisms you use to encourage and support employees in job- and career-related development/learning objectives.

(3) How does your employee performance management system, including feedback to employees, support high performance?

(4) How do your compensation, recognition, and related reward/incentive practices reinforce high performance?

(5) How do you ensure effective communication, cooperation, and knowledge/skill sharing across work units, functions, and locations, as appropriate?

(6) How do you identify characteristics and skills needed by potential employees; how do you recruit and hire new employees? How do you take into account key performance requirements, diversity of your community, and fair workforce practices?

Notes:

N1. The term employees refers to the organization's permanent, temporary, and part-time personnel, as well as any contract employees supervised by the organization. Employees include managers and supervisors at all levels. Contract employees supervised by a contractor should be addressed in Item 6.3.

N2. The term work design refers to how employees are organized and/or organize themselves in formal and informal, temporary, or longer-term units. The term job design refers to responsibilities, authorities, and tasks of individuals. In some work systems, jobs might be shared by a team, based upon cross-training.

N3. Compensation and recognition include promotions and bonuses that might be based upon performance, skills acquired, and other factors. Recognition includes monetary and nonmonetary, formal and informal, and individual and group recognition.

This Item addresses how approaches to work and job design, compensation, employee performance management, and recognition enable and encourage all employees to contribute effectively. The Item is concerned not only with current and near-term performance objectives, but also with individual and organizational learning—enabling adaptation to change.

This Item calls for information on work and job design. The basic aim of such design should be to enable employees to exercise discretion and decision making, leading to individual initiative, flexibility, innovation, knowledge and skill sharing, and rapid response to the changing requirements of the marketplace. Examples of approaches to create flexibility in work and job design might include simplification of job classifications, cross-training, job rotation, and changes in work layout and work locations. Approaches also might entail using technology and changing the flow of information to support local decision making.

Effective job design and flexible work organizations are necessary, but may not be sufficient to ensure high performance. High performance work systems require information systems, education, and appropriate training to ensure that information flow supports the job and work designs. Also important is effective communication across functions and work units to ensure a focus on customer requirements and to ensure an environment of encouragement, trust, and mutual commitment. In some cases, teams might involve individuals in different locations linked via computers or conferencing technology.

The Item calls for information on how managers and supervisors motivate employees and encourage employees to develop and utilize their full potential. Some high performance organizations are addressing these needs via career and learning objectives, developed jointly with employees.

The Item also calls for information on employee compensation, recognition, and related reward/incentive practices. It is important that they reinforce high performance, including job design, a focus on customer satisfaction, and learning. To be effective, compensation, recognition, and incentives might need to be based, wholly or in part, upon demonstrated skills and/or evaluation by peers in teams and networks as well as individually.

Compensation, recognition, and incentive approaches might include profit sharing and compensation based on skill building, use of new skills, demonstrations of self-learning, and knowledge sharing. The approaches might take into account linkages to customer retention or other performance objectives.

Compensation, recognition, and other approaches to recognize desired behaviors are essential to align and optimize the work of the organization. The best strategies, if not aligned throughout the organization, do not usually produce the desired results.

In the face of a continually shrinking pool of highly skilled workers, leading edge organizations find it more important than ever before to profile, recruit, and hire good employees. The power that comes from new insights and different viewpoints is enhanced by attracting a diverse workforce—a workforce at least as diverse as the community within which the organization works.

5.1 Work Systems

How the organization's work and job design, and compensation and recognition approaches, career progression, recruitment, and diversity practices enable and encourage all employees to contribute effectively to achieving high performance

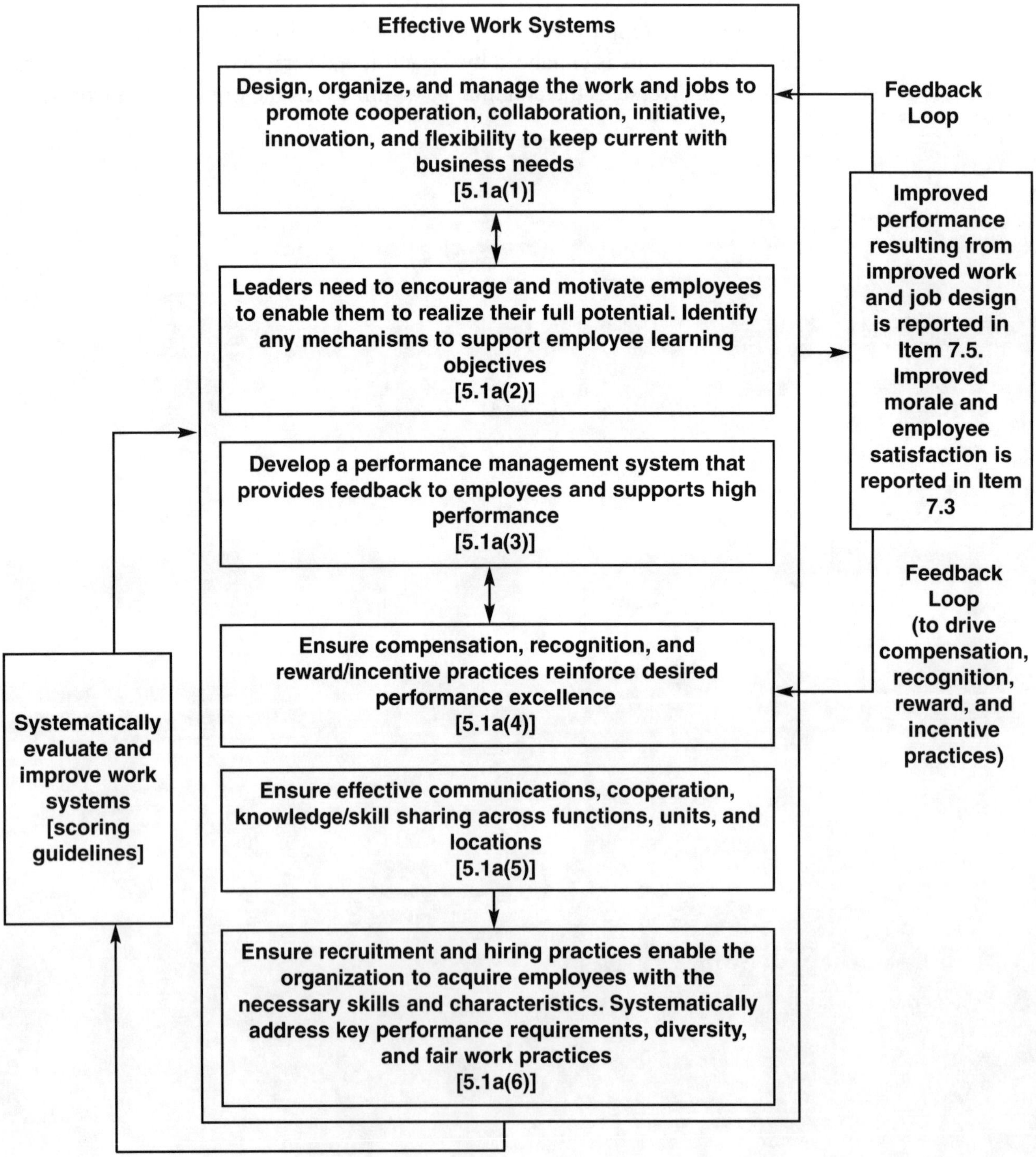

5.1 Work Systems Item Linkages

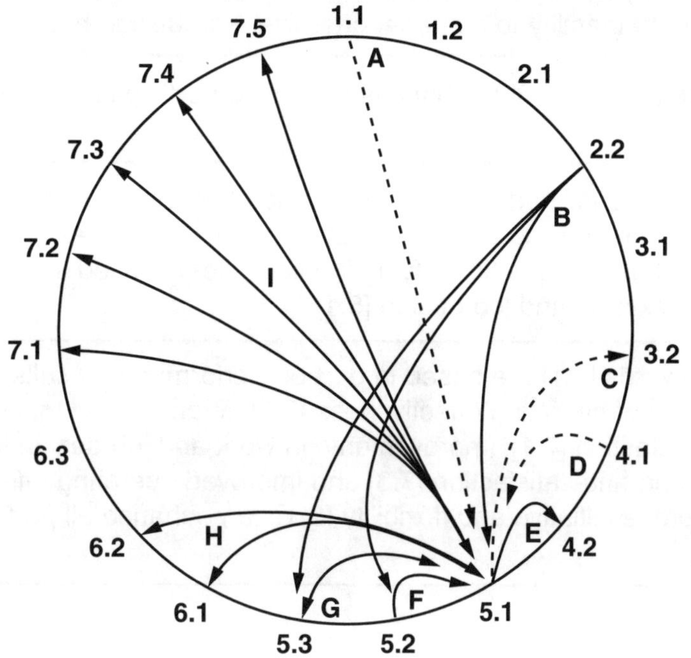

	Nature of Relationship
A	Leaders at all levels [1.1] set the policies and role model actions essential to improving work and job design to enhance employee performance, initiative, self-direction, and involvement in quality improvement [5.1].
B	Human resource development plans and goals [2.2] address ways to improve employee performance and involvement [5.1], training [5.2], and satisfaction and well-being [5.3].
C	Improved flexibility and self-direction [5.1] can enhance the effectiveness of customer-contact employees [3.2a].
D	Key comparison data [4.1] are often used to improve work systems, and reward and recognition [5.1].
E	Information regarding work systems effectiveness, design effectiveness, and employee involvement and recognition [5.1] is used to gain a better understanding of operational performance and organizational capabilities [4.2].

Continued on next page

	Nature of Relationship (continued)
F	Effective training [5.2] is critical to enable employees or managers at all levels to improve skills and improve their ability to manage, organize, and design better work processes [5.1].
G	An improved work climate [5.3b] enhances employee participation, self-direction, and initiative [5.1] and vice versa.
H	High-performance, streamlined work systems, and effective compensation and recognition [5.1] are essential to improving operational and support processes [6.1 and 6.2]. In addition, the analysis of work processes (identifying inefficiencies) is used to inform or drive the improvements in flexibility and job design [5.1].
I	Recognition or rewards [5.1] are based in part on performance results [Category 7], particularly in areas of operating effectiveness [7.5], financial and market performance [7.2], and customer satisfaction [7.1]. Improvements in work and job design [5.1] result in improved employee motivation and satisfaction [7.3] and improved operating effectiveness [7.5]. Processes to improve initiative and flexibility [5.1] can enhance all performance results [Category 7].

5.1 Work Systems—Sample Effective Practices

A. Work Systems

- Fully using the talents of all employees is a basic organizational value.
- Managers use cross-functional work teams to break down barriers, improve effectiveness, and meet goals.
- Teams have access to data and are authorized to make decisions about their work.
- Employee opinion is sought regarding work design and work processes.
- Prompt and regular feedback is provided to teams regarding their performance. Feedback covers both results and team process.
- Although lower-performing organizations use teams for special improvement projects (while the "regular work" is performed using traditional approaches), higher-performing organizations use teams and self-directed employees as the way regular work is done.
- Self-directed or self-managed work teams are used throughout the organization. They have authority over matters such as budget, hiring, and team membership and roles.
- A systematic process is used to evaluate and improve the effectiveness and extent of employee involvement.
- Many indicators of employee involvement effectiveness exist, such as the improvements in time or cost reduction produced by teams.
- The performance management system provides feedback to employees that supports their ability to contribute to a high performing organization.
- Compensation, recognition, and rewards/incentives are provided for generating improvement ideas. Also, a system exists to encourage and provide rapid reinforcement for submitting improvement ideas.
- Compensation, recognition, and rewards/incentives are provided for results, such as for reductions in cycle time and exceeding target schedules with error-free products or services at less-than-projected cost.
- Employees, as well as managers, participate in creating the compensation, recognition, and rewards/incentives practices and help monitor its implementation and systematic improvement.
- The organization evaluates its approaches to employee performance and compensation, recognition, and rewards to determine the extent to which employees are satisfied with them, the extent of employee participation, and the impact of the system on improved performance (reported in Item 7.3).
- Evaluations are used to make improvements. The best organizations have several improvement cycles. (Many improvement cycles can occur in one year.)

- Performance measures exist for employee involvement, self-direction, and initiative. Goals for these measures are expressed in measurable terms. These measurable goals form at least a good part of the basis for performance recognition.
- Recognition, reward/incentives, and compensation are influenced by customer satisfaction ratings as well as other performance measures.

5.2 Employee Education, Training, and Development (25 points) Approach/Deployment Scoring

Describe how your organization's education and training support the achievement of your business objectives, build employee knowledge, skills, and capabilities, and contribute to improved employee performance.

Within your response, include answers to the following questions:

a. Employee Education, Training, and Development

(1) How does your education and training approach balance short- and longer-term organizational and employee needs, including development, learning, and career progression?

(2) How do you design education and training to keep current with business and individual needs? Include how job and organizational performance are used in education and training design and evaluation.

(3) How do you seek and use input from employees and their supervisors/managers on education and training needs, expectations, and design?

(4) How do you deliver and evaluate education and training? Include formal and informal education, training, and learning, as appropriate.

(5) How do you address key developmental and training needs, including diversity training, management/leadership development, new employee orientation, and safety, as appropriate?

(6) How do you address performance excellence in your education and training? Include how employees learn to use performance measurements, performance standards, skill standards, performance improvement, quality control methods, and benchmarking, as appropriate.

(7) How do you reinforce knowledge and skills on the job?

Notes:

Education and training delivery [5.2a(4)] might occur inside or outside the organization and involve on-the-job, classroom, computer-based, distance learning, and/or other types of delivery (formal or informal).

This Item addresses how the organization develops the workforce via education, training, and on-the-job reinforcement of knowledge and skills. Development is intended to meet ongoing needs of employees and a high performance workplace that must accommodate to change.

Education and training requirements address the knowledge and skills employees need to meet their overall work and personal objectives, including career progression, and the organization's need for leadership development of employees. Depending upon the nature of the organization's work and the employees' responsibilities and stage of development, education and training needs might vary greatly. As a result, both the organization's and employee's short- and longer-term needs are to be considered. Examples include leadership and knowledge sharing skills, communications, teamwork, problem solving, interpreting and using data, meeting customer requirements, process analysis, process simplification, waste reduction, cycle time reduction, error-proofing, priority setting based upon cost and benefit data, and other training that affects employee effectiveness, efficiency, and safety. Education also might include basic skills such as reading, writing, language, and arithmetic.

The Item calls for information on how education and training are designed, delivered, reinforced, and evaluated, with special emphasis upon on-the-job application of knowledge and skills. The Item emphasizes the importance of the involvement of employees and their managers in the design of training, including clear identification of specific needs. This involves job analysis—understanding the types and levels of the skills required and the timeliness of training. Determining specific education and training needs might include use of organizational assessment or employee self-assessment to determine and/or compare skill levels for progression within the organization or elsewhere.

In addressing performance excellence, education and training must include elements that promote excellence throughout the organization. This may include training leaders on the techniques and elements of the Performance Excellence Criteria. It might also include developing the leadership and problem-solving skills of employees and managers (not *just* managers).

Education and training delivery might occur inside or outside the organization and involve on-the-job, classroom, computer-based, distance learning, or other types of delivery. This includes the use of developmental assignments within or outside the organization to enhance employees' career opportunities and employability.

The Item also emphasizes the evaluation of education and training. Such evaluation might take into account managers' evaluation, employees' self-evaluation, and peer evaluation of value received through education and training relative to needs identified in design. Evaluation might also address factors such as the effectiveness of education and training delivery, impact on work unit and organizational performance, costs of delivery alternatives, and benefit/cost ratios.

Although the Item does not explicitly require information on training for customer-contact employees, such training is increasingly important. It usually entails:

- Acquiring key knowledge and skills, including knowledge of products and services;
- Listening to customers;
- Soliciting comments from customers;
- Anticipating and handling problems or failures ("recovery");
- Developing skills in customer retention; and
- Learning how to effectively manage expectations.

5.2 Employee Education, Training, and Development

How the organization's education and training addresses business objectives, building employee knowledge, skills, and capabilities, and contributes to improving employee performance

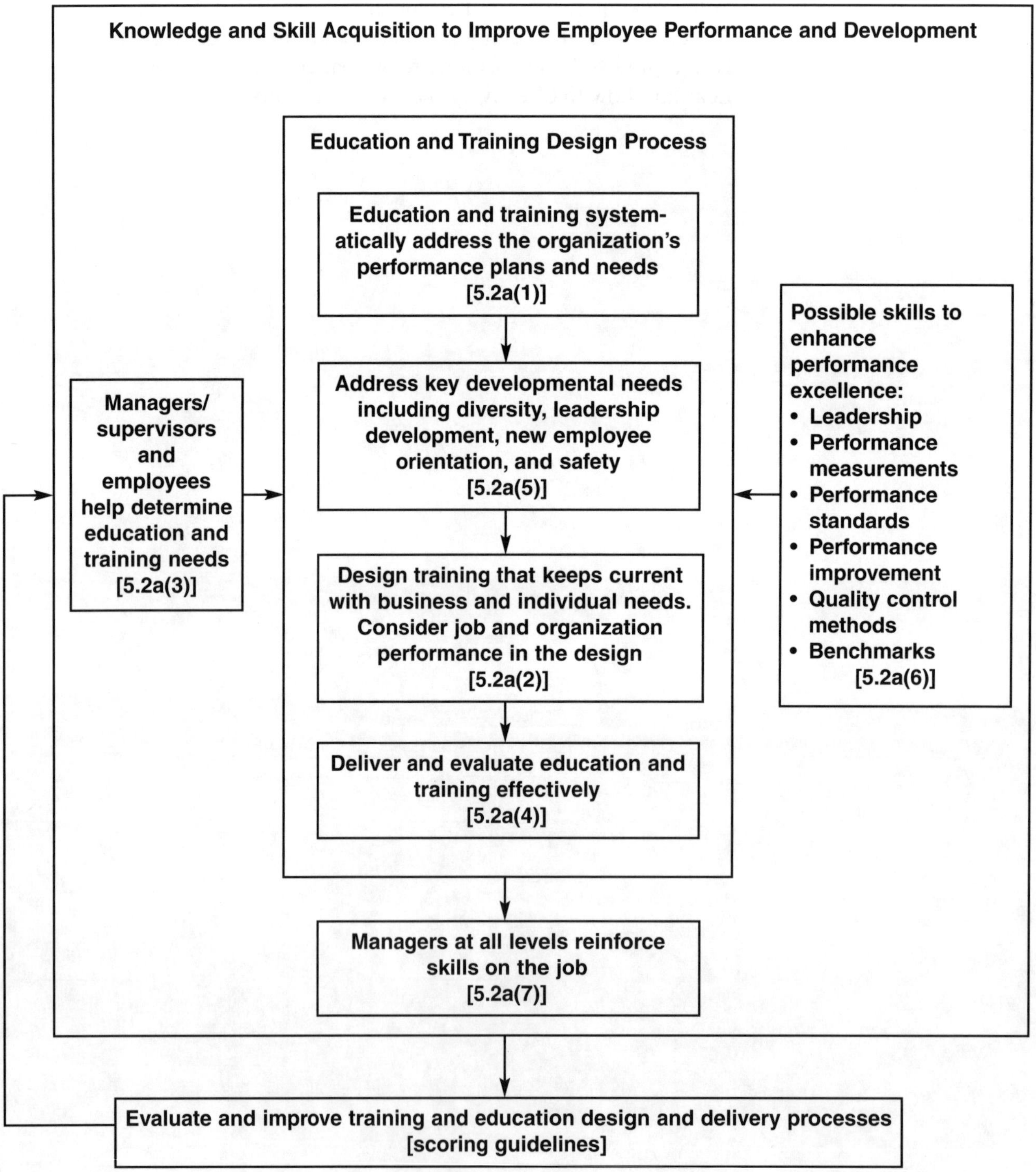

5.2 Employee Education, Training, and Development Item Linkages

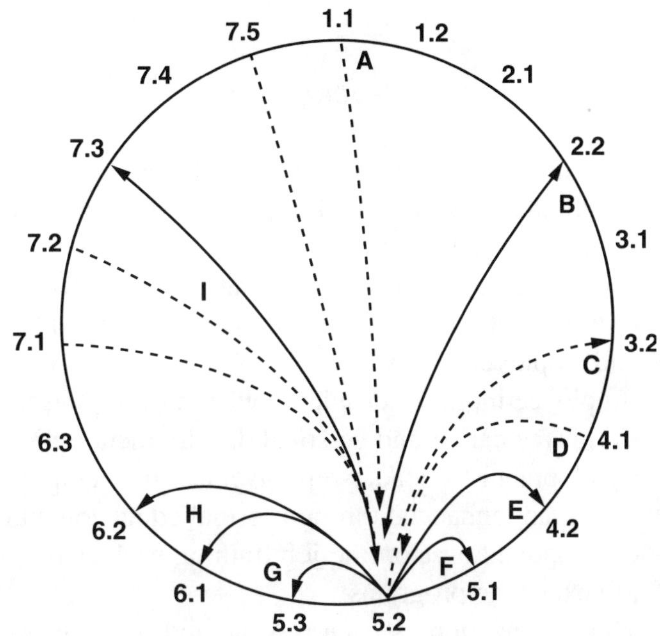

Nature of Relationship	
A	Leaders at all levels [1.1] reinforce training on the job to ensure its effectiveness [5.2].
B	Human resource development plans [2.2a] are used to help align training [5.2] to support the organizational goals [2.2b].
C	Training [5.2] can enhance capabilities of customer-contact employees and strengthen customer relationships [3.2a].
D	Key measures and benchmarking data [4.1] are used to improve training [5.2].
E	Information regarding training effectiveness [5.2] is analyzed [4.2].
F	Effective training [5.2] enables employees and managers at all levels to improve skills and their ability to manage, organize, and design better work processes [5.1].
G	Effective training [5.2] is often critical to maintaining and improving a safe, healthful work environment [5.3a].
H	Training [5.2] is essential to improving work in process effectiveness and innovation [6.1 and 6.2].
I	Results of improved training and development [5.2] are reported in 7.3. In addition, customer satisfaction [7.1], financial and market [7.2], and operational performance and product and service quality results [7.5] are monitored, in part, to assess training effectiveness [5.2].

5.2 Employee Education, Training, and Development—Sample Effective Practices

A. Employee Education Training and Development

- Systematic needs analyses are conducted by managers and employees to ensure that skills required to perform work are routinely assessed, monitored, and maintained.
- Clear linkages exist between strategic objectives and the education and training that are provided. Skills are developed based on work demands and employee needs.
- Employee input is considered when developing training plans.
- Employee career and personal development options, including development for leadership, diversity, new employee orientation, and safety, are enhanced through formal education and training. Some development uses on-the-job training such as rotational assignments or job exchange programs.
- The organization uses various methods to deliver training to ensure that it is suitable for employee knowledge and skill levels.
- Training is linked to work requirements, which managers reinforce on the job. Just-in-time training is preferred (rather than just-in-case training) to help ensure that the skills will be used immediately after training.
- Employee feedback on the appropriateness of the training is collected and used to improve course delivery and content.
- The organization systematically evaluates training effectiveness on the job. Performance data are collected on individuals and groups at all levels to assess the impact of training.
- Employee satisfaction with courses is tracked.
- Training design and delivery is systematically refined and improved based on these evaluations.

5.3 Employee Well-Being and Satisfaction (25 points) Approach/Deployment Scoring

Describe how your organization maintains a work environment and an employee support climate that contribute to the well-being, satisfaction, and motivation of all employees.

Within your response, include answers to the following questions:

a. Work Environment

How do you address and improve workplace health, safety, and ergonomic factors? How do employees take part in identifying these factors and in improving workplace safety? Include performance measures and/or targets for each key environmental factor. Also include significant differences, if any, based on different work environments for employee groups and/or work units.

b. Employee Support Climate

(1) How do you enhance your employees' work climate via services, benefits, and policies? How are these enhancements selected and tailored to the needs of different categories and types of employees, and to individuals, as appropriate?

(2) How does your work climate consider and support the needs of a diverse workforce?

c. Employee Satisfaction

(1) How do you determine the key factors that affect employee well-being, satisfaction, and motivation?

(2) What formal and/or informal assessment methods and measures do you use to determine employee well-being, satisfaction, and motivation? How do you tailor these methods and measures to a diverse workforce and to different categories and types of employees? How do you use other indicators such as employee turnover, absenteeism, grievances, and productivity to assess and improve employee well-being, satisfaction, and motivation?

(3) How do you relate assessment findings to key business results to identify work environment and employee support climate improvement priorities?

Notes:

N1. Approaches for enhancing employees' work climate [5.3b(1)] might include: counseling; career development and employability services; recreational or cultural activities; non–work-related education; day care; job rotation and/or sharing; special leave for family responsibilities and/or for community service; home safety training; flexible work hours; outplacement; and retiree benefits (including extended health care).

Continued on next page

N2. Specific factors that might affect employee well-being, satisfaction, and motivation [5.3c(1)] include: effective employee problem or grievance resolution; safety factors; employee views of management; employee training, development, and career opportunities; employee preparation for changes in technology or the work organization; work environment and other work conditions; workload; cooperation and teamwork; recognition; benefits; communications; job security; compensation; and equal opportunity.

N3. Measures and/or indicators of well-being, satisfaction, and motivation [5.3c(2)] might include: safety; absenteeism; turnover; turnover rate for customer-contact employees; grievances; strikes; other job actions; insurance costs; worker's compensation claims; and results of surveys. Results relative to such measures and/or indicators should be reported in Item 7.3.

This Item addresses the work environment, the employee support climate, and how they are tailored to support the well-being, satisfaction, and motivation of all employees.

Area 5.3a calls for information regarding a safe and healthful work environment to show how the organization includes such factors in its planning and improvement activities. Important factors in this Area include establishing appropriate measures and targets and recognizing that employee groups might experience very different environments.

Area 5.3b calls for information on the organization's approach to enhance employee well-being, satisfaction, and motivation based upon a holistic view of employees as key stakeholders. The Area emphasizes the need to consider a variety of services, facilities, activities, and opportunities to address the needs of different employee groups and to tailor these to their well-being, satisfaction, and motivation. Increasingly, the needs of a diverse workforce have to be addressed.

Most organizations, regardless of size, have many opportunities to contribute to employee well-being, satisfaction, and motivation. Examples of services, facilities, activities, and other opportunities are: personal and career counseling; career development and employability services; recreational or cultural activities; formal and informal recognition; non–work-related education; day care; special leave for family responsibilities and/or for community service; home safety training; flexible work hours; outplacement; and retiree benefits, including extended health care. Also, these services might include career enhancement activities such as skills assessments, helping employees develop learning objectives and plans, and conducting employability assessments.

As the workforce becomes more diverse (including employees that may work in other countries for multinational companies) it becomes more important to consider and support the needs of those employees with different services.

Area 5.3c calls for information on how the organization determines employee well-being, satisfaction, and motivation. The Area recognizes that many factors might affect employees. Although satisfaction with pay and promotion potential is important, these factors might not be adequate to assess the overall climate for motivation and high performance. For this reason, the organization might need to consider a variety of factors that might affect well-being, satisfaction, and motivation, such as: effective employee problem or grievance resolution; safety; employee views of leadership and management; employee development and career opportunities; employee preparation for changes in technology or work organization; work environment; workload; cooperation and teamwork; recognition; benefits; communications; job security; compensation; diversity; and capability to provide required services to customers.

In addition to formal or informal survey results, other measures and/or indicators of well-being, satisfaction, and motivation might include safety, absenteeism, turnover, turnover rate for customer-contact employees, grievances, strikes, and worker's compensation claims. Declining rates of employees participating in satisfaction surveys voluntarily may indicate growing dissatisfaction with the survey or that leaders do not use the survey results to drive improvements. Further understanding of these factors could be developed through exit interviews with departing employees.

Area 5.3c also addresses how the information and data on the well-being, satisfaction, and motivation of employees are actually used in identifying improvement priorities. Priority setting might draw upon human resource results presented in Item 7.3 and might involve addressing employee problems based on impact on organizational performance.

Factors inhibiting motivation need to be prioritized and addressed. Failure to address these factors is likely to result in even more problem symptoms and adversely affect the results (Item 7.3).

5.3 Employee Well-Being and Satisfaction

How the organization maintains a work environment and employee support climate that supports the well-being, satisfaction, and motivation of employees

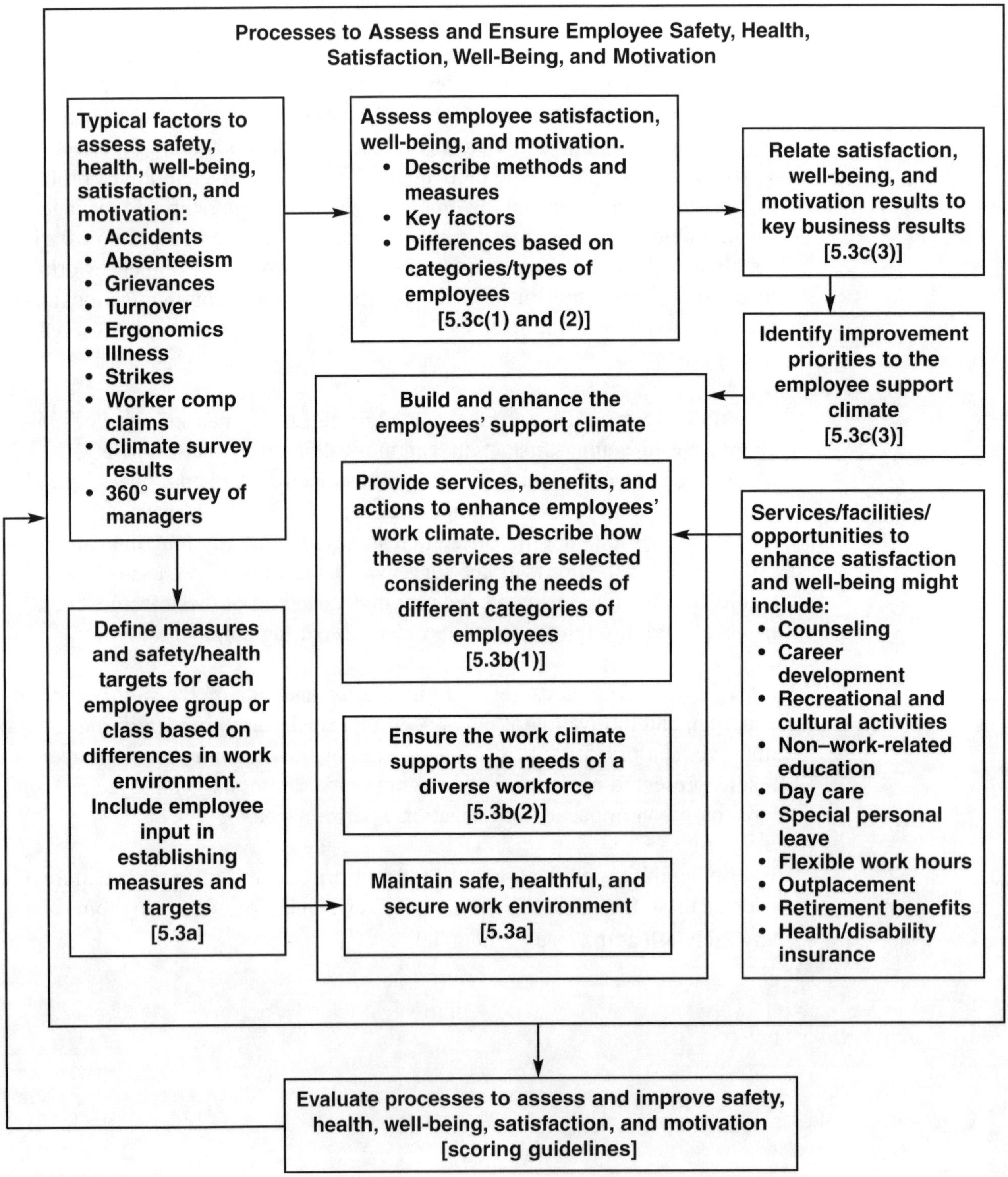

5.3 Employee Well-Being and Satisfaction Item Linkages

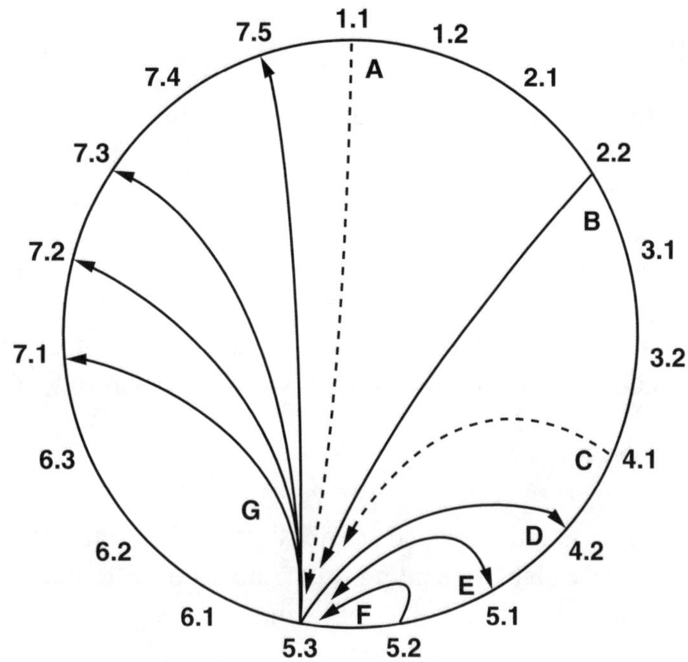

Nature of Relationship	
A	Leaders at all levels [1.1] have responsibility for enhancing employee morale and well-being [5.3].
B	Human resource development plans [2.2a] address morale and well-being concerns [5.3].
C	Key benchmarking data [4.1] are used to design processes to enhance employee morale and well-being [5.3].
D	Information regarding employee well-being and morale [5.3c] is used to gain a better understanding of problems and performance capabilities [4.2].
E	High morale [5.3] enhances employee participation, self-direction, and initiative [5.1], and vice versa.
F	Training systems [5.2] enhance employee development, leading to improved employee morale and well-being [5.3].
G	Systems that enhance employee satisfaction and well-being [5.3] can boost performance [7.2 and 7.5] and customer satisfaction [7.1]. Specific results of employee well-being and satisfaction systems are reported in 7.3.

5.3 Employee Well-Being and Satisfaction—Sample Effective Practices

A. Work Environment

- Quality activities consider issues relating to employee health, safety, and workplace environment. Plans exist to optimize these conditions and eliminate adverse conditions.
- Root causes for health and safety problems are systematically identified and eliminated. Corrective actions are communicated widely to help prevent the problem in other parts of the organization.
- Targets are set and reviewed for all key health, safety, and ergonomic factors affecting the employees' work environment.

B. Employee Support Climate

- Special activities and services are available for employees. These can be quite varied, depending on the needs of different employee categories. Examples include the following:
  - Flexible benefits plan including health care, on-site day care, dental, portable retirement, education (both work and non–work-related), maternity, paternity, and family illness leave.
  - Group purchasing power program where the number of participating merchants is increasing steadily.
  - Special facilities for employee meetings to discuss their concerns.
- Senior leaders build a work climate that addresses the needs of a diverse workforce. Recruitment and training are tools to enhance the work climate.

C. Employee Satisfaction

- Key employee satisfaction opinion indicators are gathered periodically based on the stability of the organization (organizations in the midst of rapid change conduct assessments more frequently).
- On-demand electronic surveys are available for quick response and tabulations any time managers need employee satisfaction feedback.
- Satisfaction data are derived from employee focus groups, e-mail data, employee satisfaction survey results, turnover, absenteeism, stress-related disorders, and other data that reflect employee satisfaction. (A key employee satisfaction indicator is one that reflects conditions affecting employee morale and motivation.)

- Managers use the results of these surveys to focus improvements in work systems and enhance employee satisfaction. Actions to improve satisfaction are clearly tied to assessments so employees understand the value of the assessment, and the improvement initiative does not appear random or capricious.
- Employee satisfaction indicators are correlated with drivers of business success to help identify where resources should be placed to provide maximum business benefit.
- Methods to improve how employee satisfaction is determined are systematically evaluated and improved. Techniques to actually improve employee satisfaction and well-being are, themselves, evaluated and refined consistently.

6 Process Management—85 Points

The **Process Management** Category examines the key aspects of your organization's process management, including customer focused design, product and service delivery, support, and supplier and partnering processes involving all work units.

Process Management is the focal point within the Criteria for all key work processes. Built into the Category are the central requirements for efficient and effective process management—effective design, a prevention orientation, linkage to suppliers and partners, operational performance, cycle time, and evaluation and continuous improvement.

Flexibility, cost reduction, and cycle time reduction are increasingly important in all aspects of process management and organizational design. In simplest terms, flexibility refers to the ability to adapt quickly and effectively to changing requirements. Depending on the nature of the organization's strategy and markets, flexibility might mean rapid changeover from one product to another, rapid response to changing demands, or the ability to produce a wide range of customized services. Flexibility might demand special strategies such as implementing modular designs, sharing components, sharing manufacturing lines, and providing specialized training. Flexibility also increasingly involves outsourcing decisions, agreements with key suppliers, and novel partnering arrangements.

Cost and cycle time reduction often involve many of the same process management strategies as achieving flexibility. Thus, it is crucial to utilize key measures for these requirements in overall process management.

Process management contains three Items that evaluate the management of product and service processes, support processes, and supplier and partnering processes.

Product and Service Processes

- Design, develop, and introduce products and services to meet customer requirements, operational performance requirements, and market requirements
- Ensure a rapid, efficient, trouble-free introduction
- Manage and continuously improve operating processes

Support Processes

- Design, develop, and introduce products and services to meet customer requirements, operational performance requirements, and market requirements
- Manage and continuosly improve support processes

Supplier and Partnering Performance

- Ensure performance requirements are met, minimize supplier cost, and help suppliers improve performance and their ability to help you

6.1 Product and Service Processes (55 points) Approach/Deployment Scoring

Describe how your organization manages key product and service design and delivery processes.

Within your response, include answers to the following questions:

a. *Design Processes*

(1) What are your design processes for products/services and their related production/delivery processes?
(2) How do you incorporate changing customer/market requirements into product/service designs and production/delivery systems and processes?
(3) How do you incorporate new technology into products/services and into production/delivery systems and processes, as appropriate?
(4) How do your design processes address design quality and cycle time, transfer of learning from past projects and other parts of the organization, cost control, new design technology, productivity, and other efficiency/effectiveness factors?
(5) How do you ensure that your production/delivery process design accommodates all key operational performance requirements?
(6) How do you coordinate and test design and production/delivery processes to ensure capability for trouble-free and timely introduction of products/services?

b. *Production/Delivery Processes*

(1) What are your key production/delivery processes and their key performance requirements?

Continued on next page

(2) How does your day-to-day operation of key production/delivery processes ensure meeting key performance requirements?
(3) What are your key performance measures and/or indicators used for the control and improvement of these processes? Include how real-time customer input is sought, as appropriate.
(4) How do you improve your production/delivery processes to achieve better process performance and improvements to products/services, as appropriate? How are improvements shared with other organizational units and processes, as appropriate?

Notes:

N1. Product and service design, production, and delivery differ greatly among organizations, depending upon many factors. These factors include the nature of the products and services, technology requirements, issues of modularity and parts commonality, customer and supplier relationships and involvement, and product and service customization. Responses to Item 6.1 should address the most critical requirements for your business.

N2. Responses to Item 6.1 should include how customers and key suppliers and partners are involved in design processes, as appropriate.

N3. Results of operational improvements in product and service design and delivery processes should be reported in Item 7.5. Results of improvements in product and service performance should be reported in Item 7.1.

This Item examines how the organization designs, introduces, and improves its products and services. It also examines how production/delivery processes are operated and improved. The trouble-free introduction of new products and services is important to the organization's overall performance. This requires effective coordination, starting early in the product and service design phase. The Item also examines organizational learning through a focus on how learnings in one process or work unit are replicated and added to the knowledge base of other projects or work units. This is a proactive form of "internal" benchmarking.

Area 6.1a calls for information on the design of products and services, and their production/delivery processes. Aspects of this design include:

- How changing customer and market requirements and technology are incorporated into product and service designs and production/delivery processes;
- How new technology is incorporated into products/services and production/ delivery processes. Customer questions, complaint data (from Item 3.2) are used in this delineation; and

- How design and production/delivery processes are coordinated to ensure trouble-free and timely introduction and delivery of products and services.

Design approaches could differ significantly depending upon the nature of the products/services—whether the products/services are entirely new, modified slightly, or involve major process changes. Responses should reflect the key requirements for the products and services. Factors that might need to be considered in design include: health; safety; long-term performance; environmental impact; "green" manufacturing; measurement capability; process capability; manufacturability; maintainability; supplier capability; and documentation needed (if any) to ensure design processes are consistently followed. Effective design must also consider cycle time and productivity of production and delivery processes. This might involve detailed mapping of manufacturing or service processes and redesigning ("reengineering") those processes to achieve efficiency, as well as to meet changing customer requirements.

Organizations with suppliers that are crucial to design and delivery should also consider, at the design stage, how these suppliers might contribute to or disrupt the success of the product or service launch. Overall, effective design must take into account all stakeholders in the value chain from key suppliers to dealers and distributors. If many design projects are carried out in parallel, or if the organization's products utilize parts, equipment, and facilities used for other products, coordination of resources might be a major concern, and might offer means to significantly reduce unit costs and time to market. This coordination should be addressed in responding to Area 6.1a.

Coordination of design processing involves many work units and/or individuals whose performance materially affects overall process outcome. This might include groups such as research and development (R&D), marketing, design, and product/process engineering.

Area 6.1b calls for information on the management and improvement of key production/delivery processes. The information required includes a description of the key processes and their specific requirements, and how performance relative to these requirements is determined and maintained. Specific reference is made to key performance measurements and customer interactions. This requires the identification of critical points in processes for measurement, observation, or interaction. The intent is that these activities occur at the earliest points possible in processes to minimize problems that may result from deviations from expected performance. Expected performance frequently requires setting performance levels or standards to guide ongoing decision making. When deviations occur, prompt corrective action is required to restore the performance of the process to its design specifications. Depending on the nature of the process, the correction could involve technical and/or human factors. Proper correction involves changes at the source (root cause) of the deviation. Such corrective action should minimize the likelihood of this type of variation occurring anywhere else in the organization. The sooner a problem is known, the sooner it can be eliminated. Accordingly, real-time, in-process measures should be taken to minimize delay in finding, fixing, and preventing problems from recurring.

When customer interactions are involved, differences among customers must be considered in evaluating how well the process is performing. This might entail specific or general contingencies, depending on the customer information gathered. This is especially true of professional and personal services.

Area 6.1b calls for information on how processes are improved to achieve better performance. Better performance means not only better quality from the customers' perspective but also better financial and operational performance—such as productivity—from the organization's perspective. A variety of process improvement approaches are commonly used. These include:

- Sharing successful strategies across the organization;
- Process analysis and research (e.g., process mapping, optimization experiments, and error proofing);
- Research and development results;
- Benchmarking;
- Using alternative technology; and
- Using information from customers of the processes—within and outside the organization.

Process improvement approaches might utilize financial data to evaluate alternatives and set priorities. Together, these approaches offer a wide range of possibilities, including complete redesign ("reengineering") of processes.

6.1 Product and Service Processes

How products and services as well as production/delivery processes are designed, managed, and improved

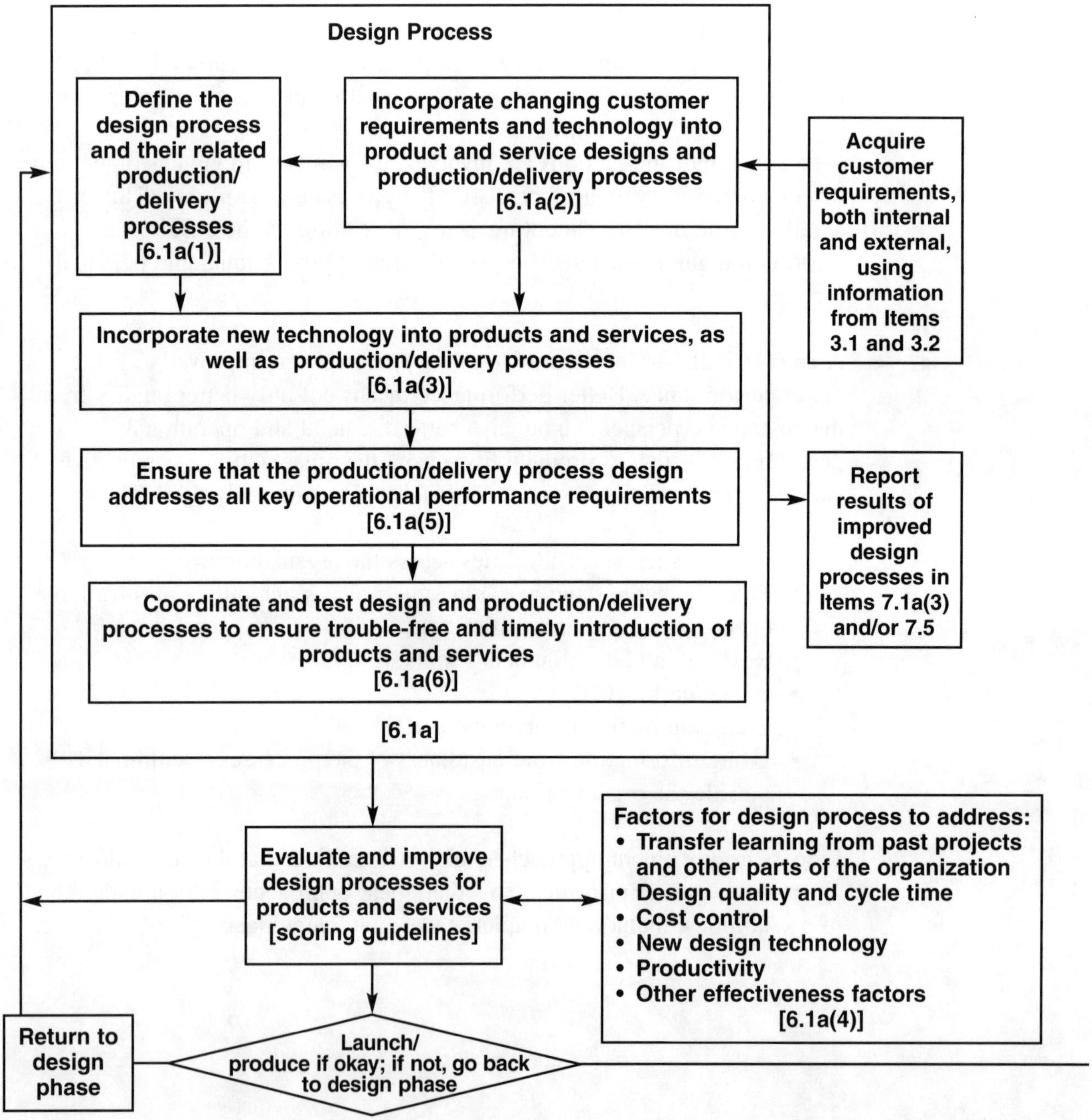

continued on next page

continued from previous page

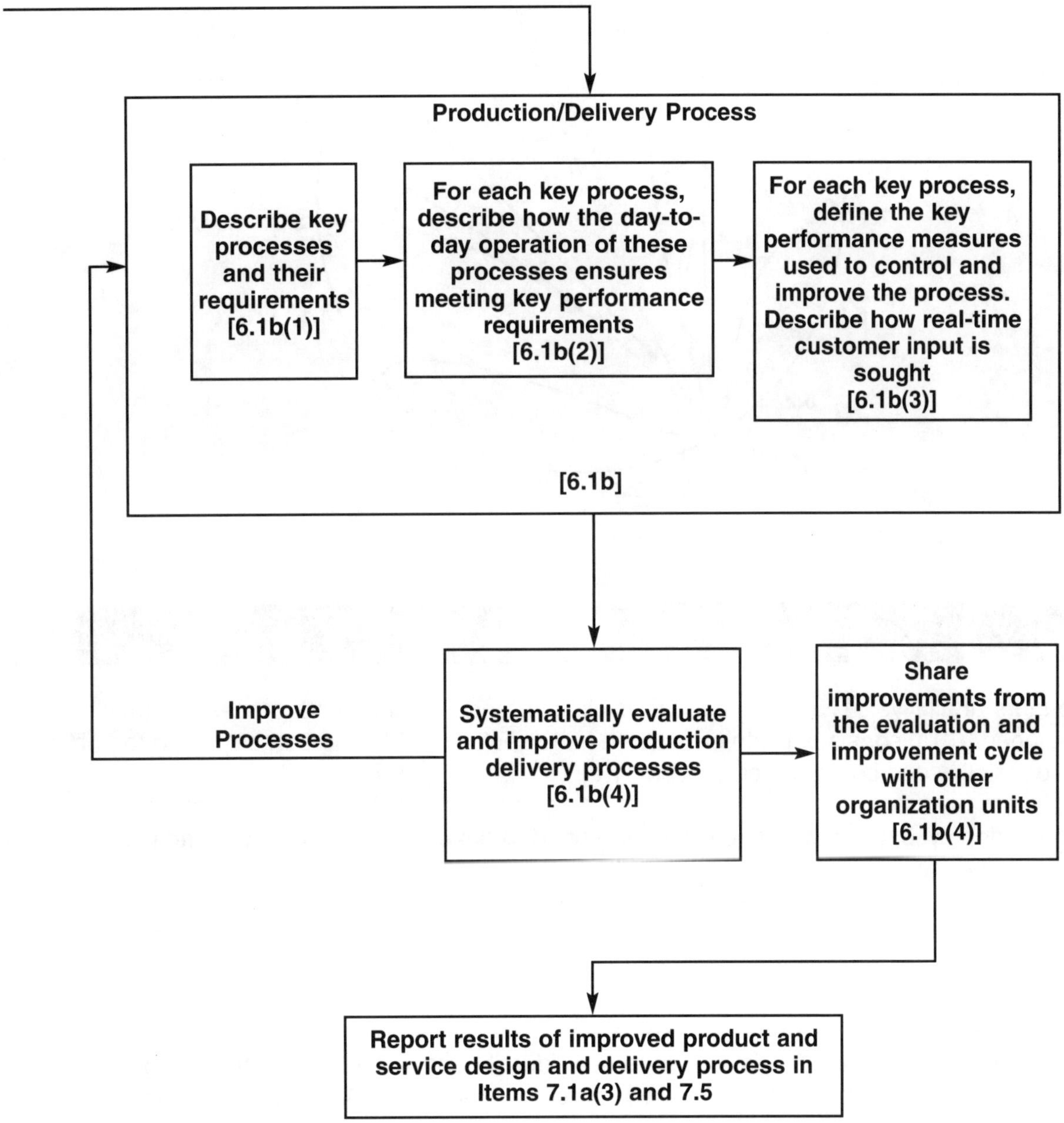

6.1 Product and Service Processes Item Linkages

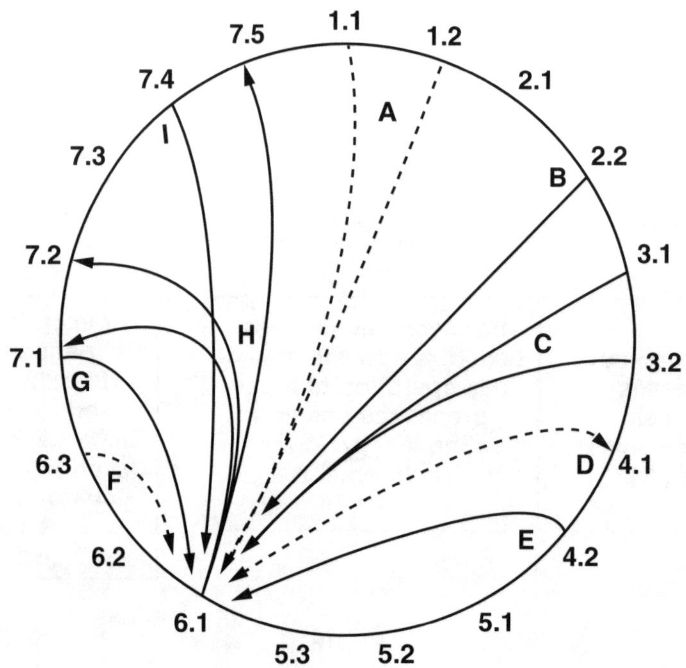

Nature of Relationship	
A	Leaders at all levels [1.1] have a responsibility for ensuring that work processes are designed [6.1a] consistent with organizational objectives, including those relating to public responsibility and corporate citizenship [1.2].
B	Goals, deployed to the workforce [2.2], are used to drive and align actions to achieve improved performance [6.1].
C	Information about customer requirements [3.1] and information from customer hot lines (complaints) through customer-contact employees [3.2a] is used to design or modify products and services to better meet requirements.
D	Critical work processes [6.1] are used to help identify and prioritize benchmarking or comparison targets [4.1]. Benchmarking and comparison data [4.1] are used to improve work processes [6.1].

Continued on next page

Nature of Relationship (continued)	
E	Priorities for work process improvements [6.1] are set based on performance data analysis [4.2].
F	Effective management of supplier and partner performance [6.3] can result in improved operations processes [6.1] by reducing error, rework, and delay.
G	Information about customer satisfaction [7.1] is used to target improvement efforts in product and service design and development processes [6.1].
H	Processes ensure that products and services are designed to meet customer requirements and have a trouble-free introduction [6.1a], and address product and service production and delivery [6.1b], product and service operating performance [7.1a(3) and 7.5], and financial results [7.2].
I	Information about supplier performance [7.4] is essential to the design and implementation of new, modified, or customized products and services [6.1a].

6.1 Product and Service Processes—Sample Effective Practices

A. Design Processes

- A systematic, iterative process (such as quality function deployment) is used to maintain a focus on the voice of the customer and convert customer requirements into product or service design, production, and delivery.
- Product design requirements are systematically translated into process specifications, with measurement plans to monitor process consistency.
- The work of various functions is coordinated to bring the product or service through the design-to-delivery phases. Functional barriers between units have been eliminated organization-wide.
- Concurrent engineering is used to operate several processes (for example, product and service planning, R&D, manufacturing, marketing, supplier certification) in parallel as much as possible, rather than operating in sequence. All activities are closely coordinated through effective communication and teamwork.
- Internal process capacity and supplier capability, using measures such as C_{pk}, are reviewed and considered before production and delivery process designs or plans are finalized.
- Market, design, production, service, and delivery reviews occur at defined intervals or as needed.
- Steps are taken (such as design testing or prototyping) to ensure that the production and delivery process will work as designed, and will meet customer requirements.
- Design processes are evaluated and improvements have been made so that future designs are developed faster (shorter cycle time), at lower cost, and with higher quality, relative to key product or service characteristics that predict customer satisfaction.

B. Production/Delivery Processes

- Performance requirements (from Item 6.1a, design processes, and Item 3.1, customer requirements) are set using facts and data and are monitored using statistical or other process control techniques.
- Production and service delivery processes are measured and tracked. Measures (quantitative and qualitative) should reflect or assess the extent to which customer requirements are met, as well as production consistency.

- For processes that produce defects (out-of-control processes), root causes are quickly and systematically identified and corrective action is taken to prevent their recurrence.
- Corrections are monitored and verified. Improvements are shared throughout the organization.
- Processes are systematically reviewed to improve productivity, reduce cycle time and waste, and increase quality.
- Tools are used—such as flowcharting, work redesign, and reengineering—throughout the organization to improve work processes.
- Benchmarking, competitive comparison data, or information from customers of the process (in or out of the organization) are used to gain insight to improve processes.

6.2 Support Processes (15 points) Approach/Deployment Scoring

Describe how your organization manages its key support processes.

Within your response, include answers to the following questions:

a. Support Processes

(1) What are your key support processes?

(2) How do you determine key support process requirements, incorporating input from internal and/or external customers, as appropriate? What are the key operational requirements (such as productivity and cycle time) for the processes?

(3) How do you design these processes to meet all the key requirements?

(4) How does your day-to-day operation of key support processes ensure meeting key performance requirements? How do you determine and use in-process measures and/or customer feedback in your support processes?

(5) How do you improve your support processes to achieve better performance and to keep them current with business needs and directions, as appropriate? How are improvements shared with other organizational units and processes, as appropriate?

Notes:

N1. Support processes are those that support the organization's products/services design and delivery processes, and business operations. For many organizations, this might include information and knowledge management, finance and accounting, facilities management, research and development (R&D), administration, and sales/marketing. The key support processes to be included in Item 6.2 are unique to each organization and how it operates. Focus should be on the most important processes not addressed in Items 6.1 and 6.3.

N2. Results of improvements in key support processes and key support process performance results should be reported in Item 7.5.

This Item applies requirements to the support area that are similar to those for operations (Item 6.1). Accordingly, this Item addresses how the organization designs, implements, operates, and improves its support processes. Support processes are those that support the organization's product and service design and delivery processes, but are not usually designed in detail with the products and services themselves, because their requirements usually do not depend significantly upon product and service characteristics.

Support process design requirements are usually driven by internal requirements, and they must be coordinated and integrated to ensure efficient and effective linkage and performance. Support processes might include finance and accounting, software services, sales, marketing, public relations, information services, human resources, legal services, plant and facilities management, research and development, and secretarial and other administrative services.

The Item also calls for information on how the organization maintains the performance consistency of the key support processes. Key support processes and their principal requirements must be well-defined, including key in-process measurements and customer interactions. These principal requirements are similar to those in Area 6.1b.

Item 6.2 also calls for information on how the organization improves and keeps its key support processes current with business needs and directions, and how improvements are shared with other organizational units or processes. Four possible improvement approaches are:

- Process analysis and research;
- Benchmarking;
- Use of alternative technology; and
- Use of information from customers of the processes—within and outside the organization.

Together, these approaches offer a wide range of possibilities, including complete redesign ("reengineering") of processes.

6.2 Support Processes

How key support processes are designed, managed, and improved

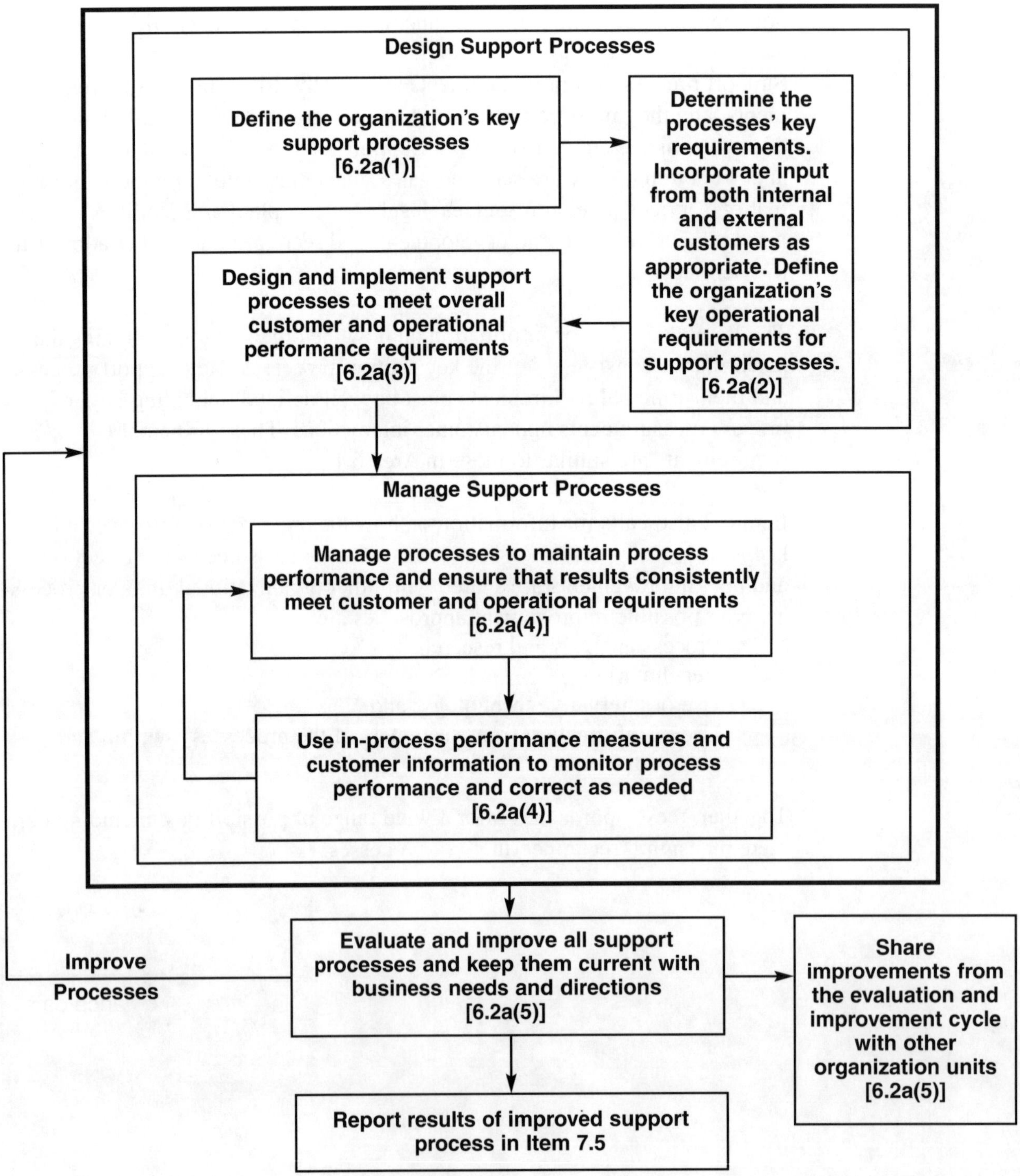

6.2 Support Processes Item Linkages

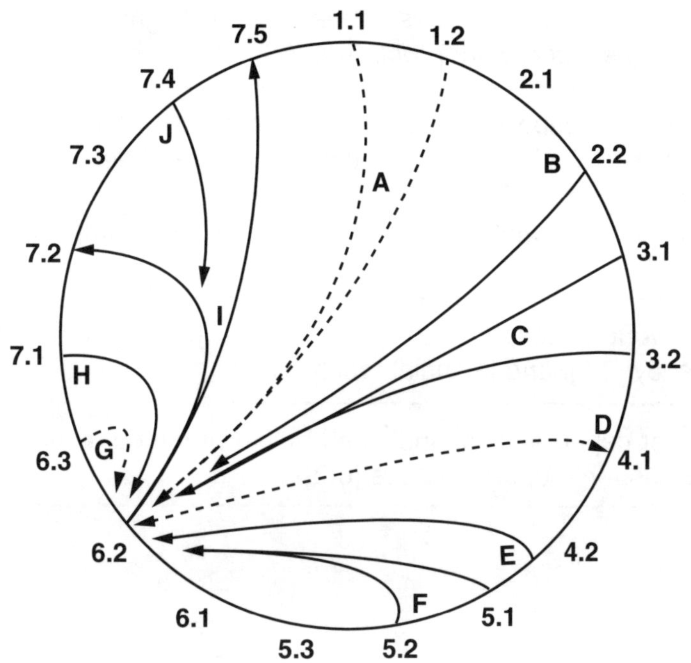

Nature of Relationship	
A	Leaders at all levels [1.1] ensure that support processes [6.2] are aligned with organization priorities, including regulatory and public responsibilities [1.2].
B	Goals deployed to the workforce [2.2], are used to drive and align actions to achieve improved support performance [6.2].
C	Information about customer requirements [3.1] and from customer contact personnel [3.2a] is used to identify improvement opportunities in support work processes [6.2].
D	Critical work processes in the support area [6.2] are used to help identify and prioritize benchmarking targets [4.1]. Benchmarking data [4.1] are used to improve support work processes [6.2].
E	Priorities for support work processes improvement [6.2] are set based on performance data and analysis [4.2].

Continued on next page

	Nature of Relationship (continued)
F	High performance flexible work systems and effective recognition [5.1] and training [5.2] are essential to improving support work processes [6.2].
G	Effective management of supplier and partner performance [6.3] may be required to improve support work processes [6.2] by reducing rework, error, and delay.
H	Information about customer satisfaction [7.1] is used to target improvement efforts in support work processes [6.2].
I	Improved support work processes [6.2] produce better product and service quality, operational efficiency [7.5], and financial results [7.2].
J	Supplier and partner capabilities, as indicated by performance results [7.4], are considered in the design process for support services [6.2].

6.2 Support Processes—Sample Effective Practices

A. Support Processes

- A formal process exists to understand internal customer requirements, translate those requirements into efficient service processes, and measure their effectiveness.
- Specific improvements in support services are made with the same rigor and concern for the internal and external customer as improvements in core operating processes.
- All key support services are subject to continuous review and improvements in performance and customer satisfaction.
- Systems to ensure process performance are maintained, and customer requirements are met. In-process measures are defined and monitored to ensure early alert of problem.
- Root causes of problems are systematically identified and corrected for processes that produce defects.
- Corrections are monitored and verified. Processes used and results obtained should be systematic and integrated throughout the organization.
- Support processes are systematically reviewed to improve productivity, reduce cycle time and waste, and increase quality. Ideas are shared throughout the organization.
- Work process simplification or improvement tools are used with measurable sustained results.
- Stretch goals are used to drive higher levels of performance.
- Benchmarking, competitive comparison data, or information from customers of the process (in or out of the organization) are used to gain insight to improve processes.

6.3 Supplier and Partnering Processes (15 points) Approach/Deployment Scoring

Describe how your organization manages its key supplier and/or partnering interactions and processes.

Within your response, include answers to the following questions:

a. Supplier and Partnering Processes

(1) What key products/services do you purchase from suppliers and/or partners?

(2) How do you incorporate performance requirements into supplier and/or partner process management? What key performance requirements must your suppliers and/or partners meet to fulfill your overall requirements?

(3) How do you ensure that your performance requirements are met? How do you provide timely and actionable feedback to suppliers and/or partners? Include the key performance measures and/or indicators and any targets you use for supplier and/or partner assessment.

(4) How do you minimize overall costs associated with inspections, tests, and process and/or performance audits?

(5) How do you provide business assistance and/or incentives to suppliers and/or partners to help them improve their overall performance and to improve their abilities to contribute to your current and longer-term performance?

(6) How do you improve your supplier and/or partner processes, including your role as supportive customer/partner, to keep current with your business needs and directions? How are improvements shared throughout your organization, as appropriate?

Notes:

N1. Supplier and partnering processes might include processes for supply chain improvement and optimization, beyond direct suppliers and partners.

N2. If your organization selects preferred suppliers and/or partners based upon volume of business or criticality of their supplied products and/or services, include selection criteria in the response.

N3. Results of improvements in supplier and partnering processes and supplier/partner performance results should be reported in Item 7.4.

This Item addresses how the organization designs, implements, operates, and improves its supplier and partnering processes and relationships. It also addresses supplier and partner performance management and improvement.

The term "supplier" refers to other organizations outside the company, as well as other units of the parent organization that provide goods and services (except for those units that are considered "support" and covered in Item 6.2).

Suppliers' and partners' goods and services may be used at any stage in the production, design, delivery, and use of the organization's products and services. Thus, suppliers include businesses such as distributors, dealers, warranty repair services, transportation, contractors, and franchises, as well as those that provide materials and components. Suppliers also include service suppliers, such as health care, training, and education providers.

The Item places particular emphasis on the unique relationships that organizations are building with key and preferred suppliers, including establishing partnering relationships. For many organizations, these suppliers and partners are an increasingly important part of achieving not only high performance and lower-cost objectives, but also strategic objectives. For example, they might provide unique design, integration, and marketing capabilities.

The key performance requirements for suppliers and partners must be defined by the organization. These requirements are the principal factors involved in the organization's purchases, such as quality, delivery, and price. Processes for determining whether or not these requirements are met might include audits, process reviews, receiving inspections, certification, testing, and rating systems.

The organization must develop plans and take action to improve the ability of suppliers and partners to contribute to achieving your organization's performance goals. These plans and actions might include one or more of the following:

- Improving your own procurement and supplier management processes (including seeking feedback from suppliers and internal customers);
- Changing supplier selection leading to a reduction in the number of suppliers and enhancement of partnership agreements;
- Joint planning;
- Rapid information and data exchanges;
- Use of benchmarking and comparative information;
- Customer-supplier teams;
- Providing training to suppliers and partners;
- Long-term agreements;
- Incentives; and
- Recognition.

6.3 Supplier and Partnering Processes

How the supplier and partnering process, relationship, and performance are designed, managed, and improved

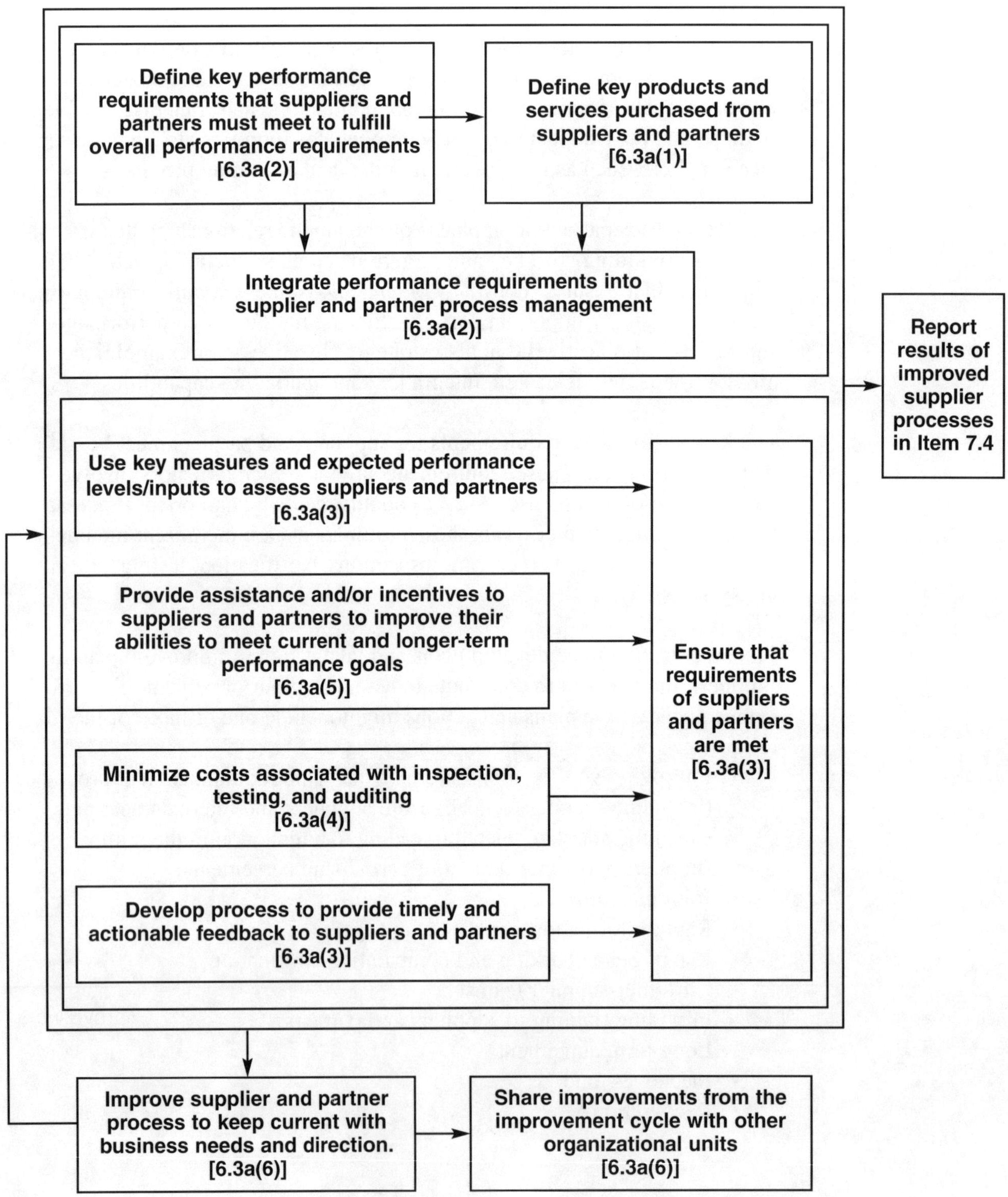

6.3 Supplier and Partnering Processes Item Linkages

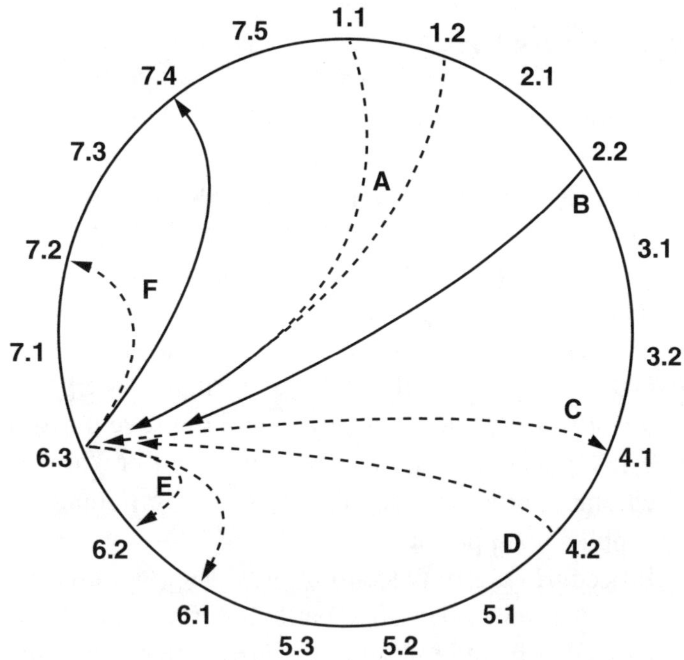

	Nature of Relationship
A	Leaders at all levels [1.1] who interact with suppliers and partners have a responsibility to ensure systematic improvement of performance on key indicators [6.3] and ensure that suppliers and partners do not act in a manner inconsistent with the organization's commitment to the public, including regulatory compliance [1.2].
B	Goals [2.2], deployed through the key supplier chain, are used to drive improved supplier performance [6.3] in critical areas.
C	Problems and issues with supplier performance [6.3] are used to help identify and prioritize benchmarking targets [4.1]. Benchmarking and comparison data [4.1] are used to improve supplier performance initiatives [6.3].
D	Data are analyzed [4.2] to help improve supplier and partner work processes and performance [6.3].
E	Improved supplier performance [6.3] may be required to, and typically helps to, improve work processes [6.1 and 6.2].
F	Improved supplier processes [6.3] result in better supplier performance [7.4] and possibly better financial performance [7.2].

6.3 Supplier and Partnering Processes—Sample Effective Practices

A. Supplier and Partnering Processes

- Performance requirements are clearly defined in measurable terms and communicated to suppliers.
- Decisions on which suppliers are selected are driven by measurable performance characteristics of the supplier's capabilities to achieve high levels of performance excellence and exceed requirements, rather than primarily on price.
- Measures of expected supplier performance are in place.
- Data on supplier and partner performance are provided to suppliers frequently so that they can adjust and improve performance rapidly.
- The organization has a system in place to review and improve its own procurement processes and processes for communicating with and selecting suppliers and partners.
- Procedures are in place to improve supplier and partner performance (for example, fewer defective parts, less rework and scrap, faster response time) that include training or certification programs. The organization systematically helps its key suppliers improve their own performance and capabilities. This information is shared throughout the organization.
- Actions are taken to reduce unnecessary costs—such as incoming inspection, testing, or audits—by improving the internal performance systems of suppliers and partners.

7 Business Results—450 Points

The **Business Results** Category examines your organization's performance and improvement in key business areas—customer satisfaction, product and service performance, financial and marketplace performance, human resource results, supplier and partner results, and operational performance. Also examined are performance levels relative to competitors.

The Business Results Category provides a results focus that encompasses the customer's evaluation of the organization's products and services, overall financial and market performance, and results of all key processes and process improvement activities. Through this focus, the Criteria's dual purposes—superior value of offerings as viewed by customers and the marketplace, and superior organizational performance reflected in operational and financial indicators—are maintained. Category 7 thus provides "real-time" information (measures of progress) for evaluation and improvement of processes, products, and services, aligned with overall organizational strategy. Item 4.2 calls for analysis of business results data and information to determine overall organizational performance.

The Category of business results evaluates the organization's performance and improvement in areas important to business success.

Current levels and improvement trends for

- Customer satisfaction and dissatisfaction and product and service quality broken out by appropriate customer groups and market segments
- Financial and marketplace performance
- Human resource performance broken out by employee types and categories as appropriate
- Supplier and partner performance
- Operational performance

Include appropriate comparative data—define what "good" means.

7.1 Customer Focused Results (115 points) Results Scoring

Summarize your organization's customer focused results, including customer satisfaction and product and service performance results. Segment your results by customer groups and market segments, as appropriate. Include appropriate comparative data.

Provide data and information to answer the following questions:

a. Customer Focused Results

(1) What are your current levels and trends in key measures and/or indicators of customer satisfaction, dissatisfaction, and satisfaction relative to competitors?

(2) What are your current levels and trends in key measures and/or indicators of customer loyalty, positive referral, customer-perceived value, and/or customer relationship building, as appropriate?

(3) What are your current levels and trends in key measures and/or indicators of product and service performance?

Notes:

N1. Customer satisfaction and dissatisfaction results reported in this Item should relate to determination methods and data described in Item 3.2.

N2. Measures and/or indicators of customer satisfaction relative to competitors might include objective information and data from customers and independent organizations.

N3. Comparative performance of products and services and product/service performance measures that serve as indicators of customer satisfaction should be included in 7.1a(3).

N4. The combination of direct customer measures/ indicators in 7.1a(1) and 7.1a(2) with product and service performance measures/indicators in 7.1a(3) provides an opportunity to determine cause and effect relationships between product/service attributes and evidence of customer satisfaction, loyalty, positive referral, etc.

This Item addresses the results of most significance to assessing the organization's customer-related performance—customer satisfaction, customer dissatisfaction, customer satisfaction relative to competitors, and product/service performance. The Item calls for the use of all relevant data and information to help explain or define the organization's performance as viewed by the customer. Relevant data and information include: customer satisfaction and dissatisfaction; retention, gains, and losses of customers and customer accounts; positive customer referrals; customer complaints and warranty claims; customer-perceived value based on quality and price; and competitive awards, ratings, and recognition from customers and independent organizations.

For 1999, the Performance Excellence Criteria also seek relevant data and information pertaining to product and service performance measures, especially those that serve as *predictors* of customer satisfaction. (Note: This type of result was previously reported in Item 7.5.) Taken together, these product and service features are derived from the customer-related "listening posts." If properly selected, improvements in the features should show a strong, positive correlation with customer and marketplace improvement indicators. The correlation between product/service performance and customer indicators is a critical management tool—a device for defining and focusing on key quality and customer requirements and for identifying product/service differentiators in the marketplace. The results reported in Item 7.1 might reveal emerging or changing market segments, the changing importance of requirements, or even the potential obsolescence of products and/or services. (These data and correlations are analyzed as a part of Item 4.2, and monitored by leaders in Item 1.1b.)

Product/service performance appropriate for inclusion might be based upon one or more of the following:

- Internal (organizational) measurements;
- Field performance;
- Data collected by the organization or for the organization;
- Customer surveys on product and service performance; and
- Attributes that cannot be accurately assessed through direct measurement (e.g., ease of use) or when variability in customer expectations makes the customer's perception the most meaningful indicator (e.g., courtesy).

7.1 Customer Focused Results

The organization's customer satisfaction and customer dissatisfaction results using indicators of product/service performance that tend to be predictors of customer satisfaction

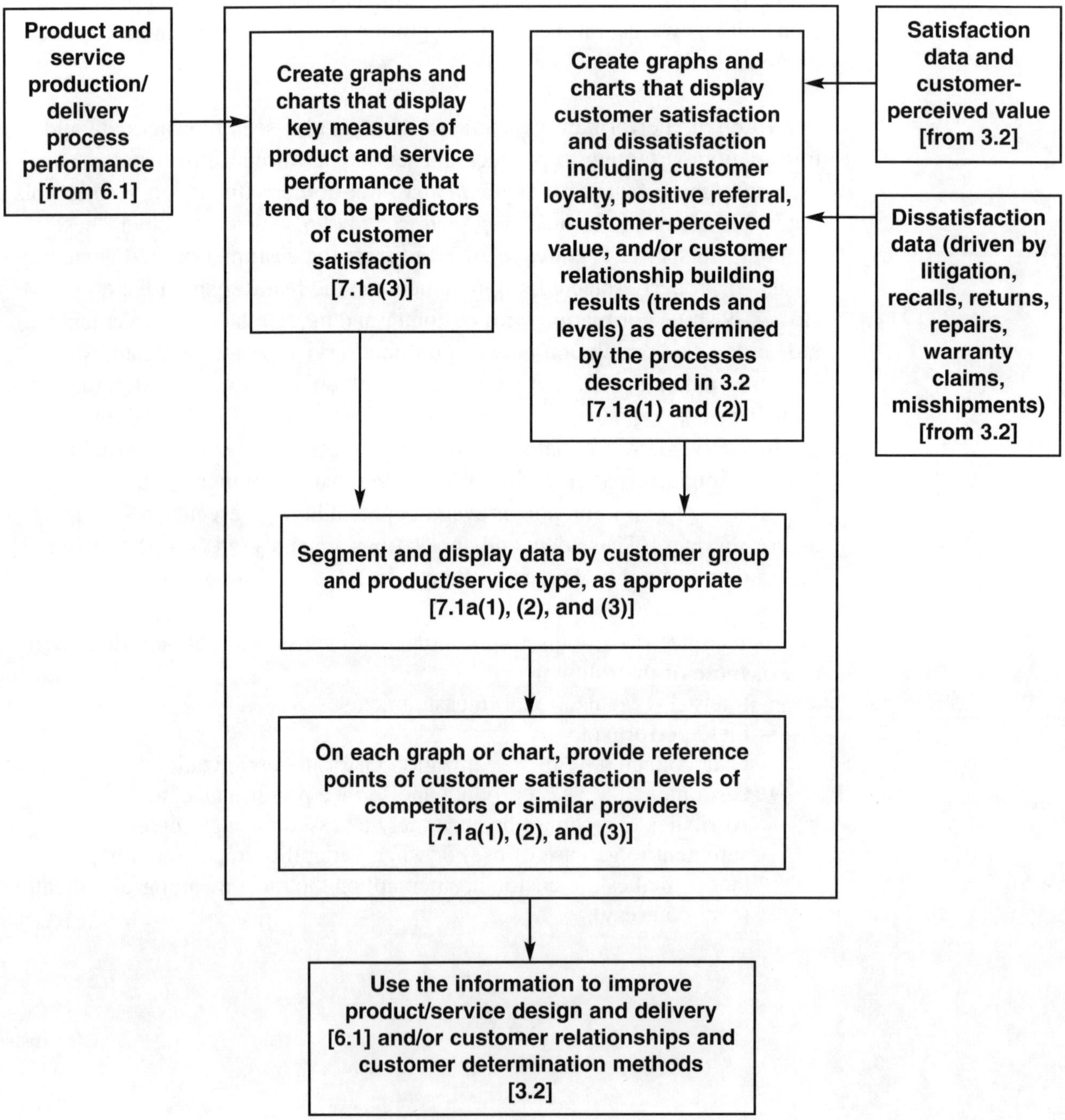

7.1 Customer Focused Results Item Linkages

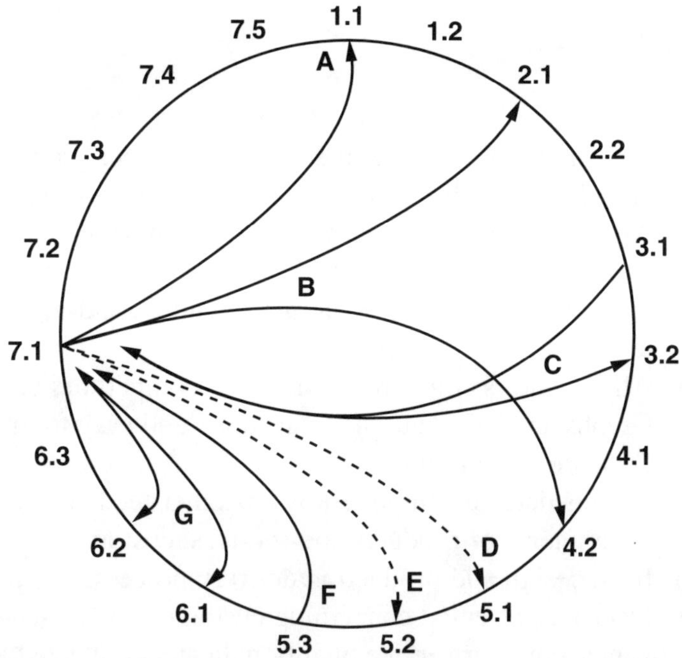

	Nature of Relationship
A	Data on levels of satisfaction of customers and indicators of product/service performance [7.1] are monitored by leaders at all levels [1.1].
B	Data on customer satisfaction and product/service performance indicators [7.1] are collected and used to analyze operational performance [4.2], and for strategic planning [2.1].
C	Processes used to gather intelligence about current customer requirements [3.1], strengthen customer relations [3.2a], and determine customer satisfaction [3.2b] are used to produce customer satisfaction results data [7.1]. In addition, customer satisfaction results [7.1] are used to set customer contact requirements (service standards) [3.2a].
D	Recognition and rewards [5.1b] may be based, in part, on customer satisfaction results [7.1].
E	Customer satisfaction data [7.1] are monitored, in part, to assess training effectiveness [5.2].
F	Systems to enhance employee satisfaction and well-being [5.3] can produce higher levels of customer satisfaction [7.1], especially from customer-contact employees.
G	Data on satisfaction or dissatisfaction of customers [7.1] are used to help design products and services and to improve operational [6.1] and support [6.2] processes. Design and production/delivery processes [6.1] have a direct effect on customer satisfaction/dissatisfaction results [7.1].

7.1 Customer Focused Results—Sample Effective Results

A. Customer Focused Results

- Trends and indicators of customer satisfaction and dissatisfaction (including complaint data), segmented by customer groups, are provided in graph and chart form for all key measures. Multiyear data are provided.
- All indicators show steady improvement. (Indicators include data collected in Area 3.2b such as customer assessments of products and services, customer awards, and customer retention, and in Item 6.1 such as quality levels and on-time delivery.)
- All indicators compare favorably to competitors or similar providers.
- Graphs and information are accurate and easy to understand.
- Data are not missing.
- Results data are supported by customer feedback, customers' overall assessments of products and services, customer awards, and indicators from design and production/delivery processes of products and services.
- Data are presented concerning customer dissatisfaction for the most relevant product or service quality indicators collected through the processes described in Item 3.2b (some of which may be referenced in the business overview).
- Operational data are presented that correlate with, and help predict, customer satisfaction. These data show consistently improving trends and levels that compare favorably with competitors.

7.2 Financial and Market Results (115 points) Results Scoring

Summarize your organization's key financial and marketplace performance results, segmented by market segments, as appropriate. Include appropriate comparative data.

Provide data and information to answer the following questions:

a. ***Financial and Market Results***

(1) What are your current levels and trends in key measures and/or indicators of financial performance, including aggregate measures of financial return and/or economic value, as appropriate?

(2) What are your current levels and trends in key measures and/or indicators of marketplace performance, including market share/position, business growth, and new markets entered, as appropriate?

Note:

Aggregate measures such as return on investment (ROI), asset utilization, operating margins, profitability, profitability by market/customer segment, liquidity, debt to equity ratio, value added per employee, and financial activity measures are appropriate for responding to 7.2a(1).

This Item addresses those factors that best reflect the organization's financial and marketplace performance. Measures reported in this Item will frequently be those key financial and market measures tracked by senior leadership on an ongoing basis to gauge overall performance and often used to determine incentive compensation for senior leaders. Measures of financial performance might include return on equity, return on investment, operating margins, pre-tax profit margin, earnings per share, profit forecast reliability, and other liquidity and financial activity measures. Marketplace performance could include market share measures of business growth, new product and geographic markets entered, and percent new product sales, as appropriate. Comparative data for these measures might include industry best, best competitor, industry average, and appropriate benchmarks from outside your industry.

7.2 Financial and Market Results

Results of improvement efforts using key measures and/or indicators of financial and market performance

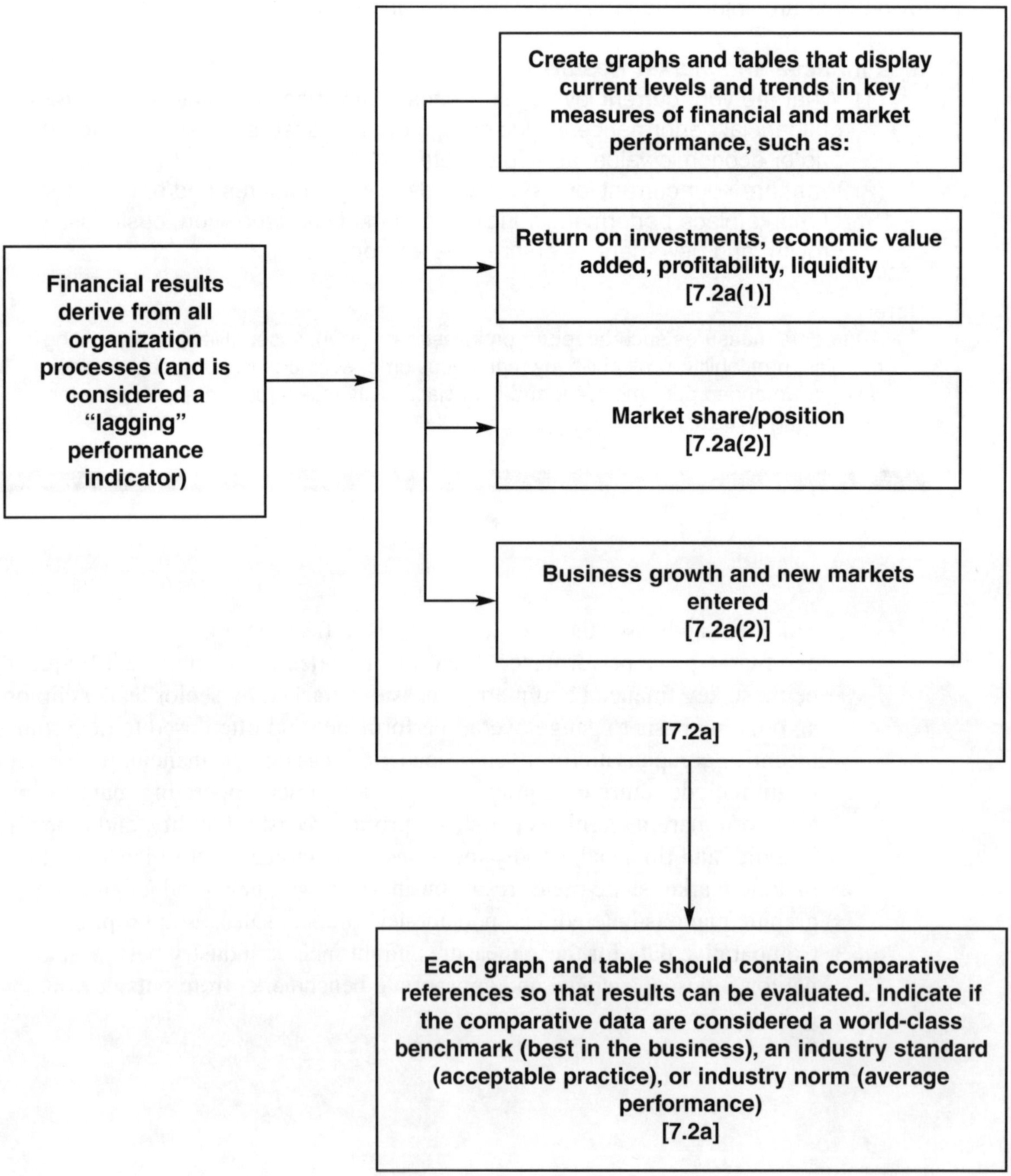

7.2 Financial and Market Results Item Linkages

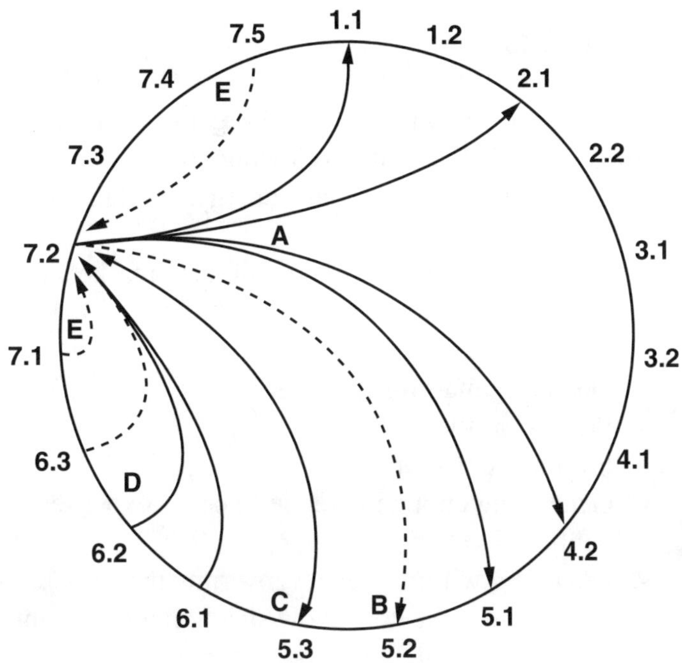

Nature of Relationship	
A	Financial and market results data [7.2] are used for strategic planning [2.1], leadership monitoring and decision making [1.1], and analysis [4.2], and may be used as a basis for compensation, recognition, and reward [5.1].
B	Financial data [7.2] are monitored, in part, to assess training effectiveness [5.2].
C	Employee morale and well-being [5.3] affect financial performance results [7.2], and vice-versa.
D	Financial and market results [7.2] are enhanced by improvements in product and service processes [6.1], support processes [6.2], and supplier and partner processes [6.3].
E	Organization-specific results [7.1a(3) and 7.5] form the basis for financial and market results [7.2].

7.2 Financial and Market Results—Sample Effective Results

A. Financial and Market Results

- Key measures and indicators of organization market and financial performance address the following areas:
  - Effective use of materials, energy, capital, and assets;
  - Asset utilization;
  - Market share, business growth, new markets entered, and market shifting;
  - Return on equity;
  - Operating margins;
  - Pre-tax profit;
  - Earnings per share;
  - Generating enough revenue to cover expenses (not-for-profit and public sector); and
  - Operating within budget (government sector).
- Measures and indicators show steady improvement.
- Important financial and market data are presented.
- Comparative data include industry best, best competitor, and other appropriate benchmarks.

7.3 *Human Resource Results (80 Points)*
Results Scoring

Summarize your organization's human resource results, including employee well-being, satisfaction, development, and work system performance. Segment your results by types and categories of employees, as appropriate. Include appropriate comparative data.

Provide data and information to answer the following questions:

a. Human Resource Results

(1) What are your current levels and trends in key measures and/or indicators of employee well-being, satisfaction and dissatisfaction, and development?

(2) What are your current levels and trends in key measures and/or indicators of work system performance and effectiveness?

Notes:

N1. Results reported in this Item should relate to activities described in Category 5. The results should be responsive to key process needs described in Category 6, and the company action plans and related human resource plans described in Item 2.2.

N2. For appropriate measures of employee well-being and satisfaction, see Notes to Item 5.3. Appropriate might include innovation and suggestion rates, courses completed, learning, on-the-job performance improvements, and cross-training.

N3. Appropriate measures and/or indicators of work system performance and effectiveness might include job and job classification simplification, job rotation, work layout, and changing supervisory ratios.

This Item addresses the organization's human resource results—those relating to employee well-being, satisfaction, development, motivation, and work system performance and effectiveness.

Results reported could include generic and business- or organization-specific factors. Generic factors include safety, absenteeism, turnover, and satisfaction. Business- or organization-specific factors include results commonly used in the industry or created by the organization for purposes of tracking progress.

Results reported might include input data, such as extent of training, but the main emphasis should be placed on measures of effectiveness. Results reported for work system performance should include those relevant to the organization and might include measures of improvement in job classification, job rotation, work layout, and changes in local decision making.

The Item calls for comparative information so that results can be evaluated meaningfully against competitors or other relevant external measures of performance. For some measures, such as absenteeism and turnover, local or regional comparisons also are appropriate. The Item also calls for segmentation of results by different employee groups, as appropriate.

7.3 Human Resource Results

Results of human resource improvement efforts using key measures and/or indicators of such performance

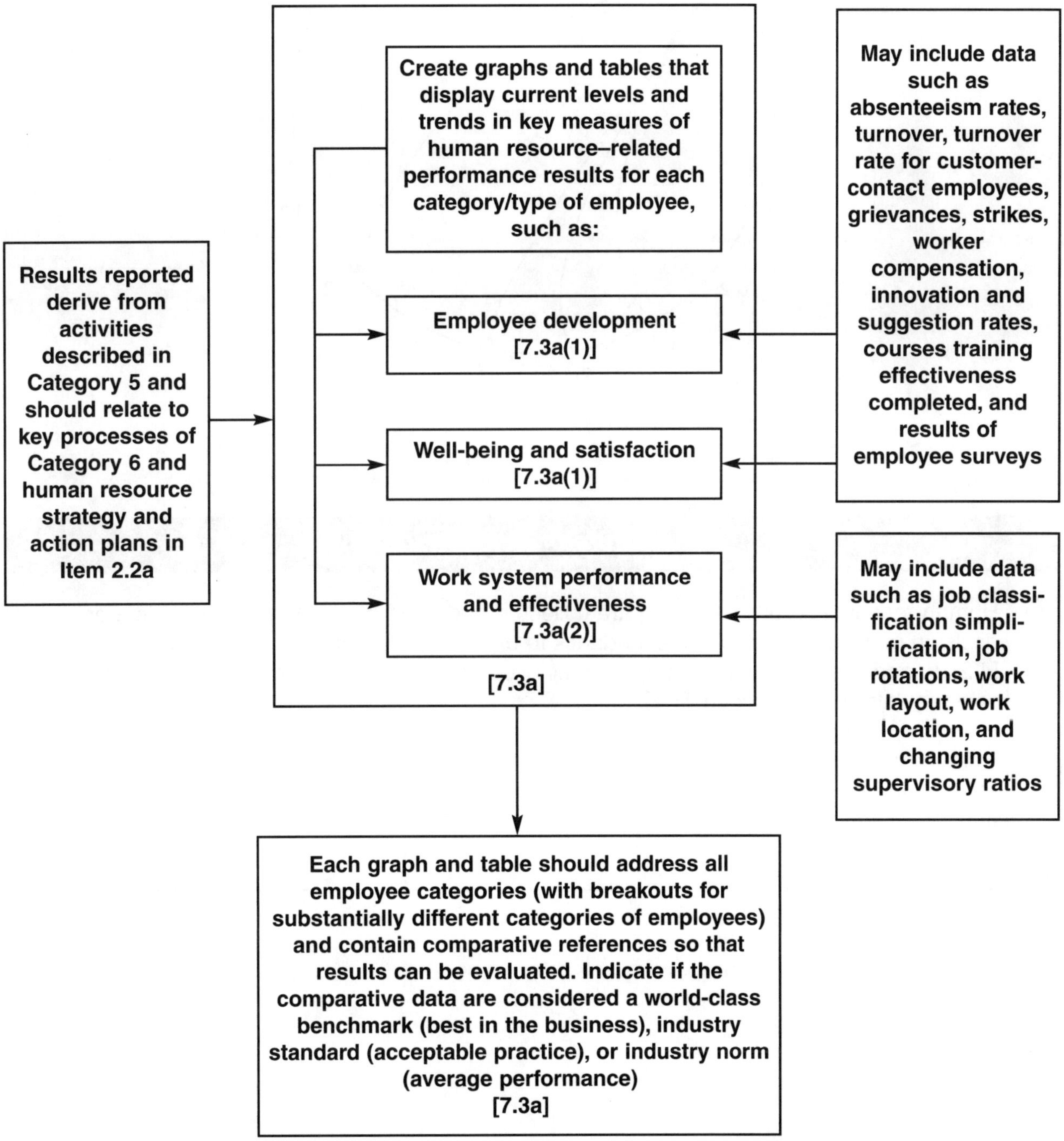

7.3 Human Resource Results Item Linkages

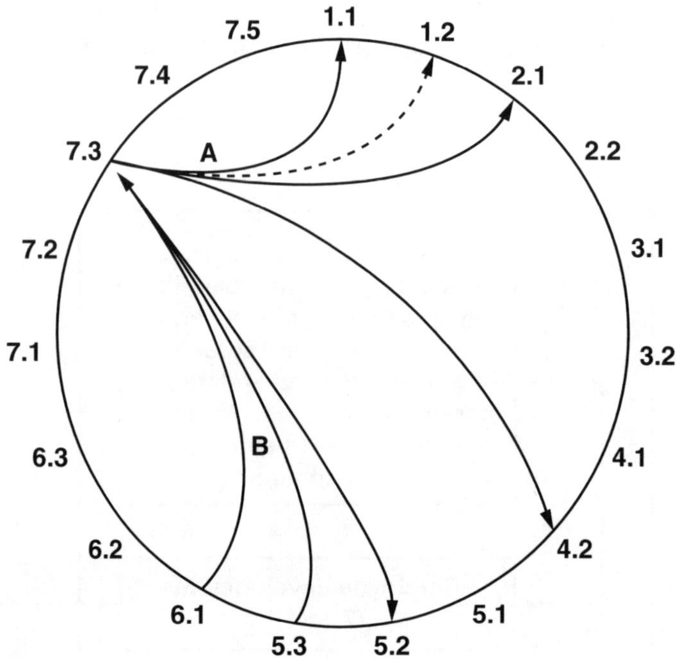

	Nature of Relationship
A	Human resource results data [7.3] are collected and used for planning [2.1], for leader decision making [1.1], to provide feedback to organizational managers [1.1], and analysis [4.2]. In addition, results in the area of employee safety [7.3] are used to ensure compliance with regulatory requirements [1.2].
B	Human resource results derive from and are enhanced by improving work systems and enhancing flexibility and by strengthening employee recognition systems [5.1], training [5.2], and well-being and satisfaction [5.3]. In addition, human resource results data [7.3] are monitored, in part, to assess training effectiveness [5.2].

7.3 Human Resource Results—Sample Effective Results

A. Human Resource Results

- The results reported in Item 7.3 derive from activities described in Category 5 and the Human Resource Plans and Goals from Item 2.2a.
- Multiyear data are provided to show sustained performance.
- All results show steady improvement.
- Data are not missing—if human resource results data are declared important, they are reported.
- Comparison data for benchmark or competitor organizations are reported.
- Trend data are reported for employee satisfaction with working conditions, safety, retirement package, and other employee benefits. Satisfaction with management is also reported.
- Trends for declining absenteeism, grievances, employee turnover, strikes, and worker compensation claims are reported.
- Data are reported for all employee categories.

7.4 Supplier and Partner Results (25 Points) Results Scoring

Summarize your organization's key supplier and partner results. Include appropriate comparative data.

Provide data and information to answer the following question:

a. ***Supplier and Partner Results***
What are your current levels and trends in key measures and/or indicators of supplier and partner performance? Include your performance and/or cost improvements resulting from supplier and partner performance and performance management.

Note:
Results reported in this Item should relate directly to processes and performance requirements described in Item 6.3.

This Item addresses current levels and trends in key measures and/or indicators of supplier and partner performance as well as performance of the supplier management process, such as cost reductions. Suppliers and partners provide "upstream" and/or "downstream" materials and services. The focus should be on the most critical requirements from the point of view of your organization—the "buyer" of the products and services. Data reported should reflect results by whatever means they occur—via improvements by suppliers and partners and/or through selection of better performing suppliers and partners. Measures and indicators of performance should relate to the principal factors involved in your organization's purchases, e.g., quality, delivery, and price.

Data reported also should reflect how suppliers and partners have contributed to your organization's performance goals. Results reported could include cost savings; reductions in scrap, waste, or rework; and cycle time or productivity enhancements.

The Item calls for comparative information so that results reported can be meaningfully evaluated against competitors or other relevant external measures of performance.

7.4 Supplier and Partner Results

Results of supplier and partner performance improvement efforts using key measures and/or indicators of such performance

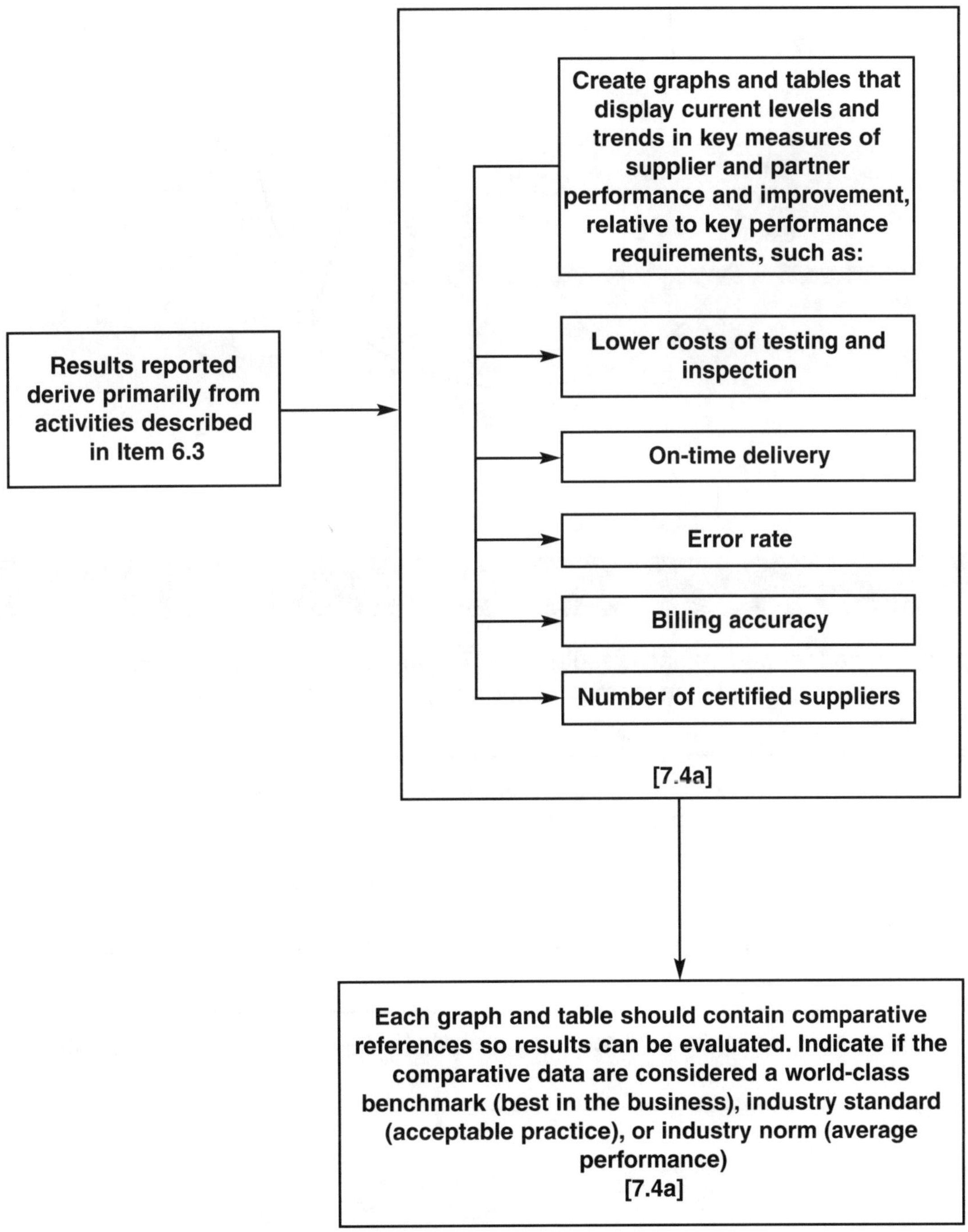

7.4 Supplier and Partner Results Item Linkages

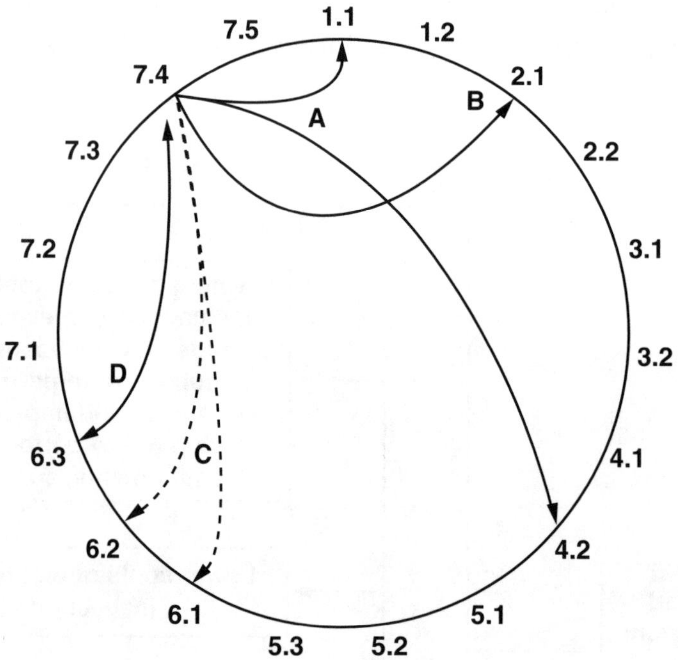

Nature of Relationship	
A	Supplier and partner performance results data [7.4] are collected and used to provide feedback to organizational managers [1.1], for analysis [4.2] relative to supplier and partner performance.
B	Supplier and partner performance results [7.4] are used to determine supplier capabilities during the strategic planning process [2.1].
C	Supplier and partner capabilities as reflected in the results data [7.4] are considered in the product and service processes [6.1] and support processes [6.2] to help determine the overall process capability of the organization to deliver products and services that meet customer requirements.
D	Processes to improve supplier and partner capability [6.3a] affect supplier and partner results [7.4].

7.4 Supplier and Partner Results—Sample Effective Results

A. Supplier and Partner Results

- Results are broken out by key suppliers or supplier types as appropriate. Data are presented using the measures and indicators of supplier performance described in the Business Overview, Item 6.3 and relevant goals in Area 2.2b.
- If the organization's supplier management efforts include factors such as building supplier partnerships or reducing the number of suppliers, data related to these efforts are included in responses.
- Supplier performance measures include defect rate, on-time delivery, and number of certified suppliers.
- Multiyear data are provided to demonstrate steady improvement.
- Data are not missing—all data declared to be important are reported.
- Comparison data for suppliers of benchmark or competitor organizations are reported.
- Data are broken out by meaningful supplier categories to demonstrate consistent improvement in each category.

7.5 Organizational Effectiveness Results (115 Points) Results Scoring

Summarize your organization's key operational performance results that contribute to the achievement of organizational effectiveness. Include appropriate comparative data.

Provide data and information to answer the following questions:

a. Organizational Effectiveness Results

(1) What are your current levels and trends in key measures and/or indicators of key design, production, delivery, and support process performance? Include productivity, cycle time, and other appropriate measures of effectiveness and efficiency.

(2) What are your results for key measures and/or indicators of regulatory/legal compliance and citizenship? What are your results for key measures and/or indicators of accomplishment of organizational strategy?

Notes:

N1. Results reported in Item 7.5 should address key organizational requirements and progress toward accomplishment of key organizational performance goals as presented in the Business Overview, and in Items 1.1, 2.2, 6.1, and 6.2. Include results not reported in Items 7.1, 7.2, 7.3, and 7.4.

N2. Results reported in Item 7.5 should provide key information for analysis (Item 4.2) and review (Item 1.1) of organizational operational performance and should provide the operational basis for customer results (Item 7.1) and financial and market results (Item 7.2).

N3. Regulatory/legal compliance results reported in Item 7.5 should address requirements described in Item 1.2.

This Item addresses key performance results not covered in Items 7.1 through 7.4 that contribute significantly to the organization's goals—customer satisfaction, product and service quality, operational effectiveness, and financial/marketplace performance. The Item encourages the use of any unique measures the organization has developed to track performance in important areas.

Results should reflect key process performance measures. Measures of productivity and operational effectiveness in all key areas—product/service delivery areas and support areas—are appropriate for inclusion. Results of compliance with regulatory/legal requirements should be reported.

Measures and/or indicators of operational effectiveness could include the following: environmental improvements reflected in emissions levels, waste stream reductions, by-product use, and recycling; responsiveness indicators such as cycle time, lead times, and set-up times; process assessment results such as customer assessment or third-party assessment (such as ISO 9000); and business-specific indicators such as innovation rates, innovation effectiveness, cost reductions through innovation, time to market, product/process yield, complete and accurate shipments, and measures of strategic goal achievement.

The Item calls for comparative information so that results reported can be evaluated against competitors or other relevant external measures of performance. These comparative data might include industry best, best competitor, industry average, and appropriate benchmarks from outside your industry. Such data might be derived from independent surveys, studies, laboratory testing, or other sources.

7.5 Organizational Effectiveness Results

Results of improvement efforts that contribute to achievement of operational effectiveness

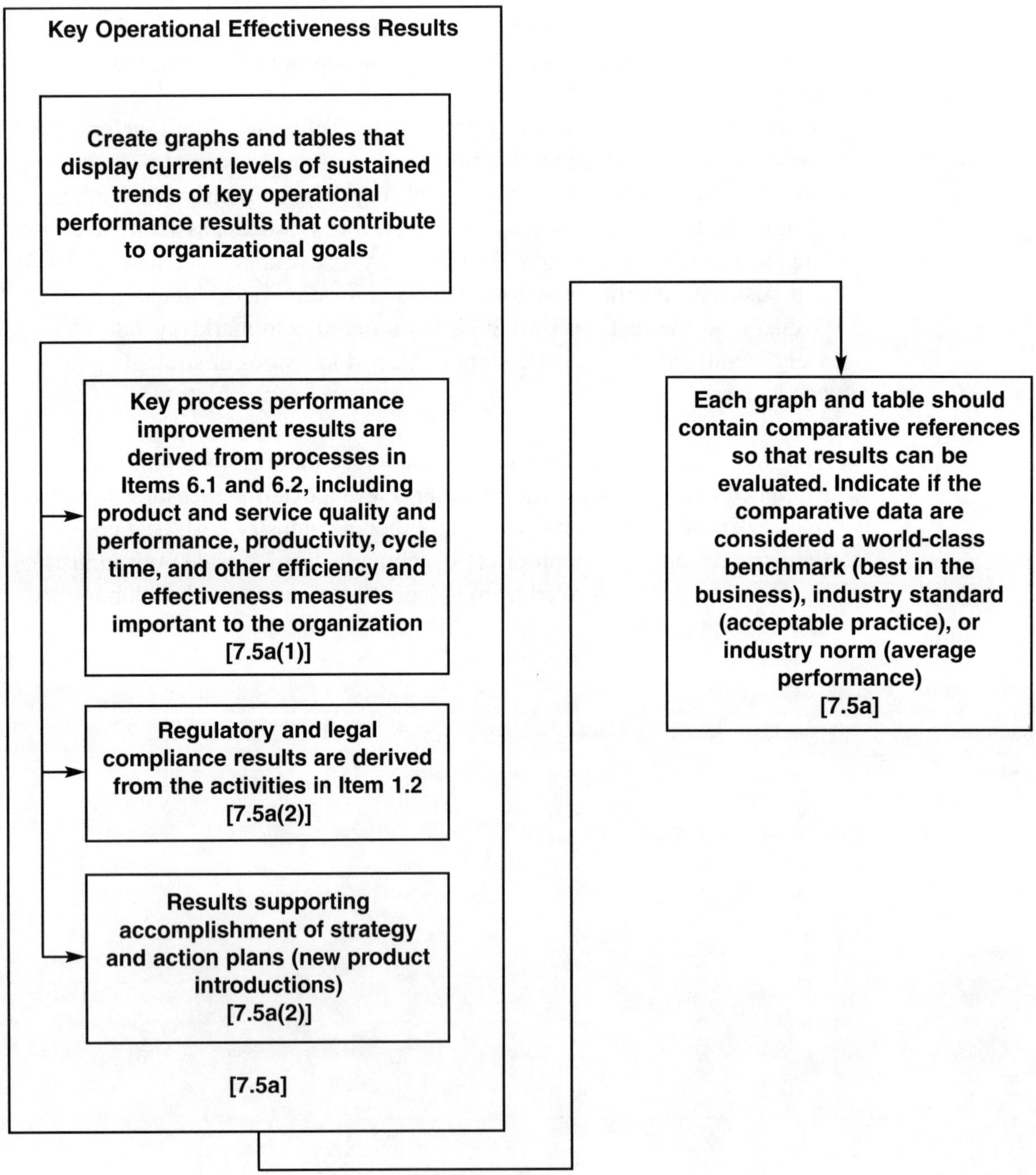

7.5 Organizational Effectiveness Results Item Linkages

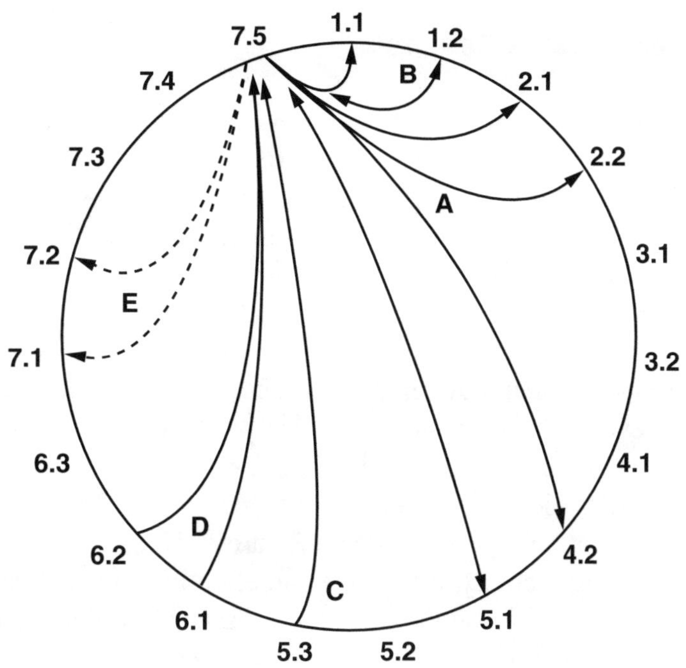

	Nature of Relationship
A	Product and service quality characteristics and operational performance results data [7.5] are collected and used for planning [2.1], goal setting [2.2], management, monitoring, and decision making [1.1], analysis [4.2], and reward and recognition determination [5.1]. In addition, processes to improve employee initiative and flexibility [5.1] can enhance performance results [7.5].
B	Regulatory and legal compliance resulting from the activities in Item 1.2 should be reported in 7.5. In addition, these results are monitored to determine if process changes are needed.
C	Employee morale and well-being [5.3] affect product and service quality results [7.5].
D	Designing products and services to meet customer requirements, improved operational performance [6.1], and support performance [6.2] affect product and service quality [7.5].
E	Organization effectiveness results [7.5] provide the basis for financial and market results [7.2] and customer focused results [7.1].

7.5 Organizational Effectiveness Results—Sample Effective Results

A. Organizational Effectiveness Results

- Indices and trend data are provided in graph and chart form for all operational performance measures identified in 6.1, 6.2, 1.2, relevant organizational goals (2.2), and the key business factors identified in the business overview and not reported elsewhere in Category 7. Multiyear data are reported.
- Most to all indicators show steady improvement.
- Product and service quality measures and indicators address requirements such as accuracy, timeliness, and reliability. Examples include defect levels, repeat services, meeting product or service delivery or response times, and availability levels. However, if these measures predict customer satisfaction, they should be moved to Item 7.1.
- Operational performance measures address
  - Productivity, efficiency and effectiveness such as productivity indices, human resource utilization, waste reduction, energy efficiency, and product/service design improvement measures
  - Public responsibilities such as environmental improvements
  - Cycle time reductions
- Comparative data include industry best, best competitor, industry average, and appropriate benchmarks. Data are also derived from independent surveys, studies, laboratory testing, or other sources.
- Data are not missing. (For example, do not show a steady trend from 1992 to 1998, but leave out 1994.)
- Data are not aggregated since aggregation tends to hide poor performance by blending it with good performance. Break out and report trends separately.

Tips on Preparing a Baldrige Award Application

Preparing the Business Overview

The Business Overview is an outline of your organization. It should address what is most important to the organization, key influences on how it operates, and where it is headed. The Business Overview is a statement of what is relevant and important to your organization and its performance. Many organizations make a mistake in preparing a superficial Business Overview. It is a statement about the organization that helps examiners understand key components of your business. It should be carefully and completely developed and fully address all the required elements. The Business Overview helps you and the examiners focus on key business performance requirements and business results. It is used by the examiners and judges in all stages of application review and during the site visit.

Guidelines for Preparing the Business Overview

The Business Overview consists of five sections as follows:

Basic Description of Your Organization
This section should provide information on the following:

- Your products and services;
- The size and location(s) of your organization and whether it is publicly or privately owned;
- Your organizational culture: purpose, vision, mission, and values, as appropriate;
- Your major markets: local, regional, national, or international; and principal customer types, such as consumers, other businesses, and government;
- Your employee base, including number, types, educational level, bargaining units, and special safety requirements;
- Your major equipment, facilities, and technologies used; and
- Regulatary environment affecting you: occupational health and safety, environmental, financial and product, etc.

If your organization is a subunit of a larger organization, describe:

- The organizational relationship to your "parent" and percent of employees the subunit represents;

- How your products and services relate to those of your "parent" and/or other units of the "parent" organization; and
- Key support services, if any, that your "parent" organization provides.

Customer and Market Requirements

This section should provide information on:

- Key customer and market requirements (for example, on-time delivery, low defect levels, price demands, and after-sales services) for products and services.
- Briefly describe all important requirements, and note significant differences, if any, in requirements among customer groups and/or market segments. (Note any special relationships, such as partnerships, with customers or customer groups.)

Supplier and Partnering Relationships

This section should provide information on:

- Types and numbers of suppliers of goods and services;
- The most important types of suppliers, dealers, and other businesses; and
- Any limitations, special relationships, or special requirements that may exist with some or all suppliers and partners.

Competitive Situation

This section should provide information on:

- Numbers and types of competitors;
- Your position (relative size, growth) in the industry;
- Principal factors that determine competitive success, such as productivity growth, cost reduction, and product innovation; and
- Changes taking place that affect competition, such as growing global competition.

Business Directions

This section should provide information, as appropriate, on:

- Major new thrusts, such as changes in products or entry into new markets or segments;
- New business alliances;
- Introduction of new technologies;
- Changes in strategy; and
- Unique factors.

Page Limit The Business Overview is limited to five pages.

1999 Criteria Response Guidelines

The guidelines given in this section are offered to assist Criteria for Performance Excellence users in responding most effectively to the requirements of the 19 Criteria Items. Writing an application for the Baldrige Award involves responding to these requirements in 50 or fewer pages.

The guidelines are presented in three parts:

- General Guidelines regarding the Criteria booklet, including how the Items are formatted;
- Guidelines for Responding to Approach/Deployment Items; and
- Guidelines for Responding to Results Items.

General Guidelines

Review the Item format and understand how to respond to the Item requirements.
The Item format shows the different parts of Items, the significance of each part, and where each part is placed. It is especially important to understand the Areas to Address and the Item Notes.

Item requirements are presented in question format, sometimes with modifying statements. Responses to an Item should contain answers to all questions and modifying statements; however, each question need not be separately answered. Responses to multiple questions within a single Area to Address may be grouped as appropriate to the organization. The Appendix to this book contains a restatement of the Criteria in declarative sentences, not questions. Many have found this makes it easier to understand the many different requirements that are embedded in the Criteria.

Start by preparing the Business Overview.
The Business Overview is the most appropriate starting point for writing an application. The Business Overview is intended to help everyone—including Criteria users/application writers and reviewers—to understand what is most relevant and important to the organization's business.

In addition, read the information describing the linkages, sample effective practices, and process flow diagrams presented in this book. In particular, be certain to understand how the various requirements of the Criteria are integrated into a comprehensive management system.

Guidelines for Responding to Approach/Deployment Items

The Criteria focus on key performance results. However, results by themselves offer little diagnostic value. For example, if some results are poor or are improving at rates slower than the competition's, it is important to understand why this is so and what might be done to accelerate improvement.

The purpose of Approach/Deployment Items is to permit diagnosis of the organization's most important processes—the ones that enable fast-paced performance improvement and contribute to key business results. Diagnosis and feedback depend heavily upon the processes and systems that are in place. For this reason, it is important to respond to these Items by providing key process information.

Understand the Meaning of "How"

Items requesting information on approach include questions that begin with the word "how." Responses should outline key process information such as methods, measures, deployment, and evaluation/improvement/learning factors. Responses lacking such information, or merely providing an example, are referred to in the Scoring Guidelines as anecdotal information and are worth little to nothing.

Show What and How

Describe your system for meeting the requirements of each item. Ensure that methods, processes, and practices are fully described. Use flowcharts to help examiners visualize your key processes.

It is important to give basic information about what the key processes are and how they work. Although it is helpful to include who performs the work, merely stating who does not permit diagnosis or feedback related to the central issue of how the process works. For example, stating that "customer satisfaction data are analyzed by the Customer Service Department" does not permit diagnosis or feedback, because from this information, it is impossible to determine if the approach is systematic, consistently applied, evaluated, refined, or widely used. A meaningful analysis of strengths and opportunities for improvement cannot be provided.

Show That Activities Are Systematic

Ensure that the response describes a systematic approach, not merely an anecdotal example.

Systematic approaches are repeatable, predictable, and involve the systematic use of data and information for evaluation, subsequent improvement, and learning. In other words, the approaches are consistent over time, build in learning and evaluation, and show maturity. Scores above 50 percent rely on clear evidence that approaches are systematic, evaluated, and refined.

Show Deployment

Ensure that the response gives clear and sufficient information on deployment. For example, one must be able to distinguish from a response whether an approach described is used in one, some, most, or all parts of the organization.

Deployment can be shown compactly by using summary tables that outline what is done in different parts of the organization. This is particularly effective if the basic approach is described in a narrative.

Show Focus, Consistency, and Integration

The response demonstrates that the organization is focused on key processes and on improvements that offer the greatest potential to improve business performance and accomplish organization action plans.

There are four important factors to consider regarding integration:

- The Business Overview should make clear what is important;
- The Strategic Planning Category, including the strategic objectives and action plans, should highlight areas of greatest focus and describe how deployment plan and strategy alignment is accomplished;
- Descriptions of organizational-level analysis and review (Items 4.2 and 1.1) should show how the organization analyzes and reviews performance information to set priorities; and
- The Process Management Category should highlight product, service, support, and supplier processes that are key to overall performance.

Integrating systems required in the Approach/Deployment Items and tracking corresponding measures in the Results Items should improve business performance.

Respond Fully to Item Requirements

Ensure that the response fully addresses all important parts of each Item and each Area to Address. Missing information will be interpreted by examiners as a gap in approach and/or deployment. All areas should be addressed and checked in final review. Individual components of an Area to Address may be addressed individually or together.

Cross-Reference When Appropriate

Each Item response should, as much as possible, be self-contained. However, some responses to different Items might be mutually reinforcing. It is then appropriate to refer to the other responses, rather than to repeat information. In such cases, key process information should be given in the Item requesting this information. For example, employee education and training should be described in detail in Item 5.2. References elsewhere to education and training would then reference, but not repeat, this detail.

Use a Compact Format

Applicants should make the best use of the 50 application pages permitted. Use flowcharts, tables, and "bulletized" presentation of information.

Refer to the Scoring Guidelines

The evaluation of item responses is accomplished by consideration of the Criteria Item requirements and the maturity of the organization's approaches, breadth of deployment, and strength of the improvement process relative to the scoring guidelines. Therefore, applicants need to consider both the Criteria and the scoring guidelines in preparing responses. In particular, remember that in order to score over 50 percent, organizations must demonstrate consistent evaluation and corresponding improvements. The Scoring Guidelines make this requirement applicable to *all* Items in Categories 1 through 6. Even if the details of the Item do not ask for a description of techniques, it will help the examiners give you full credit for your processes if an explanation is provided to show how the processes are evaluated and refined.

Guidelines for Responding to Results Items

The Baldrige Criteria place great emphasis on results. All Results Items remain in Category 7 for 1999. Items 7.1, 7.2, 7.3, 7.4, and 7.5 call for results related to all key requirements, stakeholders, and goals.

Focus on Reporting Critical Results

Results reported should cover the most important requirements for business success, highlighted in the Business Overview, and the Strategic Planning and Process Management categories, and included in responses to other Items, such as Human Resource Focus (Category 5) and Process Management (Category 6).

Four key requirements for effective presentation of results data include the following:

- Trends show directions of results and rates of change;
- Performance levels show performance on some meaningful measurement scale;
- Comparisons show how trends or levels compare with those of other, appropriately selected organizations; and
- Breadth of results show that all important results are included.

No Minimum Time

No minimum period of time is required for trend data. However, results data might span five years or more for some results. Trends might be much shorter for some of the organization's more recent improvement activities. Because of the importance of showing deployment and focus, new data should be included even if trends and comparisons are not yet well established. However, it may be better to report four quarterly measures covering a one-year period than two measures for beginning and end of year. The four measures help to demonstrate a sustained trend (if one exists).

Compact Presentation

Many results can be reported compactly by using graphs and tables. Graphs and tables should be labeled for easy interpretation. Results over time or compared with others should be "normalized"—presented in a way (such as use of ratios) that takes into account various size factors. For example, reporting safety trends in terms of lost workdays per 100 employees would be more meaningful than total lost workdays, if the number of employees has varied over the time period, or if you are comparing your results to organizations varying in size from yours.

Link Results with Text

Descriptions of results and the results themselves should be close together in the application. Trends that show a significant positive or negative change should be explained. Use figure numbers that correspond to Items. For example, the third figure for Item 7.1 should be 7.1-3. (See the example below.)

The following graph illustrates data an applicant might present as part of a response to Item 7.1, Customer Focused Results. In the Business Overview and in Item 3.1, the applicant has indicated on-time delivery as a key customer requirement.

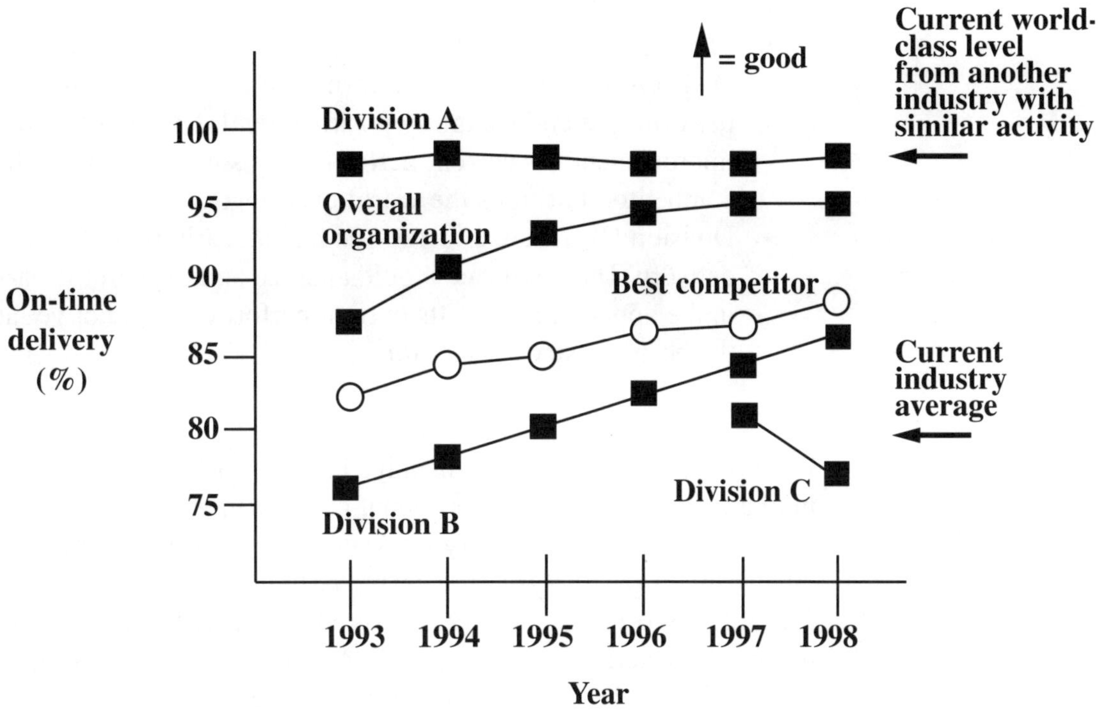

Figure 7.1-3 On-Time Delivery Performance

Using the graph, the following characteristics of clear and effective data presentation are illustrated.

- A figure number is provided for reference to the graph in the text.
- Both axes and units of measure are clearly labeled.
- Trend lines report data for a key business requirement—on-time delivery.
- Results are presented for several years.
- Appropriate comparisons are clearly shown.
- The organization shows, using a single graph, that its three divisions separately track on-time delivery.

- If different segments or components exist, show each as a separate measure. Avoid aggregating data when the segments are meaningful.
- An upward-pointing arrow appears on the graph, indicating that increasing values are "good." (A downward-pointing arrow would indicate that decreasing values are "good.")

To help interpret the scoring guidelines, the following comments on the graphed results in the sample above would be appropriate.

- The current overall organization performance level is very good to excellent. This conclusion is supported by the comparison with competitors and with a world-class level.
- The organization exhibits an overall excellent improvement record.
- Division A is the current performance leader—showing sustained high performance and a slightly positive trend. Division B shows rapid improvement. Its current performance is near that of the best industry competitor, but trails the world-class level.
- Division C—a new division—is having early problems with on-time delivery. The applicant should analyze and explain the early problems in the application text. Its current performance is not yet at the level of the best industry competitor.

Complete Data

Be sure that results data are displayed for all relevant customer, financial, market, human resource, operational performance, and supplier performance characteristics. If you identify relevant performance measures and goals in other parts of the analysis (for example, Items 1.2, 2.1, 2.2, 3.1, 3.2, 4.1, 4.2, 5.1, 5.2, 5.3, 6.1, 6.2, and 6.3), be sure to include the results of these performance characteristics in Category 7. As each relevant performance measure is identified in the assessment process, create a blank chart and label the axes. Define all units of measure, especially if they are industry-specific or unique to the applicant. As data are collected, populate the charts. If expected data are not provided in the application, examiners may assume that the trends or levels are not good. Missing data drive the score down in the same way that poor trends do.

Break Out Data

This point, mentioned earlier, bears repeating: avoid aggregating the data. Where appropriate, break data into meaningful components. If you serve several different customer groups, display performance and satisfaction data for each group. As the following graph demonstrates, only one of the three trends is positive, although the average is positive. Examiners will seek component data when aggregate data are reported. Presenting aggregate data instead of meaningful component data is likely to reduce the score.

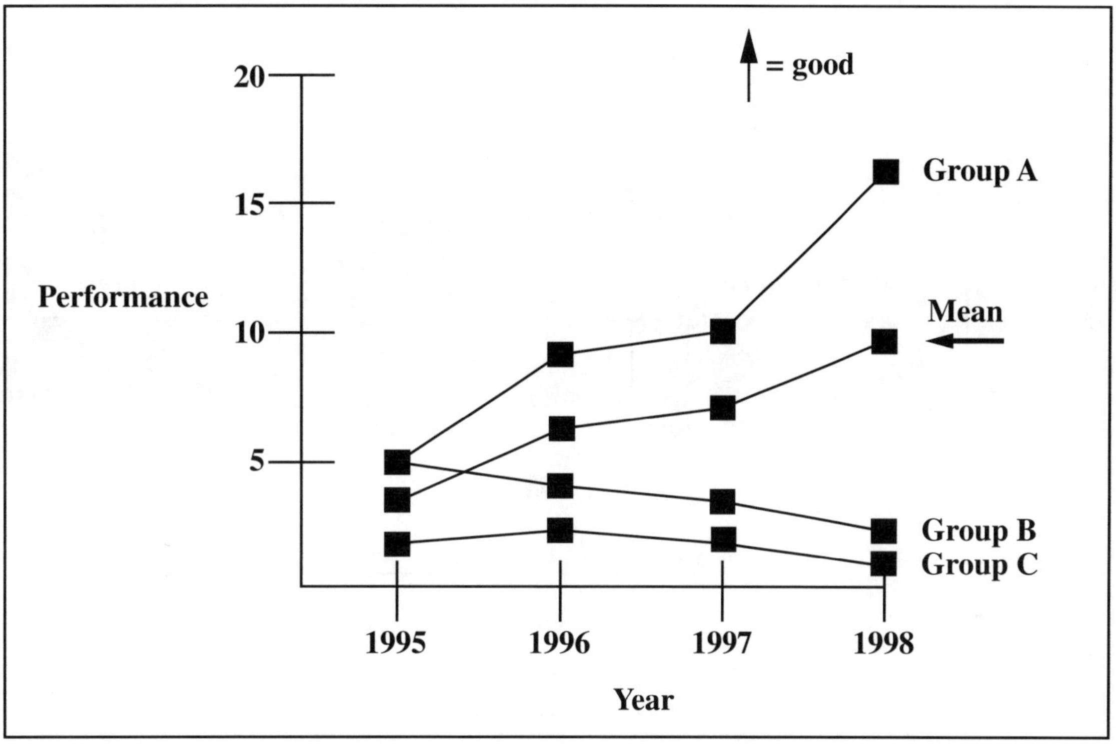

The Importance of Criteria Notes

Several items are followed by one or more notes that offer some insight and explanation about the Item. Often these notes suggest activities or measures that other organizations have used to meet the requirements of the Item. There are many ways to manage a high performance system that are not included in the notes. Notes are considered suggestions and *not* requirements.

Data and Measures

Comparison data are required for all items in Category 7. These data are designed to demonstrate how well the organization is performing. To judge performance excellence, one must possess comparison data. In the following chart, performance is represented by the line connecting the squares. Clearly the organization is improving, but how "good" is it? Without comparison data, answering that question is difficult.

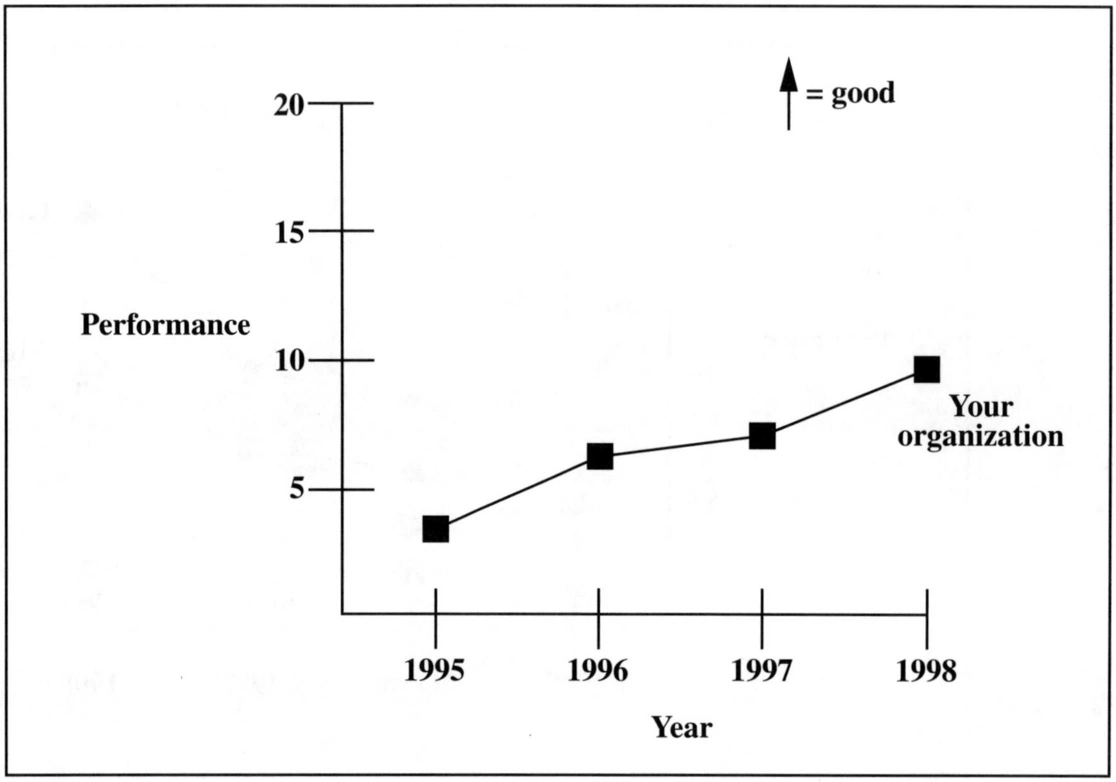

Now consider the chart with comparison data added.

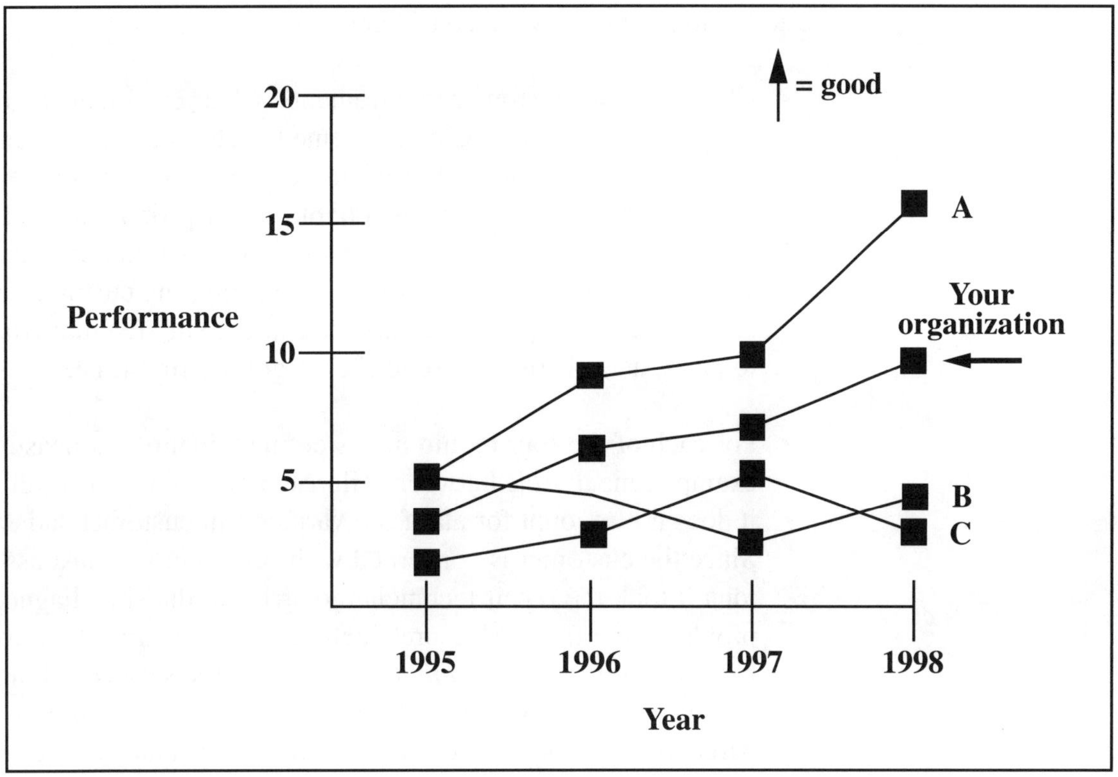

Note the position of three hypothetical comparisons, represented by the letters A, B, and C. Consider the following two scenarios.

- If **A** represents the industry average and both **B** and **C** represent area competitors, examiners would conclude that your organization's performance was substandard, even though it is improving.

- If **A** represents a best-in-class (benchmark) organization and **B** represents the industry average, examiners would conclude that your organizational performance is very good.

In both scenarios, the organizational performance remained the same, but the examiner's perception of it changed based on changes in comparison data.

Measures

Agreeing on relevant measures is a difficult task for organizations in the early phases of quality and performance improvement. The task is easier if the following guidelines are considered.

- Clearly define customer requirements. Clear customer requirements are easier to measure. Clearly defined customer requirements require probing and suggesting. For example, the customer of a new computer wants the equipment to be reliable. After probing to find what "reliable" means, we discover that (1) the customer expects it to work all of the time. If it does stop working, the customer expects fast service—(2) prompt appearance at the site, (3) immediate access to parts, and (4) the ability to fix it right the first time.

- For each of the four requirements defined, identify a measure. For example, mean time between failures is one indicator of reliability, but it does not account for all of the variation in customer satisfaction. Since the customer is concerned with run time, we must assess how long it took the repair technician to arrive at the site, diagnose the problem, and fix it. Measures include *time in hours, days, weeks* between failures, *time in minutes* between the service call and the computer regaining capability (time to fix), *time in minutes* waiting for parts, and the associated costs in terms of cash and worker effort.

- Collect and report data. Several charts might be required to display these factors, or one chart with several lines.

Scoring System

The scoring of responses to Criteria Items (Items) and Award applicant feedback are based on three evaluation dimensions:

- Approach;
- Deployment; and
- Results.

Criteria users need to furnish information relating to these dimensions. Specific factors for these dimensions are described as follows:

Approach

Approach refers to how you address the Item requirements—the method(s) used. The factors used to evaluate approaches include:

- Appropriateness of the methods to the requirements;
- Effectiveness of use of the methods. Degree to which the approach:
  - is systematic, integrated, and consistently applied;
  - embodies evaluation/improvement/learning cycles; and
  - is based on reliable information and data.
- Alignment with organizational needs; and
- Evidence of innovation.

Deployment

Deployment refers to the extent to which your approach is applied to all requirements of the Item. The factors used to evaluate deployment include:

- Use of the approach in addressing Item requirements relevant to your organization; and
- Use of the approach by all appropriate work units.

Results

Results refers to outcomes in achieving the purposes given in the Item. The factors used to evaluate results include:

- Current performance;
- Performance relative to appropriate comparisons and/or benchmarks;
- Rate, breadth, and importance of performance improvements; and
- Linkage of results measures to key customer, market, process, and action plan performance requirements identified in the Business Overview and in Approach/Deployment Items.

Item Classification and Scoring Dimensions are classified according to the kinds of information and/or data you are expected to furnish relative to the three evaluation dimensions. The two types of Items and their designations are

1. Approach/Deployment (for all Items in Categories 1–6)
2. Results (for all Items in Category 7)

Approach and deployment are linked to emphasize that descriptions of Approach should always indicate the Deployment—consistent with the specific requirements of the Item. Although Approach and Deployment dimensions are linked, feedback to Award applicants reflects strengths and/or opportunities for improvement in either or both dimensions.

Results Items call for data showing performance levels and trends on key measures and/or indicators of organizational performance. However, the evaluation factor, "breadth" of performance improvements, is concerned with how widespread your improvement results are. This is directly related to the Deployment dimension. That is, if improvement processes are widely deployed, there should be corresponding results. A score for a Results Item is thus a weighted composite based upon overall performance, taking into account the breadth of improvements and their importance.

Importance as a Scoring Factor

The three evaluation dimensions described above are critical to evaluation and feedback. However, evaluation and feedback also considers the importance of your reported Approach, Deployment, and Results to your key business factors. The areas of greatest importance should be identified in the Business Overview and in the narrative for Items such as 2.1 (Strategy Development), 2.2 (Strategy Deployment), 3.1 (Customer and Market Knowledge), 3.2 (Customer Satisfaction and Relationship), 4.1 (Measurement of Organizational Performance), 5.1 (Work Systems), 5.3 (Employee Wellbeing and Satisfaction), 6.1 (Product and Service Processes), and 7.5 (Organizational Effectiveness Results). Your key customer requirements and key strategic objectives and action plans are particularly important.

Assignment of Scores to Your Responses

Baldrige Award Examiners observe the following guidelines in assigning scores to applicants' responses:

- All Areas to Address should be included in the Item response. Also, responses should reflect what is important to the organization;
- In assigning a score to an Item, an Examiner first decides which scoring range (e.g., 50 percent to 60 percent) best fits the overall Item response.

Overall "best fit" does not require total agreement with each of the statements for that scoring range. Actual score within the range depends upon an Examiner's judgment of the closeness of the Item response in relation to the statements in the next higher and next lower scoring ranges;

- An Approach/Deployment Item score of 50 percent represents an approach that meets the basic objectives of the Item and that is deployed to the principal activities and work units covered in the Item. Higher scores reflect maturity (cycles of improvement), integration, and broader deployment; and
- A Results Item score of 50 percent represents a clear indication of improvement trends and/or good levels of performance in the principal results areas covered in the Item. Higher scores reflect better improvement rates and/or levels of performance, and better comparative performance as well as broader coverage.

	Approach/Deployment	Results
0%	• No systematic approach evident; anecdotal information	• No results or poor results in areas reported
10% to 20%	• Beginning of a systematic approach to the basic purposes of the Item • Major gaps exist in deployment that would inhibit progress in achieving the basic purposes of the Item • Early stages of a transition from reacting to problems to a general improvement orientation	• Some improvements and/or early good performance levels in a few areas • Results not reported for many to most areas of importance to the organization's key business requirements
30% to 40%	• A sound, systematic approach, responsive to the basic purposes of the Item • Approach is deployed, although some areas or work units are in early stages of deployment • Beginning of a systematic approach to evaluation and improvement of basic Item processes	• Improvements and/or good performance levels in many areas of importance to the organization's key business requirements • Early stages of developing trends and obtaining comparative information • Results reported for many to most areas of importance to the organization's key business requirements
50% to 60%	• A sound, systematic approach, responsive to the overall purposes of the Item • Approach is well deployed, although deployment may vary in some areas or work units • A fact-based, systematic evaluation and improvement process is in place for basic Item processes • Approach is aligned with basic organizational needs identified in the other Criteria Categories	• Improvement trends and/or good performance levels reported for most areas of importance to the organization's key business requirements • No pattern of adverse trends and no poor performance levels in areas of importance to the organization's key business requirements • Some trends and/or current performance levels—evaluated against relevant comparisons and/or benchmarks—show areas of strength and/or good to very good relative performance levels • Business results address most key customer, market, and process requirements
70% to 80%	• A sound, systematic approach, responsive to the multiple requirements of the Item • Approach is well deployed, with no significant gaps • A fact-based, systematic evaluation and improvement process and organizational learning/sharing are key management tools; clear evidence of refinement and improved integration as a result of organizational-level analysis and sharing • approach is well integrated with organizational needs identified in the other Criteria Categories	• Current performance is good to excellent in areas of importance to the organization's key business requirements • Most improvement trends and/or current performance levels are sustained • Many to most trends and/or current performance levels—evaluated against relevant comparisons and/or benchmarks—show areas of leadership and very good relative performance levels • Business results address most key customer, market, process, and action plan requirements
90% to 100%	• A sound, systematic approach, fully responsive to all the requirements of the Item • approach is fully deployed without significant weaknesses or gaps in any areas or work units • A very strong, fact-based, systematic evaluation and improvement process and extensive organizational learning/sharing are key management tools; strong refinement and integration, backed by excellent organizational-level analysis and sharing • Approach is fully integrated with organizational needs identified in the other Criteria Categories	• Current performance is excellent in most areas of importance to the organization's key business requirements • Excellent improvement trends and/or sustained excellent performance levels in most areas • Evidence of industry and benchmark leadership demonstrated in many areas • Business results fully address key customer, market, process, and action plan requirements

Supplementary Scoring Guidelines

Author's note: *Many examiners and organizations have found the official scoring guidelines to be vague, although they have been improved considerably this year. The guidelines, presented in 20 percent increments, may increase the difficulty of reaching consensus on a score and increase scoring variation. To resolve this problem, I developed the following supplemental scoring guidelines. Many state award programs have used these guidelines for several years and found that they make the consensus process easier and produce comparable scores.*

Approach/ Deployment

1. For each Approach/Deployment Item, first determine the appropriate level on the approach scale. This sets the upper possible score the applicant may receive on the Item.
2. Then read the corresponding level on the deployment scale. For example, if the approach level is 40 percent, read the 40 percent standard on the deployment scale where one would expect "several work units are in the early stages of deployment," and "progress in achieving the primary purposes of the Item is not inhibited." If that is the case, the final score is 40 percent.
3. However, if the deployment score is lower than the approach score then it establishes the lower range of possible final scores for the Item. The actual final score will be between the low and high scores. For example, if "many major gaps exist and progress is significantly inhibited," the lowest possible score would be 10 percent. This final score must be between 40 and 10 percent (e.g., 10, 20, 30, or 40 percent).
4. Never increase an approach score based on better deployment.
5. Scoring Approach/Deployment Items are presented on the pages immediately following this scoring section.

Results

1. For Results Items, base your assessment only on the standards described on the results scale. *Do not consider approach or deployment standards at all.*
2. Determine the extent to which performance results are positive, complete, and at high levels relative to competitors or similar providers or an industry standard.
3. To determine the extent to which all important results are reported, examiners should develop a list of the key measures the applicant indicates are important. Start with the measures listed in the overview section. Then add to the key measures list based on key data reported in Item 2.1 and the goals in 2.2, as well as measures that may be mentioned in Categories 5 and 6. Key measures can be reported anywhere in an application.

Score	Approach	Deployment
0%	No systematic approach evident; anecdotal information	Anecdotal, undocumented.
10%	Early beginning of a systematic approach consistent with the basic purposes of the Item is somewhat evident. Mostly reactive approach to problems. Many key requirements of the Item not addressed. In the earliest stages of transitioning from reacting to problems to a general improvement orientation.	Many major gaps exist in deployment. Progress in achieving basic purposes of Item is significantly inhibited.
20%	A partially systematic but beginning approach consistent with the basic purposes of the Item is evident. Generally reactive to problems. Some key requirements of the Item not addressed. In the early stages of transitioning from reacting to problems to a general improvement orientation.	Some major gaps exist in deployment. Progress in achieving basic purposes of Item is noticeably inhibited.
30%	A sound systematic approach responsive to the basic purposes of the Item is somewhat evident. A few key requirements of the Item not addressed. Beginning of a systematic approach to evaluation but little, if any improvement of basic Item processes is evident. Random improvements may have been made.	The approach is generally deployed although several units are in the earliest stages of deployment. Progress in achieving primary purposes of Item is minimally inhibited.
40%	A sound systematic approach responsive to the basic purposes of the Item is clearly in place. Several minor requirements of the Item are not addressed. Beginning of a systematic approach to evaluation and improvement of basic Item processes is evident. Random improvements may have been made.	The approach is deployed although several units are in the early stages of deployment. Progress in achieving primary purposes of Item is not inhibited.
50%	A sound systematic approach responsive to the overall purposes of the Item is fully developed. Some minor requirements of the Item are not addressed. Fact-based improvement system is in place for basic Item processes that includes process evaluation in key areas (but no refinements are in place). Random improvements may have been made. The approach is aligned with some basic organization needs identified in the other Criteria Categories.	No major gaps in deployment exist that inhibit progress in achieving primary purposes of Item although deployment may vary in some areas or work units. Some work units still in the early stages of deployment.
60%	A sound systematic approach responsive to the overall purposes of the Item is clearly in place. A few minor requirements of the Item not addressed. Fact-based improvement system is in place for the basic requirements of the Item including at least one evaluation and improvement cycle completed, including some systematic refinement based on the evaluation in key areas. The approach is aligned with most basic organization needs identified in the other Criteria Categories.	No major gaps in deployment exist that inhibit progress in achieving primary purposes of Item although deployment may vary in some areas or work units. A few work units still in the early stages of deployment.
70%	A sound systematic approach, responsive to many of the multiple purposes of the Item is clearly in place. Organizational learning and sharing are frequently used management tools at many levels. Some systematic evaluation and evidence of refinements and improved integration result from organization-level analysis and learning. The approach is aligned and well integrated with many overall organization needs identified in the other Criteria Categories.	Approach is well deployed with some work units in the middle to advanced. No significant gaps exist that inhibit progress in achieving the purposes of Item.
80%	A sound systematic approach, responsive to most of the multiple purposes of the Item is clearly in place. Organizational learning and sharing are frequently used management tools at most levels. Considerable systematic evaluation and evidence of refinements and integration result from organization-level analysis and learning. The approach is aligned and well integrated with most overall organization needs identified in the other Criteria Categories.	Approach is well deployed with many work units in the advanced stages. No gaps exist that inhibit progress in achieving the purposes of Item.
90%	A sound systematic approach, responsive to all of the multiple purposes of the Item is in place. Considerable systematic evaluation and extensive refinements and improved organizational sharing and learning are key management tools at most levels. Some innovative processes are evident with strong refinement and integration supported by substantial organization-level analysis and sharing.	Approach is fully deployed with most work units in the advanced stages. No significant gaps or weaknesses exist in any areas or work units.
100%	A sound systematic approach, fully responsive to all of the multiple purposes of the Item is clearly in place. Considerable systematic evaluation and clear evidence of extensive refinements and improved organizational sharing and learning are key management tools at all levels. Many innovative processes are evident with strong refinement and integration supported by excellent organization-level analysis and sharing.	Approach is fully deployed with most to all work units in the advanced stages. No significant gaps or weaknesses exist in any areas or work units.

Score	Scoring Results
0%	**No results** or poor results in areas reported.
10%	Results not reported for most areas of importance to the organization's key requirements. Limited positive results and/or limited good performance levels are evident for a few areas.
20%	Results not reported for many areas of importance to the organization's key requirements. Some positive results and/or early good performance levels are evident for a few of these areas.
30%	Results are reported for many areas of importance to the organization's key requirements. Improvements and/or good performance levels are evident for many areas of importance to the organization's key requirements. Early stages of developing trends but little or no comparative information has been obtained.
40%	Results are reported for most key areas of importance to the organization's key requirements. Improvements and good performance levels are evident for many areas of importance to the organization's key requirements. Early stages of developing trends and obtaining comparative information.
50%	Results are reported for most key customer, process, and action plan requirements. Some positive trends and/or good performance levels—evaluated against relevant comparisons or benchmarks—show a few areas of strength or good relative performance levels. No pattern of adverse trends and no poor performance levels in areas of importance to key organization requirements.
60%	Results are reported for most customer, process, and action plan requirements. Many positive trends and/or good performance levels—evaluated against relevant comparisons and benchmarks—show some areas of strength and good relative performance levels. No pattern of adverse trends and no poor performance levels in areas of importance to key organization requirements.
70%	Results are reported for most key customer, process, and action plan requirements. Current performance is good in many areas important to key organization requirements. Most improvement trends and/or current performance levels are sustained and many of these—evaluated against relevant comparisons and/or benchmarks—show some areas of leadership and very good relative performance levels.
80%	Results are reported for most key customer, process, and action plan requirements. Current performance is excellent in many areas important to key organization requirements. Most improvement trends and/or current performance levels are sustained and most of these—evaluated against relevant comparisons and/or benchmarks—show areas of leadership and very good relative performance levels.
90%	Results fully address key customer, process, and action plan requirements. Current performance is excellent in most areas important to key organization requirements. Most improvement trends or current performance levels are sustained and most of these—evaluated against relevant comparisons or benchmarks—show areas of education sector leadership or benchmark leadership in many areas.
100%	Results fully address key customer, process, and action plan requirements. Current performance is excellent in most areas important to key organization requirements. Excellent improvement trends and current performance levels are sustained and—evaluated against relevant comparisons and benchmarks—show education sector leadership or benchmark leadership in many areas.

Approach/Deployment Terms

Systematic Look for evidence of a system—a repeatable, predictable process that is used to fulfill the requirements of the Item. Briefly describe the system. Be sure to explain *how* the system works. You must communicate the nature of the system to people who are not familiar with it. This is essential to achieve the 30 percent scoring threshold.

Integrated Determine the extent to which the system is integrated or linked with other elements of the overall management system. Show the linkages across categories for key themes such as those displayed earlier for each Item.

Consider the extent to which the work of senior leader is integrated. For example,

1. Senior executives (Item 1.1) are responsible for shaping and communicating the organization's vision, values, and expectations throughout the leadership system and workforce.
2. They develop relationships with key customers (Item 3.2) and monitor customer satisfaction (Item 7.1) and organization performance (Items 7.2, 7.3, 7.4, and 7.5).
3. This information, when properly analyzed (Item 4.2), helps them plan better and make more informed decisions to optimize customer satisfaction and operational and financial performance.
4. With this in mind, senior executives participate in strategy development (Item 2.1) and ensure the alignment of the workplace to achieve organizational goals (Item 2.2).
5. Senior executives may also become involved in supporting new structures to improve employee performance (Item 5.1), training effectiveness (Item 5.2), and employee well-being and satisfaction (Item 5.3).

Similar relationships (linkages) exist between other items. Highlight these linkages to demonstrate integration.

Prevention-Based Prevention-based systems are characterized by actions to minimize or prevent the recurrence of problems. In an ideal world, all systems would produce perfect products and flawless service. Since that rarely happens, high performing organizations are able to act quickly to recover from a problem (fight the fire) and then take action to identify the root cause of the problem and prevent it from surfacing again. The nature of the problem, its root cause, and appropriate corrective action is communicated to all relevant employees so that they can implement the corrective action in their area before the problem arises.

Continuous Improvement

Continuous improvement is a bedrock theme. It is the method that helps organizations keep their competitive edge. Continuous improvement involves evaluation and improvement of processes crucial to organizational success. Evaluation and improvement completes the high performance management cycle. Continuous improvement evaluations can be complex, data-driven, statistical processes, or as simple as a focus group discussing what went right, what went wrong, and how it can be done better. The key to optimum performance lies in the pervasive evaluation and improvement of all processes. By practicing systematic, pervasive, continuous improvement, time becomes the organization's ally. Consistent evaluation and refinement practices with correspondingly good deployment can drive the score to 60 percent or 70 percent, and higher.

Complete

Each Item contains one or more areas to address. Many areas to address contain several parts. Failure to address all areas and parts can push the score lower. If an area to address or part of an area does not apply to your organization, it is important to explain why. Otherwise, examiners may conclude that the system is incomplete.

Anecdotal

If your assessment describes a process that is essentially anecdotal and does not systematically address the Criteria, it is worth very little (0 to 10 points).

Deployment

The extent to which processes are widely used by organization units affects scoring. For example, a systematic approach that is well integrated, evaluated consistently, and refined routinely may be worth 70 percent to 90 percent. However, if that process is not in place in all key parts of the organization, the 70 percent to 90 percent score will be reduced, perhaps significantly, depending on the nature and extent of the gap.

Major gaps are expected to exist at the 0 to 20 percent level. At the 30 percent and higher levels, no major gaps exist, although some units may still be at the early stages of development. At the 70 percent to 80 percent level, no major gaps exist and the approach is well integrated with organizational needs identified in other parts of the Criteria.

Summary

For each Item examined, the process is rated as follows:

- Anecdotal: 0 to 10 percent
- Systematic: 10 percent to 30 percent
- Fully developed: 40 percent
- Prevention-based and evaluated: 50 percent
- Integrated: 50 percent to 100 percent
- Refined: 60 percent to 80 percent
- Widely used, with no gaps in deployment: 70+ percent

Systematic, integrated, prevention-based, and continuously improved systems that are widely used are generally easier to describe than undeveloped systems. Moreover, describing numerous activities or anecdotes does not convince examiners that an integrated, prevention-based system is in place. In fact, simply describing numerous activities and anecdotes suggests that an integrated system does not exist. However, by tracing critical success threads through the relevant Items in the Criteria, the organization demonstrates that its system is integrated and fully deployed.

To demonstrate system integration, pick several critical success factors and show how the organization manages them. For example, trace the leadership focus on performance.

- Identify performance-related data that are collected to indicate progress against goals (Item 4.1).
- Show how performance data are analyzed (Item 4.2) and used to set work priorities (Item 1.1).
- Show how performance effectiveness is considered in the planning process (Item 2.1) and how work at all levels is aligned to increase performance (Item 2.2).
- Demonstrate the impact of human resource management (Item 5.1) and training (Item 5.2) on performance and show how both tie to the strategy and human resource plans (Item 2.2).
- Show how design, development, production, delivery, and support processes (Items 6.1 and 6.2) are enhanced to improve results.
- Report the results of improved performance (Items 7.1, 7.2, 7.3, 7.4, and 7.5).
- Determine how improved performance affects customer satisfaction levels (Item 7.1).
- Show how customer concerns (Item 3.1 and 3.2) are used to drive the selection of key measures (Item 4.1) and impact design and delivery processes (Item 6.1).

Note that the application is limited to 50 pages, not including the 5-page Business Overview. This may not be sufficient to describe in great detail the approach, deployment, results, and systematic integration of all of your critical success factors, goals, or key processes. Thus, you must pick the most important few, indicate them as such, then thoroughly describe the threads and linkages throughout the application.

Self-Assessments of Organizations and Management Systems

Baldrige-based self-assessments of organization performance and management systems take several forms, ranging from rigorous and time intensive, to simple and somewhat superficial. This section discusses the various approaches to organizational self-assessment and the pros and cons of each. Curt Reimann, the first director of the Malcolm Baldrige National Quality Award Office and the closing speaker for the 10th Quest for Excellence Conference, spoke of the need to streamline assessments to get a good sense of strengths, areas for improvement, and the vital few areas to focus leadership and drive organizational change. Three distinct types of self-assessment will be examined: the written narrative, the Likert scale survey, and the behaviorally anchored survey.

Full-Length Written Narrative

The Baldrige application development process is the most time-consuming organizational self-assessment process. To apply for the Baldrige Award, applicants must prepare a 50-page written narrative to address the requirements of the performance excellence Criteria. In the written self-assessment, the applicant is expected to describe the processes and programs it has in place to drive performance excellence. The Baldrige application process serves as the vehicle for self-assessment in most state-level quality awards. The process has not changed since the national quality award program was created in 1987 (except for reducing the maximum page limit from 85 to 50 pages).

Over the years, three methods have been used to prepare the full-length, comprehensive written narrative self-assessment.

- The most widely used technique involves gathering a team of people to prepare the application. The team members are usually assigned one of the seven Categories and asked to develop a narrative to address the Criteria requirements of that Category. The Category writing teams are frequently subdivided to prepare responses item by item. After the initial draft is complete, an oversight team consolidates the narrative and tries to ensure processes are linked and integrated throughout. Finally, top leaders review and scrub the written narrative to put the best spin on the systems, processes, and results reported.

- Another technique is similar to that described above. However, instead of subdividing the writing team according to the Baldrige Categories, the team remains together to write the entire application. In this way, the application may be more coherent and the linkages between business processes are easier to understand. This approach also helps to ensure consistency and integrity of the review processes. However, with fewer people involved, the natural "blind spots" of the team may prevent a full and accurate analysis of the management system. Finally, as with the method described above, top leaders review and scrub the written narrative.
- The third method of preparing the written narrative is the least common and involves one person writing for several days to produce the application. Considering the immense amount of knowledge and work involved, it is easy to understand why the third method is used so rarely.

With all three methods, external experts are usually involved. All four 1997 Baldrige Award recipients reported they hired consultants to help them finalize their application by sharpening its focus and clarifying linkages. In fact, the author of this book worked with two of them to do this.

Pros:

- Baldrige-winning organizations report that the discipline of producing a full-length written self-assessment (Baldrige application) helped them learn about their organization and identify areas for improvement before the site visit team arrived. The written narrative self-assessment process clearly helped focus leaders on their organization's strengths and areas for improvement—provided that a complete and honest assessment was made.
- The written narrative self-assessment also provides rich information to help examiners conduct a site visit (the purpose of which is to verify and clarify the information contained in the written self-assessment).

Cons:

- Written narrative self-assessments are extremely time- and labor-intensive. Organizations that use this approach for Baldrige or state applications or for internal organizational review, report that it requires between approximately 2,000 and 4,000 person-hours of effort—sometimes much more. People working on the self-assessment are diverted from other tasks during this period.
- Because the application is closely scrutinized and carefully scrubbed, and because of page limits it may not fully and accurately describe the

actual management processes and systems of the organization. Decisions based on misleading or incomplete information may take the organization down the wrong path.

- Although the written self-assessment provides information to help guide a site visit, examiners cannot determine the depth of deployment because only a few points of view are represented in the narrative.
- Finally, and perhaps most importantly, the discipline and knowledge required to write a meaningful narrative self-assessment is usually far greater than that possessed within the vast majority of organizations. Even the four 1997 Baldrige winners hired expert consultants to help them prepare and refine their written narrative.

Short Written Narrative

Two of the most significant obstacles to writing a useful full-length written narrative self-assessment are poor knowledge of the performance excellence Criteria and the time required to produce a meaningful assessment. If people do not understand the Criteria, it takes significantly longer to prepare a written self-assessment. In fact, the amount of time required to write an application/assessment is inversely related to the knowledge of the Criteria possessed by the writers. The difficulty associated with writing a full-length narrative has prevented many organizations from participating in state, local, or school award programs.

To encourage more organizations to begin the performance improvement journey, many state award programs developed progressively higher levels of recognition, ranging from "commitment" at the low-end, through "demonstrated progress," to "achieving excellence" of the top of the range. However, even with progressive levels of recognition, the obstacle of preparing a 50-page written narrative prevented many from engaging in the process. To help resolve this problem, several state programs permit applicants who seek recognition at the lower levels to submit a 7- to 20-page "short" written narrative self-assessment. (Most states still require applicants for the top-level award to complete a full-length written self-assessment.) The short form ranges from requiring a one page description per Category to one page per Item (hence the 7- to 20-page range in length).

Pros:

- It clearly takes less time to prepare the short form.
- Because of the reduced effort required to complete the self-assessment, states find more organizations are beginning the process of assessing and improving their performance.

Cons:

- The short form provides significantly less information to help examiners prepare for the site visit. Although it does take less time to prepare than the full-length version, the short form still requires several hundred hours of team preparation.
- The short form is usually closely scrutinized and carefully scrubbed just as its full-length cousin. This reduces accuracy and value to both the organization and examiners.
- The knowledge required to write even a short narrative prevents organizations in the beginning stages from preparing an accurate and meaningful assessment.
- Finally, there is not enough information presented in the short form to understand the extent of deployment of the systems and processes covered by the Criteria.

The Likert Scale Survey

Just about everyone is familiar with a Likert scale survey. These surveys typically ask respondents to rate, on scale 1 to 5, the extent to which they strongly disagree or strongly agree with a comment.

The following is an example of a simple Likert scale survey item:

Senior leaders effectively communicate values and customer focus.				
1	**2**	**3**	**4**	**5**
Strongly Disagree				**Strongly Agree**

A variation on the simple Likert scale survey item has been developed in an attempt to improve consistency among respondents. Brief descriptors have been added at each level as shown below in the Descriptive Likert scale survey item:

1	2	3	4	5
None	**Few**	**Some**	**Many**	**Most**
Senior leaders effectively communicate values and customer focus.				

Pros:

- The Likert scale survey is quick and easy to administer. People from all functions and levels within the organization can provide input.

Cons:

- Both the simple and the descriptive Likert scale survey items are subject to wide ranges of interpretation. One person's rating of "2" and another person's rating of "4" may actually describe the same systems or behaviors. This problem of scoring reliability raises questions about the accuracy and usefulness of both the simple and the descriptive survey techniques for conducting organizational self-assessments. After all, a quick and easy survey that produces inaccurate data still has low value. That is the main reason why states have not adopted the Likert scale survey as a tool for conducting the self-assessments, even for organizations in the beginning stages of the quality journey.

The Behaviorally Anchored Survey

A behaviorally anchored survey contains elements of a written narrative and a survey approach to conducting a self-assessment. The method is simple. Instead of brief descriptors such as "strongly agree/strongly disagree" or "none-few-some-many-most," a more complete behavioral description is presented for each level of the survey scale. Respondents simply identify the behavioral description that most closely fits the activities in the organization. A sample follows:

Translating Organizational Performance Review Findings into Improvement Targets [1.1b(2 and 3)]

To what extent do leaders systematically use the performance results to drive improvements throughout the organization?

1 Not Evident ☑	Leaders and managers do not use the review findings to anticipate problems and promote improvement and innovation. They tend to be reactive and "fight fires."
2 Beginning ☐	A few of the organization's leaders and managers use the performance results to set priorities for improvement. However, very few share the findings throughout the organization or follow up to ensure improvements are made.
3 Basically Effective ☐	Some of the organization's leaders and managers use the performance results to set priorities for improvement and even promote limited innovation in some parts of the organization. Some have also begun to monitor and follow up to ensure improvements are made.
4 Mature ☐	Many of the organization's leaders and managers consistently use the performance results to set priorities for improvement and promote innovation throughout many parts of the organization including a few key suppliers/partners and customers (as appropriate). Many leaders closely monitor progress and follow up to ensure improvements are made. The effectiveness of these processes is routinely evaluated.
5 Advanced ☐	Most of the organization's leaders and managers consistently use the performance results to set priorities for improvement and promote innovation throughout most of the organization including key suppliers/partners and customers (as appropriate). Most closely monitor progress and follow up to ensure improvements are made and sustained. The effectiveness of these processes is routinely evaluated and some improvement has resulted.

How is this done (describe the approach or method) and how widely is it used (deployment)?

Suggested action steps to improve, if needed:

Evaluating and Improving Leadership and Management Effectiveness at All Levels [1.1b(4)]	
To what extent do leaders and managers use organizational performance data and employee feedback to evaluate and improve their effectiveness?	
1 Not Evident ☐	Performance evaluations of leaders and managers include financial or cost/budget results but not employee input. Measurable improvement objectives are not usually developed for the next review cycle.
2 Beginning ☑	Performance evaluations of leaders and managers include financial, cost, and a few other organizational performance results and anecdotal employee input but no systematic employee feedback. A few measurable improvement objectives are tied to these results for the next review.
3 Basically Effective ☐	Performance evaluations of leaders and managers include financial, cost, and several other key performance results. Employee feedback based on systematic assessments (such as 360 degree or upward evaluation) is considered a little. Some measurable improvement objectives are tied to organization and—to a lesser extent—employee results for the next review.
4 Mature ☐	Performance evaluations and plans of leaders and managers include financial, cost, and many other key performance results. Employee feedback based on systematic assessments (such as 360 degree or upward evaluation) is usually considered. Many improvement objectives are tied to organizational and employee results for the next review cycle. The effectiveness of these processes is routinely evaluated.
5 Advanced ☐	Performance evaluations and plans of leaders and managers include most to all key performance results. Employee feedback based on systematic assessments (such as 360 degree or upward evaluation) is considered fully. Most improvement objectives are tied to organizational and employee results for the next review cycle. The effectiveness of these processes is routinely evaluated and some improvement has resulted.
How is this done (describe the approach or method) and how widely is it used (deployment)?	
Suggested action steps to improve, if needed:	

Since the behavioral descriptions in the survey combine the requirements of the Criteria with the standards from the scoring guidelines, it is possible to produce accurate Baldrige-based scores for Items and Categories for the entire organization and for any subgroup or division.

The following tables provide sample scores for the entire organization and for two job classifications. The chart below shows the percent scores, on a 0 to 100 scale, for each Item. This helps users determine at a glance, the relative strengths and weaknesses.

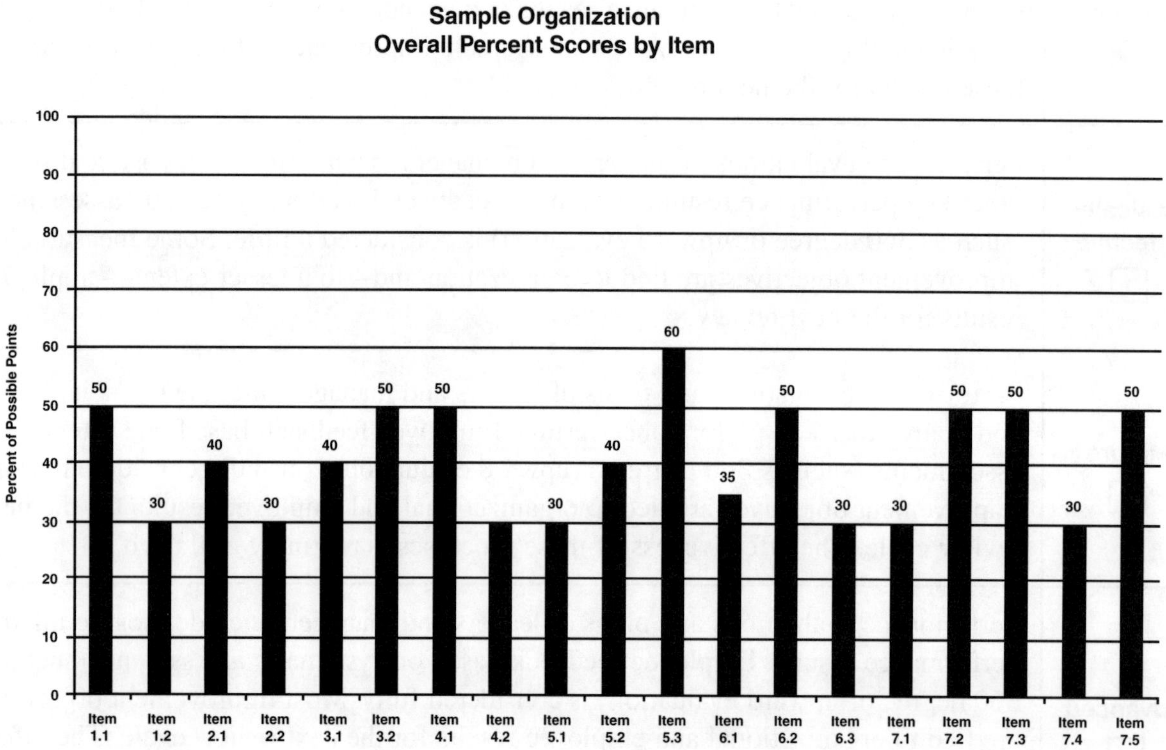

The following chart shows the ratings by subgroup, in this case, position of senior managers and supervisors. On the previous graph, Item 1.1, Leadership System reflected a rating of 50 percent. However, according to the breakout below, senior managers believe the processes are much stronger (over 60 percent) than supervisors (less than 35 percent). This typically indicates incomplete systems development or poor deployment of existing systems and processes required by the Item.

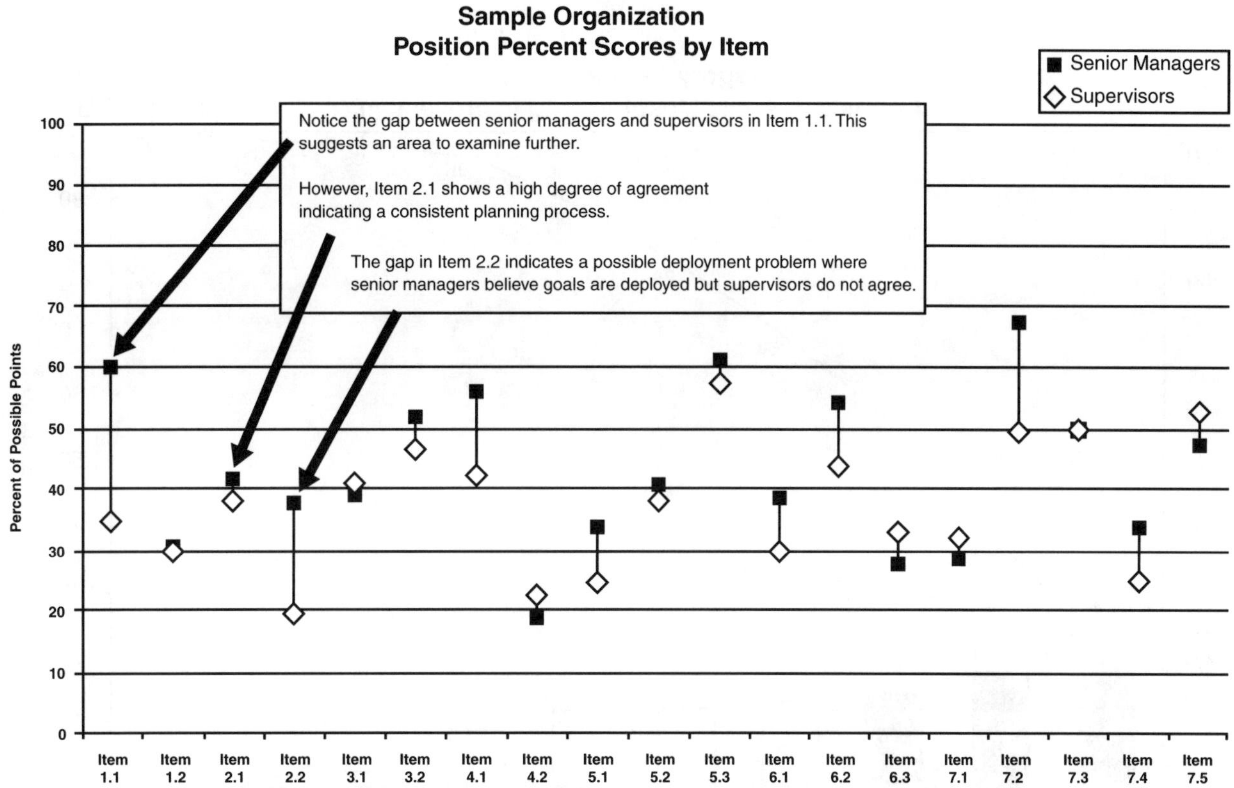

The following pareto diagram presents data reflecting the areas respondents believed were most in need of improvement. Continuing with the leadership example, it is clear that respondents believe that leaders need to do a better job of setting clear high performance expectations (Theme D), communicating vision and performance expectations (Theme E), and assessing and improving leadership performance and accountability (Theme G). This helps examiners focus on which areas in leadership may be the most important opportunities for improvement.

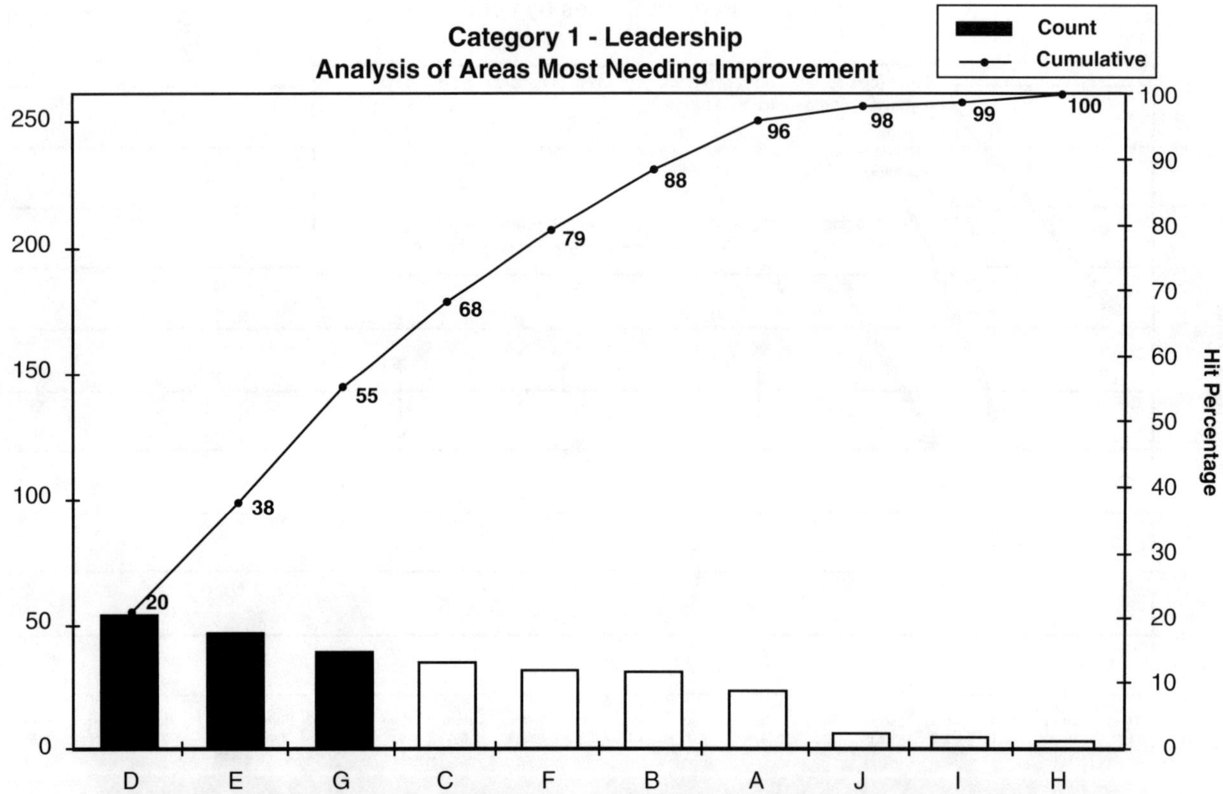

Letter Key for Category 1—Leadership			
A	Future Emphasis / Customer Orientation	F	Reviewing Organization Performance
B	Leadership Commitment to Values	**G**	**Leadership System Performance and Accountability**
C	Focus on Continuous Improvement	H	Compliance with Laws and Regulations
D	**High Performance Expectations**	I	Reducing Public Risks
E	**Communication of Vision and Performance**	J	Community Involvement

The following chart allows examiners to determine what type of employee (in this case administrator or faculty staff) identified the various improvement priorities. Look at "D" and "G" below and you will see that faculty/staff identified the need to improve these areas by a 3 to 1 margin. This tends to indicate a deployment gap and suggests that administrators are not perceived as effective as they believe themselves to be.

Priority Improvement Counts and Percentages — By Position for Leadership Category

1. Leadership

	Count												Percentage (See Chart Below)									
	A	B	C	D	E	F	G	H	I	J		Total	A	B	C	D	E	F	G	H	I	J
Supervisors	6	12	19	36	16	13	28	1	1	2		100	6	12	19	36	16	13	28	1	1	2
Senior Managers	13	12	19	15	29	23	13	1	3	2		150	9	8	13	10	19	15	9	1	2	1

Percentage of "Priority Improvement Hits"

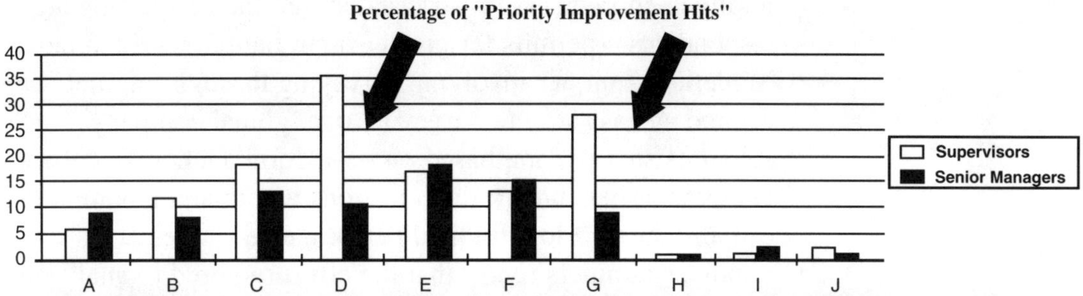

Letter Key for Category 1—Leadership			
A	Future Emphasis / Customer Orientation	F	Reviewing Organization Performance
B	Leadership Commitment to Values	**G**	**Leadership System Performance and Accountability**
C	Focus on Continuous Improvement	H	Compliance with Laws and Regulations
D	**High Performance Expectations**	I	Reducing Public Risks
E	**Communication of Vision and Performance**	J	Community Involvement

Finally, a complete report of the comments and explanations of the respondents can be prepared and used by examiners and organization leaders for improvement planning.

Pros:

- Descriptive behavioral anchors increase the consistency of rating. That is, one respondent's rating of "2" is likely to be the same as another respondent's rating of "2."

- Although completing a behaviorally anchored survey requires more reading than a Likert scale survey, the amount of time and cost required to complete it is still less than 20 percent of the time and cost required to prepare even a short written narrative.
- Because it is easy and simple to use, the behaviorally anchored survey does not impose a barrier to participation as does the written narrative. States and companies who use surveys with properly written behavioral anchors find the accuracy of the assessment to be as good and in many cases better than that achieved by the narrative self-assessment, and significantly better than Likert scale assessments. By obtaining input from a cross-section of functions and levels throughout the organization, a performance profile can be developed which not only identifies strengths and areas for improvement, but deployment gaps as well—something the written narrative assessments rarely provide.
- For organizations doing business throughout the world, the behaviorally anchored survey—translated into the native language of respondents—permits far greater input than the written narrative.
- Modern techniques involving surveying through Internet access created an easy way to survey a large, global company.
- Accurate survey data, based on behavioral anchors, can be used to compare or benchmark organizations within and among industries, and can also support longitudinal performance studies.
- Finally, examiners report that the effort required to analyze survey data and plan a site visit is about 50 percent less than the amount of effort required to analyze and prepare for a site visit based on a written narrative. Moreover, they report better information regarding deployment.

Cons:

- Organizations with highly developed performance management systems that seek to apply for top state or national recognition may prefer to practice developing the full-length narrative self-assessment because it is usually required.
- Examiners who are comfortable with the Baldrige application review process, which requires 25 or more hours to conduct an individual review of a full-length narrative self-assessment, initially find it disconcerting to develop comments and plan a site visit based on data gathered from a survey. Different training for examiners is required to develop skills at using survey data to prepare feedback and plan site visits.

NOTE: The preceding report of a behaviorally anchored self-assessment survey is administered by the National Council for Performance Excellence, Winooski, Vermont, and used with their permission. Readers may contact them by calling Wendy Steager at (800) 655-1922 or by writing to NCPE, One Main Street, Winooski, VT 05404. The Vermont Council for Quality, Minnesota Council for Quality, and Florida Sterling Award and their boards of examiners use this survey technique to assess schools, government agencies, and businesses. The behaviorally anchored survey has completely replaced the written narrative self-assessment as the application for the Vermont Quality Award as well as the Aruba National Quality Award. Examiners successfully use survey data to plan and conduct site visits in companies as well. At the same time, organization leaders use survey data for improvement planning. The Florida Sterling Award uses the behaviorally anchored survey approach for organizations in the early stages of developing performance excellence systems. Additionally, many private sector organizations are using this type of assessment for internal business evaluations.

In conclusion:

- The full-length written narrative self-assessment is costly. It provides useful information both to examiners and the organizations completing it. The process of completing the written self-assessment can help more advanced organizations to focus and work together as a team.
- The usefulness of the short form written self-assessment is marginal especially for beginning organizations; little useful information is provided to examiners and managers/employees of the organization. However, because it takes less time to complete, one of the barriers to participation is lowered.
- Concerns over the accuracy and inter-rater reliability of the simple and descriptive Likert scales make their use in conducting effective organizational assessments of management systems questionable.
- The behaviorally anchored survey combines the benefits of survey speed with the accuracy and completeness of a well-developed written narrative self-assessment. In addition, the behaviorally anchored survey can identify gaps in deployment unlike the written narrative self-assessment and is less costly and faster to administer than the written narrative.

A copy of the business, education, and health care surveys can be obtained from the National Council for Performance Excellence, One Main Street, Winooski, Vermont 05404 (800-655-1922).

The Site Visit

Introduction

Many people and organizations have asked about how to prepare for site visits. This section is intended to help answer those questions and prepare the organization for an on-site examination. It includes rules of the game for examiners and what they are taught to look for. As we all know, the best preparation for this type of examination is to see things through the eyes of the trained examiner.

Before an organization can be recommended to receive the Malcolm Baldrige National Quality Award, it must receive a visit from a team of business assessment experts from the National Board of Examiners. Approximately 25 percent to 30 percent of organizations applying for the Baldrige Award in recent years have received these site visits.

The Baldrige Award site visit team usually includes two senior examiners—one of whom is designated as team leader—and four to seven other examiners. In addition, the team is accompanied by a representative of the National Quality Award Office and a representative of ASQ—which provides administrative services to the Baldrige Award office under contract.

The site visit team usually gathers at a hotel near the organization's headquarters on the Sunday morning immediately preceding the site visit. During the day, the team makes final preparations and plans for the visit.

Each team member is assigned lead responsibility for one or more categories of the award Criteria. Each examiner is usually teamed with one other examiner during the site visit. These examiners usually conduct the visit in pairs to ensure the accurate recording of information.

Site visits usually begin on a Monday morning and last one week. By Wednesday or Thursday most site visit teams will have completed their on-site review. They retire to the nearby hotel to confer and write their reports. By the end of the week, the team must reach consensus on the findings and prepare a final report for the panel of judges.

Purpose of Site Visits

Site visits help clarify uncertain points and verify self-assessment (that is, application) accuracy. During the site visit, examiners investigate areas most difficult to understand from self-assessments, such as the following:

- Deployment—how widely a process is used throughout the organization;
- Integration—whether processes fit together to support performance excellence;
- Process ownership—whether processes are broadly owned, simply directed, or micromanaged;
- Employee involvement—whether the extent to which employees' participation in managing processes of all types is optimized; and
- Continuous improvement maturity—the number and extent of improvement cycles and resulting refinements in all areas of the organization and at all levels.

Characteristics of Site Visit Issues

Examiners look at issues that are an essential component of scoring and role model determination. They have a responsibility to:

- Clarify information that is missing or vague;
- Verify significant strengths identified from the self-assessment; and
- Verify deployment of the practices described in the self-assessment.

Examiners will:

- Concentrate on cross-cutting issues;
- Examine data, reports, and documents;
- Interview individuals and teams; and
- Receive presentations from the applicant organization.

Examiners are not permitted to conduct their own focus groups or surveys with customers, suppliers, or dealers or disrupt work processes. Conducting focus groups or surveys would violate the confidentiality agreements as well as be statistically unsound.

Typically Important Site Visit Issues

- Role of senior management in leading and serving as a role model
- Degree of involvement and self-direction of employees below upper management
- Comprehensiveness and accessibility of the information system
- Utility and validity of available data
- Extent that facts and data are used in decision making
- Degree of emphasis on customer satisfaction
- Extent of systematic approaches to work processes
- Deployment and integration of quality principles and processes
- Training effectiveness
- Use of compensation, recognition, and rewards to promote key values
- Extent that strategic plans align organizational work
- Extent of the use of measurable goals at all levels in the organization
- Evidence of evaluation and improvement cycles in all work processes and in system effectiveness
- Improvement levels in cycle times and other operating processes
- Extent of integration of all processes—operational and support
- Level of maturity of improvement initiatives
- Extent of benchmarking effort
- Level of supplier involvement in performance improvement activities
- Uncovering improvements since the submission of the application (self-assessment) and receiving up-to-date business results

Discussions with the Applicant Prior to the Site Visit

Prior to the site visit, all communication between the applicant organization and its team must be routed through their respective single points of contact. Only the team leader may contact the applicant on behalf of the site visit team prior to the site visit. This helps ensure consistency of message and communication for both parties. It prevents confusion and misunderstandings.

The team leader should provide the applicant organization with basic information about the process. This includes schedules, arrival times, and equipment and meeting room needs.

Applicant organizations usually provide the following information prior to the site visit team's final site visit planning meeting at the hotel on the day before the site visit starts:

- List of key contacts
- Organization chart
- Facility layout
- Performance data requested by examiners

The team leader, on behalf of team members, will ask for supplementary documentation to be compiled (such as results data brought up to date) to avoid placing an undue burden on the organization at the time of the site visit.

The site visit team will select sites that allow them to examine key issues and check deployment in key areas. This information may or may not be discussed with the applicant prior to the site visit. Examiners will need access to all areas of the organization.

Conduct of Site Visit Team Members (Examiners)

Examiners are not allowed to discuss findings with anyone but team members. Examiners may not disclose the following to the applicant:

- Personal or team observations and findings
- Conclusions and decisions
- Observations about the applicant's performance systems, whether in a complimentary or critical way

Examiners may not discuss the following with anyone:

- Observations about other applicants
- Names of other award program applicants

Examiners may not accept trinkets, gifts, or gratuities of any kind (coffee, cookies, rolls, breakfast, and lunch are okay), so applicant organizations should not offer them. At the conclusion of the site visit, examiners are not permitted to leave with any of the applicant's materials including logo items or catalogs—not even items usually given to visitors.

Examiners will dress in appropriate business attire unless instructed otherwise by the applicant organization.

Opening Meeting

An opening meeting will be scheduled to introduce all parties and set the structure for the site visit. The meeting is usually attended by senior executives and the self-assessment writing team. The opening meeting usually is scheduled first on the initial day of the site visit (8:30 or 9:00 A.M.). The team leader generally starts the meeting, introduces the team, and opens the site visit. Overhead slides and formal presentations are usually unnecessary.

The applicant organization usually has one hour to present any information it believes important for the examiners to know. This includes time for a tour, if necessary.

Immediately after the meeting, examiners are likely to want to meet with senior leaders and those responsible for preparing sections of the self-assessment (application).

Conducting the Site Visit

The team will follow the site visit plan, subject to periodic adjustments according to its findings.

The site visit team will need a private room to conduct frequent caucuses. Applicant representatives are not present at these caucuses. The team will also conduct evening meetings at the hotel to review the findings of the day, reach consensus, write comments, and revise the site visit report.

If, during the course of the site visit, someone from the applicant organization believes the team or any of its members are missing the point, the designated point of contact should inform the team leader or the Baldrige Award office monitor. Also, someone who believes an examiner behaved inappropriately should inform the designated point of contact, who will inform the team leader or the award office monitor.

Employees should be instructed to mark every document given to examiners with the name and work location of the person providing the document. This will ensure that it is returned to the proper person. Records should be made of all material given to team members.

Organizational personnel may not ask examiners for opinions and advice. Examiners are not permitted to provide any information of this type during the site visit.

Team Leader's Site Visit Checklist

This checklist provides a summary of activities required of site visit team leaders.

Preparation

- Size of team and length of visit determined, with starting and ending date and time selected
- All team members receive copies of consensus report
- Team notified of starting/ending times and locations
- Background information on new team members (if any) received
- Category lead and team pairing assignments made for each team member
- New team members complete review of narrative
- Site visit notebooks prepared
- Individual team members prepare assigned site visit issues
- Subteam members exchange site visit issues for comments
- Revised site visit issues received from subteams
- Site visit issues reviewed by Team Leader and comments sent to subteams
- Team asked to revise site visit themes or issues (as appropriate)

Previsit Meeting

- Examiner introductions/reintroductions
- Site visit issues and themes reviewed and approaches outlined
- Sites selected to visit and logistics reviewed
- Specific requests for first day listed (interviews and data)
- Caucus plans established

Continued on next page

Team Leader's Site Visit Checklist—continued

Conduct of Visit

- Opening presentation conducted
- Followed site visit plan
- Revised plan as required
- Caucused frequently
- Maintained records of findings
- Maintained records of applicant documents received
- Answered all selected site issues; developed information on site visit themes
- Closing meeting conducted

Site Visit Report

- Team completed site visit issues
- Team completed item and category summary forms
- Completed overall summary form
- Team initiated report
- Report copied; original given to award office representative before leaving site
- Leader kept copy, narrative, and other notes (or a back-up person has material)
- Collected and returned all applicant material prior to leaving site
- Collected all narratives, materials, and notes; sent or given to award office

Feedback Report

- Senior examiner/feedback author collected feedback points during site visit
- Senior examiner/feedback author reviewed feedback points with team during site visit report writing session
- Reviewed feedback report completed before leaving site and sent to award office

Generic Site Visit Questions

Examiners must verify or clarify the information contained in an application, whether or not the examiners have determined a process to be a strength or an area for improvement. Examiners must verify the existence of strengths as well as clarify the nature of each significant area for improvement.

Before and during the site visit review process, examiners formulate a series of questions based on the Baldrige performance excellence Criteria. Because the site visit must verify or clarify all significant aspects of the organization's performance management systems against the Criteria, it is possible to identify a series of generic questions that examiners are likely to ask during the site visit process. These questions are presented in the following section to help prepare applicants for the assessment process.

Category 1—Leadership

1. Describe the process your organization used in developing your mission, vision, and values. To top leaders: Who was involved with that process? How do you set direction and guide the organization? How do you seek future opportunities for your organization?
    - Please share with us the mission, vision, and values of this organization.
    - What are your organization's top priorities?
    - How do you ensure that all your employees know this?
    - How do you know how effective you are at communicating your commitment to the vision and values?
2. How do you, as a leader, see your role in supporting processes to ensure performance excellence?
    - How do you role model the behaviors you want your managers and other employees to emulate (follow)?
    - What do the leaders personally do to lead this organization? What do you do that visibly displays to employees throughout the organization your personal involvement and commitment to the vision and values? How do you promote innovation?
    - What percentage of your time is spent on performance review and improvement activities? How do you review performance to assess the organization's health, competitive performance, and progress? What key performance measures do senior leaders regularly review?
    - How do you ensure the organization has the capabilities to remain competitive?
    - How do top priorities and opportunities for innovation reflect organizational review findings? How do you ensure that these

priorities and opportunities for innovation are used throughout the organization? To what extent are these priorities and innovation opportunities used with key customers, suppliers and/or partners?
- What is your process for evaluating the effectiveness of the leadership system? How do you include or use employee feedback in the evaluation?
- Please identify specific examples where the senior leadership improved the leadership system as a result of these evaluations. How do managers evaluate and improve their own personal leadership effectiveness? How is employee feedback used here?

3. What are the criteria for promoting managers within the organization?
    - How are you making managers accountable for performance improvement, employee involvement, and customer satisfaction objectives?
    - What measures do you personally use to track progress toward achieving the organization's key business drivers? How often do you monitor these measures?
    - Can we see a copy of a manager's evaluation form?
    - How have you improved the process over the years of evaluating managers?
4. Share with us what you feel are the most important requirements of your key customers.
    - (Pick one of the requirements.) Which department is responsible for delivering this?
    - Please show us evidence of continuous improvement within that department.
5. What is the process used to monitor the performance of your organization? How does it relate to the organization's strategic business plan?
    - Do measurable goals exist?
    - How were the goals established?
    - How are they monitored? How often?
    - How are they key to your stakeholders' primary needs and expectations?
    - What are the key success factors (or key result areas, critical success factors, key business drivers) for your organization, and how do you use them to drive performance excellence?
6. As a corporate citizen, what is your process for contributing to and improving the environment and society?
    - What do you do to anticipate public concerns over the possible impact of your organization? What are some examples? How do you measure progress?
    - What are some ways your organization ensures that employees act in an ethical manner in all business transactions? How is this monitored to ensure compliance?

- Do you have any plans or processes for systematic evaluation and improvement in place?

Category 2—Strategic Planning

1. When was the last time the strategic plan was updated? How recent is it? Can we review a copy?
2. How did you develop this plan? What factors did you consider in the development of your strategic plan?
   - How does your strategic plan address supplier and/or partner capabilities? The competitive environment?
   - What role do your stakeholders play in the development of the strategic plan?
   - How do you identify resources needed to prepare for new opportunities and requirements? How are wishes addressed?
   - Are the strategic objectives for your organization derived from this plan? If not, from where do they come? May I see a list of your strategic objectives?
3. How do you plan for development, education, and training needs of the organization? What are the organization's human resource plans (long/short term)?
   - Summarize the organization's plans related to work design, innovation, rapid response, compensation and recognition, employee development and training, recruitment, health, safety, ergonomics, special services, and employee satisfaction.
   - How do these plans optimize the use of human resources?
   - How do these plans align to the strategic plan?
   - What are examples of changes to the human resource plans based on inputs from the strategic planning in the following areas: recruitment, training, compensation, rewards, incentives, fringe benefits, programs?
4. How do you deploy these goals, objectives, and action plans throughout the organization to ensure that work is aligned and action is taken to achieve the plan?
   - How do you ensure that organizational, work unit, and individual goals and plans are aligned?
   - How do you ensure that supplier and/or partner goals are aligned with your strategic plan?
5. What is (summarize) your process for evaluation and improvement of the strategic planning and plan deployment process, including the human resource planning process?
   - What are examples of improvements made as a result of this evaluation process? Where did they occur?
6. How has your performance relative to plan been tracked?

7. Who do you consider to be your top competitors, and how does your planned performance compare to theirs and/or simular providers?
   - How do you determine who your top competitors are?
8. What are your specific goals and objectives? Please provide a copy of your long-range performance projections. How did you go about establishing these projections? How do these projections compare with your competitors' projections for the same time period?

Category 3—Customer and Market Focus

1. How do you know what your former, current, and potential customers expect of you? How does your organization determine short- and long-term customer requirements? What are they?
   - How do you differentiate key requirements from less important requirements?
   - How do you anticipate requirements and prepare to meet them?
   - How do you evaluate and improve processes for determining customer requirements?
2. How do you provide easy access for your customers to obtain information and assistance or complain? What do you expect to learn from customer complaints?
   - What is your process of handling customer complaints? Do you monitor or track complaint data? What do you do with the information?
   - What percent of complaints are resolved at first contact? Describe the training you provide to customer-contact employees.
   - Describe your process for follow-up with customers. What do you do with feedback from customers regarding products and services? What triggers action?
   - What are the customer contact requirements or service standards? How were they determined? How do you know if standards are being met?
   - How do you evaluate and improve the customer relationship process?
   - What are some improvements you've made to the way you determine customer requirements? How did you decide they were important to make, and when were they made?
3. How often do senior managers talk to customers?
   - What do they do with this information?
4. What are your key measures for customer satisfaction and dissatisfaction? How do these measures provide information on likely future market behavior (loyalty, repurchase, and referrals)?
   - How do you measure customer satisfaction and dissatisfaction? Do you measure satisfaction/dissatisfaction for all key customer

groups/segments? What are your customer groups or segments? How do you determine them? How do you differentiate them in regard to products and services you offer? What process do you use to ensure the objectivity and validity of customer satisfaction data? What do you do with the information?
- What customer satisfaction information do you have about your competitors or benchmarks? What do you do with this information?
- How do you disseminate satisfaction/dissatisfaction information to your employees? What action do they take as a result?
- How do you know appropriate action is taken?
- How do you go about improving the way you determine customer satisfaction? Please provide some examples of how you have improved it over the past several years? When were the requirements made?

5. What processes do you use to build loyalty, positive referral, and lasting relationships with customers?
   - How do you differentiate these processes according to customer group?
6. How do you evaluate the effectiveness of processes for customer satisfaction determination and relationship enhancement? What requirements have resulted from this evaluation? When did they occur?

Category 4—Information and Analysis

1. What are the major performance indicators critical to running your organization?
2. How do you determine whether the information you collect and use for decision making is complete, timely, reliable, accessible, and accurate? What is the process you use to determine the relevance of the information to organizational goals and action plans?
   - What criteria do you use for data selection? How do you ensure that all data collected meet these criteria?
   - Describe how you obtain feedback from the users of the information. How is this feedback used to make improvements?
3. You have told us what your top priorities are. How do you benchmark against these? Please describe how needs and priorities for selecting comparisons and benchmarking are determined. Share an example of the process of prioritization.
   - How do you use competitive or comparative performance data generally?
   - How are the results of your benchmarking efforts used to set stretch targets?
   - How are the results of your benchmarking efforts used to improve work processes?

- How do you evaluate and improve your benchmarking processes?
- Show us samples of comparative studies. Picking some at random, determine: Why was the area selected? How were comparison data selected and obtained? How were data in the example used?

4. Please share with us an example of analysis of information important to your customers and your own organization's success.
    - How are data analyzed to determine relationships between customer information and financial performance; operational data and financial performance; or operational data and human resource?
    - What data and analyses do you use to understand your people, your customers, and your market?
    - How widely are these analyses used for decision making? What actions are you taking to extend the analysis across all parts of the organization?
    - What are you doing to improve the analysis process?

Category 5—Human Resource Focus

1. Do employees know and understand organization/work unit priorities? How do you determine this?
    - What do you do to ensure effective communication among employees and work units?
    - What do you do to encourage initiative and self-directed responsibility? What authority do employees have to direct their own actions and make business decisions?
    - (To employees.) What authority do you have to make decisions about resolving problems, changing process steps, and communications across departments?
    - How do you empower employees? What are some examples of processes you have used to evaluate and enhance opportunities for employees to take individual initiative and demonstrate self-directed responsibility in designing and managing their work? Show examples of actions taken and improvements made. When were they made?
2. How does the organization link recognition, reward, and compensation to achieve performance excellence objectives (e.g., customer satisfaction, performance improvement, and organization learning)? Describe your approach to employee recognition and compensation. How does your approach reinforce achievement of goals and objectives?
    - (General question for employees.) Do you feel that your contributions to the organization are recognized? How have you been recognized for contributing to achieving organization action plans?
    - What specific reward and recognition programs are utilized?
3. How do you take into account diversity in your community and fair hiring practices in your hiring and recruitment?

4. What ongoing training is provided for your employees?
   - How is your training curriculum designed and delivered? How do you integrate employee, supervisor, and manager feedback into the design of your training program? What methods are used?
   - How does your training program impact operational performance goals? How do you know your training improves your business results? Show examples.
   - What training and education do you provide to ensure that you meet the needs of all categories of employees? What training does a new employee receive to obtain the knowledge and skills necessary for success and high performance including leadership development of employees?
   - How do you address key development needs such as new employee orientation, safety, and diversity training?
   - How does training and education address performance excellence skills needed such as quality control, benchmarking, and performance measurement?
   - If applicable, how do employees in remote locations participate in training programs?
   - What is your system for improving training? Please give us some examples of improvements made and when they were made?
   - How do you identify skills and knowledge that will be needed by your employees of the future?
   - How are these skills and characteristics reflected in recruitment and hiring practices?
5. What are your standards for employee health and safety? Does your approach to health and safety address the needs of all employee groups?
   - How do you determine that you have a safe and healthy work environment? How do you measure this?
   - How are you performing against those standards? How were they derived?
   - What are your procedures for systematic evaluation and improvement?
6. How do your senior leaders, managers, and supervisors encourage employees to develop and put to use their full potential?
7. How is employee satisfaction measured? What do you do with the information?
   - What are the key areas of concern? To employees, ask: What does the organization do to enhance your career development?
   - What special services, facilities, activities, and opportunities does your organization provide employees?
   - What do you do to improve employee satisfaction systematically? Please give us some examples of improvements.

Category 6—Process Management

1. What is your process for designing new or revised products and services to ensure that customer requirements are met?
    - How do suppliers, partners, customers, and support organizations participate in the design process?
    - How are design changes handled and methods used to ensure that all changes are included?
    - How do you test new products or services before they are introduced to be sure they perform as expected?
    - How do you evaluate and improve the process for designing new products/services, including reductions in cycle time? Please provide some examples of improvements and when they were made.
2. What are your key production and delivery processes and their requirements, including quality indicators and performance?
    - What steps have you taken to improve the effectiveness/efficiency of key work processes, including cycle time?
    - What are the processes by which you deliver these products and services to ensure that customer expectations will be met or exceeded?
    - Once you determine that a process may not be meeting measurement goals or performing according to expectations, what process do you use to determine root cause and to bring about process improvement?
3. Please give an example of how a customer request or complaint resulted in an improvement of a current process or the establishment of a new process?
4. Please share with us your list of key support processes, requirements, and associated process measures, including in-process measures.
    - How is performance of support services systematically evaluated and refined? Please provide some examples.
    - What are the steps you have taken to design your key support processes? How do you determine the types of services needed? How do your support services interact with and add value to your operational processes?
    - How does your organization maintain the performance of key support services? Share some examples of processes used to determine root causes of support problems and how you prevent recurrence of problems.
5. Who are your most important (key) suppliers and partners?
    - How do you determine critical characteristics your key suppliers and/or partners must meet so that your needs are met? What are the key performance requirements? What type of assistance do you provide your suppliers and/or partners to help them meet your

requirements? Please explain how you measure your supplier's and/or partner's performance and provide feedback.

- Show how you systematically help your key suppliers and/or partners improve their performance and deliver better products and services to you at a lower cost. Please provide some examples.
- What are your supplier/partner management or procurement department goals and objectives? How do you support your suppliers and/or partners to keep products and services current with your needs? How do you measure and improve their performance? Please share with us some examples.

Category 7—Business Results

1. What are the customer satisfaction trends and performance levels at this time? [Links to Item 3.2 and 6.1]
    - Please show a breakout of data by customer group or segment.
    - How do these customer satisfaction trends and levels compare with those of your competitors or similar providers?
    - What are your current levels and trends for customer loyalty, positive referral, customer-perceived value, and relationship building?
    - What are your current levels and trends for how customers perceive your products and service performance?
2. What are the current levels and trends showing financial or marketplace performance or economic value?
    - Please provide data on key financial measures such as return on investment (ROI), operating profits (or budget reductions as appropriate), or economic value added.
    - Please provide data on market share or business growth, as appropriate. Identify new markets entered and the level of performance in those markets.
    - How do these trends compare with those of your competitors or similar providers?
3. What are the current levels and trends showing the effectiveness of your human resource practices? [Links to Category 5]
    - Please provide data on key indicators such as safety/accident record, absenteeism, turnover by category and type of employee/manager, grievances, and related litigation.
    - How do these trends compare with those of your competitors or similar providers?
4. Please show us your supplier/partner performance data trends and current levels for each key indicator such as on-time delivery, error rate, and reducing costs. [Links to Item 6.3]

- How does performance on these key indicators compare to your competitors, other providers, or benchmarks?

5. How do you measure the quality of your products and services? [Links to Item 6.1]
    - Please show us your performance data.
    - What are current levels and trends for key design, production, delivery and support process performance?
    - What are current level and trends for production and cycle time for design, delivery, and production?
    - How do you know which factors are most important to your customers? [Links to Item 3.1]
    - How does your performance on these key indicators compare to your competitors, other providers, or benchmarks?
6. How do you measure support service effectiveness and efficiency? [Links to Item 6.2]
    - Please show us your performance data.
    - How do you know what the key performance indicators should be?
    - How does your performance on these key indicators compare to your competitors, other providers, or benchmarks?
7. How do you measure operating effectiveness and efficiency?
    - Please show us your performance data.
    - How do you know what the key performance indicators should be? [Links to Items 6.1 and 6.2]
    - How does your performance on these key indicators compare to your competitors, other providers, or benchmarks?
    - What are your results for regulatory/legal compliance and citizenship? [Links to Item 1.2]
    - What are your results on accomplishment of your organizational strategy?

General Cross-Cutting Questions to Ask Employees

- Who are your customers?
- What are the organization's mission, vision, and quality values? What are your goals?
- What is the strategic plan for the organization? What are the organization's goals, and what role do you play in helping to achieve the goals?
- What kind of training do you receive? Was it useful?
- How are you involved in the work and decision making of the organization?
- Is this a good place to work? Why (or why not)?
- What activities are recognized or rewarded?

Summary of Business Eligibility Categories and Restrictions

Basic Eligibility Public Law 100-107 establishes the three business eligibility categories of the Award: manufacturing, service, and small business. Any for-profit business and some subunits headquartered in the United States or its territories, including U.S. subunits of foreign companies, may apply for the Award. Eligibility is intended to be as open as possible. For example, publicly or privately owned, domestic or foreign-owned entities, joint ventures, corporations, sole proprietorships, and holding companies may apply. Not eligible in the business category are: local, state, and federal government agencies; trade associations; professional societies; and not-for-profit organizations.

Business Award Eligibility Categories and Terms

Manufacturing Companies or some subunits that produce and sell manufactured products or manufacturing processes, and producers of agricultural, mining, or construction products.

Service Companies or some subunits that sell services.

Small Business Companies engaged in manufacturing and/or the provision of services that are comprised of 500 or fewer employees.

Subunits A subunit is a unit or division of a larger (parent) company. Subunits of companies in the manufacturing and service eligibility categories might be eligible. The subunit must have more than 500 employees, or have more than 25 percent of the employees of the parent, or have been independent prior to being acquired by its parent. In the last case, it must continue to operate largely independently under its own identity.

The subunit must be self-sufficient enough to be examined in all seven Criteria Categories, and it must be a discrete business entity that is readily distinguishable from other parts of the parent organization. It cannot be primarily an internal supplier to other units in the parent company or a business support function (sales, distribution, legal services, etc.).

NOTE: Subunits of "chain" organizations (where each unit performs a similar function or manufactures a similar product) are no longer categorically ineligible. Their eligibility is now determined by the same rules as other subunits.

Other Restrictions on Eligibility

Location

Although an applicant may have facilities outside the United States or its territories or receive support from its parent, in the event of a site visit, the applicant must ensure that the appropriate people and materials are available for examination in the United States to document the operational practices associated with all of its major business functions. In the event that the applicant receives the Award, it must be able to share information on the seven Criteria Categories at the Quest for Excellence Conference and at its U.S. facilities. Sharing beyond the Quest for Excellence Conference is on a voluntary basis.

Multiple-Application Restrictions

A subunit and its parent may not both apply for Awards in the same year. In addition, only one subunit of a company may apply for an Award in the same year in the same business eligibility category.

Future Eligibility Restrictions

If an organization or a subunit that has more than 50 percent of the total employees of the parent receives an Award, the organization and all its subunits are ineligible to apply for another Award for a period of five years. If a subunit receives an Award, that subunit and all its subunits are ineligible to apply for another Award for a period of five years. After five years, Award recipients are eligible to reapply for the Award or to reapply "for feedback only."

Eligibility Determination

To ensure that Award recipients meet all reasonable requirements and expectations in representing the Award throughout the United States, potential applicants must have their eligibility approved prior to applying for the Award. Potential applicants for the 1999 Award are encouraged to submit their Eligibility Determination Forms as early as possible after they are available, but no later than April 15, 1999. This form is contained in the *1999 Application Forms & Instructions for Business, Education, and Health Care.*

Fees for the 1999 Award Cycle

Eligibility Determination Fees

The eligibility determination fee is $100 for all potential applicants. This fee is nonrefundable.

Application Fees

Manufacturing company category—$4500
Service company category—$4500
Small business category—$1500
Supplemental sections—$1500 (NOTE: Supplemental sections fees are charges to companies that want a business unit reviewed as part of the application process and that business unit falls under another eligibility sector. For example, assume that manufacturing is the core business of an automaker. However, the automaker also operates a chain of service stations and a car rental system—both service sector companies. A supplemental section fee could be charged for this review.)

These fees cover all expenses associated with distribution and review of applications and development of feedback reports.

Site Visit Review Fees

Site visit review fees will be set when the visits are scheduled. Fees depend upon the number of examiners assigned and the duration of the visit. Site visit review fees for applicants in the small business category will be charged at one-half of the rate charged for companies in the manufacturing and service categories.

Site visit fees cover all expenses and travel costs associated with site visit participation and development of site visit reports. These fees are paid only by those applicants reaching the site visit stage.

Feedback

All applicants receive a feedback report. The feedback report—a tool for continuous improvement—is

- An assessment written by a team of leading U.S. quality and performance experts
- An applicant-specific listing of strengths and areas for improvement based on the Baldrige Award Criteria
- Used by organizations as part of their strategic planning processes to focus on their customers and to improve productivity

The report does not provide suggestions or ideas on how to improve.

The feedback report contains the Baldrige Award evaluation team's response to the written application. Length varies according to the detail presented in the written responses to the Baldrige Award Criteria. The report includes the following components:

- Background
- Application review process
- Scoring
- Distribution of numerical scores for all applicants
- Overall scoring summary of applicant
- Criteria Category scoring summary of applicant
- Details of the applicant's strengths and areas for improvement (feedback reports often contain more than150 strengths and areas for improvement)

Strict confidentiality is observed at all times and in every aspect of application review and feedback.

A survey of 1993 and 1994 Baldrige Award applicants conducted by the National Quality Award Office showed that more than 90 percent of respondents used the feedback report in their strategic and business planning processes.

Information about current and past winners and their achievements was drawn from the award office web page. General information on the National Institute of Standards and Technology is available on the World Wide Web at *http://www.nist.gov* and on the Baldrige Award program at *http://www.quality.nist.gov.*

Malcolm Baldrige National Quality Award Winners

1998 Winners

- Boeing Airlift and Tanker Programs, Long Beach, California (Manufacturing)
- Solar Turbines, Inc., San Diego, California (Manufacturing)
- Texas Nameplate Co., Inc., Dallas, Texas (Manufacturing)

Boeing Airlift and Tanker Programs. Known as A&T, Boeing Airlift and Tanker Programs designs, manufactures, and supports military transport aircraft. One of its major products is the C-17, designed to airlift large, heavy cargo to locations around the world. Based in Long Beach, Calif., A&T has 8,700 employees. In addition to other awards, A&T received the California Governor's Golden State Quality Award for management in 1996 and its Macon, Ga., facility received the Georgia Governor's Employer of the Year Award in 1998. In addition to California and Georgia, A&T also has sites in St. Louis, Mo.; Seattle, Wash.; and San Antonio, Texas; as well as at Air Force bases in Oklahoma, California, and South Carolina.

Solar Turbines, Inc. Based in San Diego, Calif., Solar Turbines designs and manufactures industrial gas turbines for power generation, natural gas compression, and pumping systems for sale in the United States and worldwide. Solar Turbines is one of the 50 largest exporters in the United States. A subsidiary of Caterpillar, Inc., Solar Turbines has 6,200 employees at 15 U.S. sites and in 23 foreign nations. In 1995, Solar Turbines received a "Best in Class" California U.S. Senate Productivity Award in large manufacturing.

Texas Nameplate Company, Inc. Founded in 1946, Texas Nameplate manufactures and sells identification and information labels used on a variety of products, including oil field equipment, truck and trailer vehicles, and electronic and computer equipment. With 66 employees, Texas Nameplate is the smallest company ever to receive the Baldrige Award. The company has two locations in Dallas, Texas. TNC received the Texas Quality Award in 1996.

1988–1998 Baldrige Award Winners and Contact Information

This section contains a list of Baldrige Award winners and key contact personnel from 1988 to 1998 as reported by NIST and the Office of Quality Programs. First the 1998 winners are presented, then the others in alphabetical order.

BOEING AIRLIFT AND TANKER PROGRAMS—1998 (Manufacturing)
Rick Fuller, Director of Communications
2401 Wandlow Road
Long Beach, CA 90807
Telephone: 562-496-5195
E-mail: richard.l.fuller@boeing.com

SOLAR TURBINES, INC.—1998 (Manufacturing)
Larry Winegrad, Director, Process and Quality Improvement
9330 Sky Park Court
San Diego, CA 92123
Telephone: 619-715-7777
E-mail: lwinegrad@cat.e-mail.com

TEXAS NAMEPLATE COMPANY, INC.—1998 (Manufacturing)
Scott Weber, Director of Administration
P.O. Box 150499
Dallas, TX 75315-0499
Telephone: 214-421-8206; 1-800-546-4161
E-mail: sweber@nameplate.com

3M DENTAL PRODUCTS DIVISION—1997 (Manufacturing)
Jim Wilson, Quality Specialist
3M Center; Building 260-2A-11
St. Paul, MN 55144
Telephone: 1-800-449-1476; Fax: 612-737-6049
www.mmm.com/dental/baldrige

ADAC LABORATORIES—1996 (Manufacturing)
Doug Keare, Vice President of Quality
540 Alder Drive
Milpitas, CA 95035
Telephone: 408-321-9100; Fax: 408-321-9686
www.adaclabs.com/pressrel/1996/101696.html

AMES RUBBER CORPORATION—1993 (Small Business)
Charles A. Roberts, Vice President, Total Quality
23-47 Ames Boulevard
Hamburg, NJ 07419
Telephone: 201-209-3200; Fax: 201-827-8893
www.amesrubber.com/totalqlt.htm

ARMSTRONG WORLD INDUSTRIES, INC. BUILDING PRODUCTS OPERATIONS—1995 (Manufacturing)
Nancy D. Hann, Baldrige Coordinator
Armstrong Building Products Operations
2500 Columbia Avenue
Lancaster, PA 17604
Telephone: 717-396-2540; Fax: 717-396-6330
ndhann@armstrong,com

AT&T CONSUMER COMMUNICATIONS SERVICES—1994 (Service)
John Braseli, District Manager
AT&T Consumer Markets Division
Room 6356F1
292 North Maple Avenue
Basking Ridge, NJ 07920
Telephone: 800-473-5047; Fax: 908-221-3015
As of 1/1/97, AT&T Consumer Communications Services became part of the new Consumer & Small Business Division of AT&T.

AT&T NETWORK SYSTEMS GROUP TRANSMISSION SYSTEMS BUSINESS UNIT—1992 (Manufacturing)
Jim Beauregard, Manager, Quality Engineering Assurance
Lucent Technologies, Inc. (including what was formerly TSBU)
1600 Osgood Street
North Andover, MA 01845
Telephone: 978-960-4309; Fax: 978-960-1660

AT&T UNIVERSAL CARD SERVICES—1992 (Service)
James Selzer, Vice President
8787 Baypine Road
Jacksonville, FL 32256
Telephone: 904-954-8896; Fax: 904-954-8720

CADILLAC MOTOR CAR COMPANY—1990 (Manufacturing)
Joseph R. Bransky, Director, Quality and Reliability
General Motors Corporation
30007 Van Dyke Ave., Room 142-37
Warren, MI 48090
Telephone: 810-492-7704; Fax: 810-492-7943
Tom Klipstine, Communications Staff
NAO Headquarters, Building 1-8
30400 Mound Road
Warren, MI 48090
Telephone: 810-986-6132; Fax: 810-986-9253

CORNING INCORPORATED TELECOMMUNICATIONS PRODUCTS DIVISION—1995 (Manufacturing)
Barbara Nazarczyk, Manager, Business Systems
Telecommunications Products Division
35 West Market Street
Corning, NY 14831
Telephone: 607-974-8473; Fax: 607-754-7517

CUSTOM RESEARCH, INC.—1996 (Small Business)
Beth Rounds, Senior Vice President
8401 Golden Valley Road
Minneapolis, MN 55427
Telephone: 612-542-0882; Fax: 612-542-0864

DANA COMMERCIAL CREDIT CORPORATION—1996 (Service)
Teressa Herbert, Director of Quality
P.O. Box 906
Toledo, OH 43697-0906
Telephone: 419-322-7500; Fax: 419-322-7721

EASTMAN CHEMICAL COMPANY—1993 (Manufacturing)
Christa Haynes, Coordinator, Corporate Information Center
431 Building 471
Kingsport, TN 37662
Telephone: 423-229-1925; Fax: 423-224-0323
www.eastman.com/corp/qual/nistemn.shtml

FEDERAL EXPRESS CORPORATION—1990 (Service)
Quality Questions and Information
Glenn Pearson, Manager, Quality and Process Improvement
1980 Nonconnah Boulevard
Memphis, TN 38132
Telephone: 901-224-2362; Fax: 901-224-2350

GLOBE METALLURGICAL, INC.—1988 (Small Business)
Norman Jennings, Quality Director
P.O. Box 157
Beverly, OH 45715
Telephone: 740-984-2361; Fax: 770-984-8635

GRANITE ROCK COMPANY—1992 (Small Business)
Dave Franceschi, Quality Services Manager
P.O. Box 50001
Watsonville, CA 95077-5001
Telephone: 408-768-2000; Fax: 408-768-2201

GTE DIRECTORIES CORPORATION—1994 (Service)
Bruce Rosenstie, Quality Service Manager
GTE Place, West Airfield Drive
P.O. Box 619810
D/FW Airport, TX 75261-9810
Telephone: 972-453-0172; Fax: 972-453-6758
www.directories.net/

IBM ROCHESTER—1990 (Manufacturing)
IBM Rochester, Quality Manager
3605 Highway 52 North
Rochester, MN 55901-7829
Telephone: 507-253-4434; Fax: 507-253-4461
www.as400.ibm.com/quality/as400.htm

MARLOW INDUSTRIES—1991 (Small Business)
Ms. Tiki Miller, Baldrige Award Coordinator
10451 Vista Park Road
Dallas, TX 75238-1645
Fax: 214-341-5212
www.marlow.com/quality.htm

MERRILL LYNCH CREDIT CORPORATION—1997 (Service)
Lee Lomax, Director of Quality & Business Improvement
4802 Deer Lake Drive East
Jacksonville, FL 32246
Telephone: 904-218-6242; Fax: 904-218-6124
Wendell Collins,Vice President-Publicity
800 Scudders Mill Road
Plainsboro, NJ 08536
Telephone: 609-282-3121; Fax: 609-282-1295
www.ml.com/woml/press_release/19971015-1.htm

MILLIKEN & COMPANY—1989 (Manufacturing)
Craig Long, Director of Quality
P.O. Box 1926, M-186
Spartanburg, SC 29304
Telephone: 864-503-2003; Fax: 864-503-2505
www.milliken.com/quality.html

MOTOROLA, INC.—1988 (Manufacturing)
Dennis Sester, Vice President and Director of Corporate Quality
1303 East Algonquin Road
Schaumburg, IL 60196
Telephone: 847-576-5516; Fax: 847-538-2663
www.mot.com

SOLECTRON CORPORATION—1991 and 1997 (Manufacturing)
Denise Co, Quality Assurance Associate
847 Gilbraltar Drive
Milpitas, CA 95035
Telephone: 408-956-6963; Fax: 408-957-2645
www.solectron.com/quality/index.html
Michael Donner, Director, Corporate Communications
847 Gilbraltar Drive
Milpitas, CA 95035
Telephone: 408-956-6688; Fax: 408-956-7699

TEXAS INSTRUMENTS INCORPORATED DEFENSE SYSTEMS & ELECTRONICS GROUP—1992 (Manufacturing)
Karen Hollingsworth, Director of Business Excellence
Raytheon Systems Company Sensor and Electronics Systems
P.O. Box 405, Mail Station 3461
Lewisville, TX 75067
Telephone: 972-462-4455; Fax: 972-462-5155

THE RITZ-CARLTON HOTEL COMPANY—1992 (Service)
Patrick Mene, Vice President of Quality
3414 Peachtree Road., N.E., Suite 300
Atlanta, GA 30326
Telephone: 404-237-5500; Fax: 404-240-9771

TRIDENT PRECISION MANUFACTURING, INC.—1996 (Small Business)
April Lusk
734 Salt Road
Webster, NY 14580-9796
Telephone: 716-265-1009; Fax: 716-265-0126
www.tridentprecision.com/quality/index.html

WAINWRIGHT INDUSTRIES, INC.—1994 (Small Business)
Michael Simms, Plant Manager
P.O. Box 640
St. Peters, MO 63376
Telephone: 314-278-5850; Fax: 314-278-8806
David A. Robbins, Vice President
P.O. Box 640
St. Peters, MO 63376
Telephone: 314-278-5850; Fax: 314-278-8806

WALLACE COMPANY—1990 (Small Business)
Assets of the Wallace Company have been acquired by Wilson Industries.

WESTINGHOUSE ELECTRIC CORP. COMMERCIAL NUCLEAR FUEL DIVISION—1988 (Manufacturing)
Ms. Meens Mutuala, Director of Quality and Environmental Systems
Westinghouse CNFD
P.O. Box 355
Pittsburgh, PA 15230
Telephone: 412-374-2292; Fax: 412-374-2334

XEROX BUSINESS SERVICES—1997 (Service)
Genny Craver
70 Linden Oaks Parkway
Rochester, NY 14625
Telephone: 716-383-6758; Fax: 716-264-5701
www.xerox.com/XBS/baldrige/

XEROX CORPORATION BUSINESS PRODUCTS & SYSTEMS—1989 (Manufacturing)
Genny Craver
Xerox Corporation
Xerox Square—18B
100 Clinton Avenue South
Rochester, NY 14644
Telephone: 716-383-6758; Fax: 716-423-6041

ZYTEC CORPORATION—1991 (Manufacturing)
Karen Scheldroup, Baldrige Office
7575 Market Place Drive
Eden Prairie, MN 55344
Telephone: 612-941-1100 x. 104; Fax: 612-903-9688

Innovative State Quality Award Practices

The Baldrige evaluation process has served for many years as *the* way to conduct quality and performance excellence reviews. However, in the past few years, several state award programs—not encumbered by statutory restrictions—have created new processes to deliver products that respond to changing business needs and meet their customer requirements better.

The Feedback Report

The feedback report is the key deliverable of the award process. Customers of the process—the applicants—want the report quickly and want the report to be accurate and actionable.

One of the more innovative approaches has been taken by Minnesota and Florida and involves site visiting every applicant/participant. This ensures that the feedback report is more accurate for everyone because it is based on expert inspection rather than self-assessment narrative. In addition, scores are provided at the Item level, not just at the Category level, to help applicants pinpoint areas of concern.

Another innovative approach involves providing an immediate oral feedback report following the site visit. The oral feedback covers the key points at the Category level.

The national quality award office has consistently ensured that feedback comments are nonprescriptive. This means that examiners may not offer suggestions about how to improve processes identified as needing improvement. However, most state-level applicants not only want immediate feedback, they also want some suggestions as to how to make some of the needed improvements.

The Florida Sterling Council provides applicants who are scoring in the lower ranges with a separate section of improvement suggestions on request. This helps these applicants focus on the vital few improvement practices that will help them on their quality journey. The Florida Sterling Council also trains examiners to become mentors who assist organizations in the early stages of quality and performance improvement systems development.

Progressive Recognition

Under the enabling legislation for the Malcolm Baldrige National Quality Improvement Act of 1987 (Public Law 100-107) the U.S. Department of Commerce, National Institute of Standards and Technology (then National Bureau of Standards) was authorized to provide up to two awards in three categories: manufacturing, service, and small business. If three equally qualified applicants presented themselves in one year and all were role models of excellence, one had to be eliminated. The level of competition is intense, and many decide not to apply because they have determined themselves to not be "good enough." Fortunately, Congress alleviated the problem somewhat, but not completely, when it authorized up to three awards instead of two.

This problem led to three innovations at the state level.

- First, many states, such as New York, Illinois, Minnesota, Florida, and others, decided that no artificial limit should be imposed on the number of awards that may be given in a year. All applicants determined by the panel of judges to be role models of performance excellence would be eligible to receive the quality award. The award moved from competition to qualification.
- Second, many states recognized that a primary purpose of the assessment and review process was to encourage development and improvement at all performance levels, not merely to recognize those organizations that made it to the top. Accordingly, several states such as Tennessee, Minnesota, Illinois, and New Mexico offer levels of awards to recognize and encourage progress.
- Third, states such as New York, Minnesota, and Florida, offer special recognition for exemplary practices of organizations that have not reached full role model status, but can offer excellent examples to others for some of their activities.

All of these innovations represent significant steps forward in our nationwide effort to restore global competitiveness in all sectors of our economy.

Glossary

Action Plans

Action plans refer to principal organization-level drivers, derived from short- and long-term strategic planning. In simplest terms, action plans are set to accomplish those things the organization must do well for its strategy to succeed. Action plan development represents the critical stage in planning when general strategies and goals are made specific so that effective organization-wide understanding and deployment are possible. Deployment of action plans requires analysis of overall resource needs and creation of aligned measures for all work units. Deployment might also require specialized training for some employees or recruitment of personnel.

An example of an action plan element for a supplier in a highly competitive industry might be to develop and maintain a price leadership position. Deployment should entail design of efficient processes, analysis of resource and asset use, and creation of related measures of resource and asset productivity, aligned for the organization as a whole. It might also involve use of a cost-accounting system that provides activity-level cost information to support day-to-day work. Unit and/or team training should include priority setting based on costs and benefits. Organization-level analysis and review should emphasize overall productivity growth. Ongoing competitive analysis and planning should remain sensitive to technological and other changes that might greatly reduce operating costs for the organization or its competitors.

Alignment

Alignment refers to consistency of plans, processes, actions, information, decisions, results, analysis, and learning to support key organization-wide goals.

Effective alignment requires common understanding of purposes and goals and use of complementary measures and information for planning, tracking, analysis, and improvement at three levels: the organizational level; the key process level; and the work unit level.

Asset Productivity

The productive use that is made of an organization's assets. An overall measure of asset productivity could be made by dividing the total sales/revenue/budget by total asset value. In addition, specific asset productivity can be determined by making similar calculations against a specific asset or set of assets, such as a specific plant, production line, or even the productivity of land assets (acreage).

Benchmarking

One process by which an organization compares its performance against that of other organizations, determines how those organizations achieved higher performance levels, and uses the information to improve its own performance. Although it is difficult to benchmark some processes directly in some businesses, many of the things one organization does are very similar to things that others do. For example, most organizations move information and tangible products, pay people, train them, appraise their performance, and more. A key to successful benchmarking is to identify the process elements of work and find others who are the best at that process.

Continuous Improvement

The ongoing improvement of products, programs, services, or processes by small increments or major breakthroughs.

Customer

An organization or person who receives or uses a product or service. The customer may be a member or part of another organization or the same organization, or an end user.

Cycle Time

Cycle time refers to time performance—the time required to fulfill commitments or to complete tasks.

Time measurements play a major role in the Criteria because of the great importance of time performance to improving competitiveness. Cycle time is used in the Criteria booklet to refer to all aspects of time performance. Other time-related terms in common use are setup time, lead time, order fulfillment time, changeover time, delivery time, and time to market.

Data

Numerical information used as a basis for reasoning, discussion, determining status, decision making, and analysis.

Effectiveness The extent to which a work process produces intended results.

Efficiency The effort or resources required to produce desired results. More efficient processes require fewer resources than do less efficient processes.

Employee Involvement A practice within an organization whereby employees regularly participate in making decisions on how their work is done, including making suggestions for improvement, planning, goal setting, and monitoring performance.

High Performance Work *High performance work,* a term used in the item descriptions and comments, refers to work approaches systematically pursuing ever-higher levels of overall performance, including quality, productivity, and time performance. High performance work results in improved service for customers and other stakeholders.

Approaches to high performance work vary in form, function, and incentive systems. Effective approaches generally include cooperation between management and the workforce, including workforce bargaining units; cooperation among work units, often involving teams; self-directed responsibility (sometimes called empowerment); individual and organizational skill building and learning; flexibility in job design and work assignments; an organizational structure with minimum layering (flattened), where decision making is decentralized and decisions are made closest to the front line; and effective use of performance measures, including comparisons. Some high performance work systems use monetary and nonmonetary incentives based on factors such as organization performance, team and/or individual contributions, and skill building. Also, some high performance work approaches attempt to align the design of organizations, work, jobs, and incentives.

Indicator When two or more measurements are required to provide a more complete picture of performance, the measurements are called *indicators.* For example, the number of complaints is an indicator of dissatisfaction, not an exclusive measure of it. Cycle time is a discrete measure of the time it takes to complete a process. However, it is only one indicator of process effectiveness. Other indicators may include measures of rework, waste, and defects.

Innovation

Innovation refers to the adoption of an idea, process, technology, or product that is considered new or new to its proposed application.

Successful organizational innovation is a multistep process that involves development and knowledge sharing, a decision to implement, implementation, evaluation, and learning. Although innovation is often associated with technological innovation, it is applicable to all key organizational processes that would benefit from breakthrough improvement and/or change.

Integrated

Refers to the interconnections between the processes of a management system. For example, to satisfy customers an organization must understand their needs, convert those needs into designs, produce the product or service required, deliver it, assess ongoing satisfaction, and adjust the processes accordingly. People need to be trained or hired to do the work, and data must be collected to monitor progress. Performing only a part of the required activities is disjointed and not integrated.

Inter-rater Reliability

The degree to which multiple raters, observing the same phenomenon, will give it the same rating. If they do, it has high inter-rater reliability; if not, it has low inter-rater reliability.

Measures

Measures refer to numerical information that quantifies (measures) input, output, and performance dimensions of processes, products, services, and the overall organization.

Performance

Performance refers to output results information obtained from processes, products, and services that permits evaluation and comparison relative to goals, standards, past results, and to others. Performance might be expressed in nonfinancial and financial terms.

Operational performance refers to performance relative to effectiveness and efficiency measures and indicators. Examples include cycle time, productivity, and waste reduction. Operational performance might be measured at the work unit level, the key process level, and the organization level.

Product and service quality refers to operational performance relative to measures and indicators of product and service requirements, derived from customer preference information. Product and service quality measures should correlate with, and allow the organization to predict, customer satisfaction. Examples of product and service quality include reliability, on-time delivery, defect levels, and service response time. For example, consider a coffee shop that serves breakfast coffee. Product and service quality indicators and measures may include time to serve; time to process payment; freshness (time between brewing and serving); bitterness (acidity measured by pH level); hot (temperature); and strong (ratio of coffee to water and grind coarseness). Taken together, these measures can predict customer satisfaction. In 1999, these results are evaluated as part of Item 7.1.

Customer focused performance refers to performance relative to measures and indicators of customers' perceptions, reactions, and behaviors, and to measures and indicators of product and service characteristics important to customers. Examples include customer retention, complaints, customer survey results, product reliability, on-time delivery, defect levels, and service response time.

Financial and marketplace performance refers to performance using measures of cost and revenue, including asset utilization, asset growth, and market share. Financial measures are generally tracked throughout the organization.

Supplier and partner performance refers to performance relative to processes and requirements of Item 6.3. The performance of suppliers and partners usually includes factors such as cost reduction, on-time delivery, error or defect rates, and specialized measures important to the customer.

Human resource performance relates to the activities in Category 5. Human resource performance measures usually include absenteeism, employee satisfaction ratings, safety incidents, turnover rates, strikes, worker grievances, and compensation claims.

Prevention-Based

Seeking the root cause of a problem and preventing its recurrence rather than merely solving the problem and waiting for it to happen again (a reactive posture).

Process

Process refers to linked activities with the purpose of producing a product or service for a customer (user) within or outside the organization. Generally, processes involve combinations of people, machines, tools, techniques, and materials in a systematic series of steps or actions. In some situations, processes might require adherence to a specific sequence of steps, with documentation (sometimes formal) of procedures and requirements, including well-defined measurement and control steps.

In many service situations, particularly when customers are directly involved in the service, process is used in a more general way—to spell out what must be done, possibly including a preferred or expected sequence. If a sequence is critical, the service needs to include information for customers to help them understand and follow the sequence. Service processes involving customers also require guidance to the providers on handling contingencies related to customers' likely or possible actions or behaviors.

Some organizations do not recognize the importance of the services they provide. Consider the coffee shop again. If the focus is only on making the best coffee and the service is poor—making customers wait too long—the coffee shop will lose customers. Delivering service value must be considered as important to success as delivering product value.

In knowledge work such as strategic planning, research, and analysis, process does not necessarily imply formal sequences of steps. Rather, the process implies general understandings regarding competent performance such as timing, options to be included, evaluation, and reporting. Sequences might arise as part of these understandings.

Productivity

Productivity refers to measures of efficiency of the use of resources. Although the term is often applied to single factors such as staffing (labor productivity), machines, materials, energy, and capital, the productivity concept applies as well to total resources used in producing outputs. Overall productivity—sometimes called *total factor productivity*—is determined by combining the productivities of the different resources used for an output. The combination usually requires taking a weighted average of the different single factor productivity measures, where the weights typically reflect costs of the resources. The use of an aggregate measure of overall productivity allows a determination of whether or not the net effect of overall changes in a process—possibly involving resource trade-offs—is beneficial.

Effective approaches to performance management require understanding and measuring single factor and overall productivity, particularly in complex cases with a variety of costs and potential benefits.

Refinement The result of a systematic process to analyze performance of a system and improve it.

Root Cause The original cause or reason for a condition. The root cause of a condition is that cause which, if eliminated, guarantees that the condition will not recur.

Service Standard (Customer Contact Requirements) A set, measurable level of performance. For example, an objective of an organization might be "prompt customer service." A customer contact requirement or service standard would stipulate how prompt the service should be—"Equipment will be repaired within 24 hours," or "The phone will be answered by a person on or before the second ring."

System A set of well-defined and well-designed processes for meeting the organization's quality and performance requirements.

Systematic Approach A process that is repeatable and predictable, rather than anecdotal and episodic. A systematic approach also integrates other approaches, to ensure high levels of efficiency, effectiveness, and alignment.

Value *Value* refers to the degree of worth relative to cost and relative to possible alternatives of a product, service, process, asset, or function.

Organizations frequently use value considerations to determine the benefits of various options relative to their costs, such as the value of various product and service combinations to customers. Organizations seek to deliver value to all their stakeholders. This frequently requires balancing value for customers and other stakeholders, such as stockholders, employees, and the community.

Waste Reduction Obtained from redesigning a product to require less material or from recycling waste to produce useful products.

Clarifying Confusing Terms

Comparative Information vs. Benchmarking

Comparative information includes benchmarking and competitive comparisons. *Benchmarking* refers to collecting information and data about processes and performance results that represent the best practices and performance for similar activities inside or outside the organization's business or industry. Competitive comparisons refer to collecting information and data on performance relative to direct competitors or similar providers.

For example, a personal computer manufacturer, ABC Micro, must store, retrieve, pack, and ship computers and replacement parts. ABC Micro is concerned about shipping response time, errors in shipping, and damage during shipping. To determine the level of performance of its competitors in these areas, and to set reasonable improvement goals, ABC Micro would gather competitive comparison data from similar providers (competitors). However, these performance levels may not reflect best practices for storage, retrieval, packing, and shipping.

Benchmarking would require ABC Micro to find organizations who carry out these processes better than anyone else and examine both their processes and performance levels—such as the catalog company L.L. Bean.

Benchmarking seeks best-practices information. Competitive comparisons look at competitors, whether or not they are the best.

Customer-Contact Employees

Customer-contact employees are any employees who are in direct contact with customers. They may be direct service providers or answer complaint calls. Whenever a customer makes contact with an organization, either in person or by phone or other electronic means, that customer forms an opinion about the organization and its employees. Employees who come in contact with customers are in a critical position to influence customers for the good of the organization, or to its detriment.

Customer Satisfaction vs. Customer Dissatisfaction

One is not the inverse of the other. The lack of complaints does not indicate satisfaction although the presence of complaints can be a partial indicator of dissatisfaction. Measures of customer dissatisfaction can include direct measures through surveys as well as complaints, product returns, and warranty claims.

Customer satisfaction and dissatisfaction are complex to assess. Customers are rarely "thoroughly" dissatisfied, although they may dislike a feature of a product or an aspect of service. There are usually degrees of satisfaction and dissatisfaction.

Data vs. Information

Information can be qualitative and quantitative. *Data* are information that lend themselves to quantification and statistical analysis. For example, an incoming inspection might produce a count of the number of units accepted, rejected, and total shipped. This count is considered *data.* These counts add to the base of *information* about supplier quality.

Education vs. Training

Training refers to learning about and acquiring job-specific skills and knowledge. *Education* refers to the general development of individuals. An organization might provide training in equipment maintenance for its workers, as well as support the education of workers through an associate degree program at a local community college.

Empowerment and Involvement

Empowerment generally refers to processes and procedures designed to provide individuals and teams the employee tools, skills, and authority to make decisions that affect their work—decisions traditionally reserved for managers and supervisors.

Empowerment as a concept has been misused in many organizations. For example, managers may pretend to extend decision authority under the guise of chartering teams and individuals to make recommendations about their work, while continuing to reserve decision-making authority to themselves.

This practice has given rise to another term—*involvement*—which describes the role of employees who are asked to become involved in decision making, without necessarily making decisions. Involvement is a practice that many agree is better than not involving them at all, but still does not serve to optimize their contribution to initiative, flexibility, and fast response.

Measures and Indicators

The award Criteria do not make a distinction between measures and indicators. However, some users of these terms prefer the term indicator (1) when the measurement relates to performance, but is not a direct or exclusive measure of such performance—for example, the number of complaints is an indicator of dissatisfaction, but not a direct or exclusive measure of it; and (2) when the measurement is a predictor (leading indicator) of some more significant performance, for example, gain in customer satisfaction might be a leading indicator of market share gain.

Operational Performance and Predictors of Customer Satisfaction

Operational performance processes and predictors of customer satisfaction are related but not always the same. Operational performance measures can reflect issues that concern customers as well as those that do not. Operational performance measures are used by the organization to assess effectiveness and efficiency, as well as predict customer satisfaction.

In the example of the coffee shop, freshness is a key customer requirement. One predictor of customer satisfaction might be the length of time, in minutes, between brewing and serving to guarantee freshness and good aroma. The standard might be 10 minutes or less to ensure satisfaction. Coffee more than 10 minutes old would be discarded.

A measure of operational effectiveness might be how many cups were discarded (waste) because the coffee was too old. The customer does not care if the coffee shop pours out stale coffee and, therefore, that measure is not a predictor of satisfaction. However, pouring out coffee does affect profitability and should be measured and minimized.

Ideally, an organization should be able to identify enough measures of product and service quality to predict customer satisfaction accurately and monitor operating effectiveness and efficiency.

Performance Requirements vs. Performance Measures

Performance requirements are an expression of customer requirements and expectations. Sometimes performance requirements are expressed as design requirements or engineering requirements. They are viewed as a basis for developing measures to enable the organization to determine, generally without asking the customer, whether the customer is likely to be satisfied.

Performance measures can also be used to assess efficiency, effectiveness, and productivity of a work process. Process performance measures might include cycle time, error rate, or throughput.

Support Services

Support services are those services that support the organization's product and service delivery core operating processes. Support services might include finance and accounting, management information services, software support, marketing, public relations, personnel administration (job posting, recruitment, payroll), facilities maintenance and management, research and development, secretarial support, and other administration services.

Of course, if an organization is in business to provide a traditional support service such as accounting, then accounting services provided to its external customers become its core work/operating process and are no longer considered a support service. Internal accounting services would continue to be considered a support service.

In the human resources area (Category 5), the Criteria require organizations to manage their human resource assets to optimize performance. However, many human resources support services might also exist such as payroll, travel, position control, recruitment, and employee services. These processes must be designed, delivered, and refined systematically according to the requirements of Item 6.2.

A similar relationship exists in the supplier area. Item 6.3 requires an organization to strengthen supplier and partner performance. This may take place through several measures including training suppliers and/or building partnerships between operating units in the organization and suppliers.

However, the details of developing work specifications, requests for quotations, and other aspects of procurement process might be assigned to a procurement department. That department would be considered a support service that must design its own products and services to meet the requirements of its internal customer and would be received as a support structure (6.2).

Activity	Where covered or described
Filling a job vacancy	6.2
Designing training to meet the overall requirements of the human resource plan	5.2
Systematically improving supplier performance	6.3
Procuring needed supplies for the computer assembly line on time	6.2

Teams and Natural Work Units

Natural work units reflect the people that normally work together because they are a part of a formal work unit. For example, on an assembly line, three or four people naturally work together to install a motor in a new car. Hotel employees who prepare food in the kitchen might constitute another natural work unit.

Teams may be formed of people within a natural work unit or may cross existing (natural) organization boundaries. To improve room service in a hotel, for example, some members of several natural work units such as the switchboard, kitchen workers, and waiters may form a special team. This team would not be considered a natural work team. It might be called a *cross-functional* work team because its members come from different functions within the organization.

Appendix A: Comparing Baldrige with the European Quality Model

The European Quality Award criteria were derived from the Malcolm Baldrige Criteria for Performance Excellence. Although there are differences in structure, both criteria contain essentially the same requirements. The European model is organized into nine groupings called criteria, each with parts and areas to address. The Baldrige model is organized into seven groupings called categories each with items and areas to address. The Baldrige requirements tend to be more detailed and specific than a comparable European Quality Award criterion. Both models have a heavy emphasis on achieving performance results that are important to business success.

The European Quality Model, as does the Baldrige Model, tells us that "customer satisfaction," "people (employee) satisfaction," and "impact on society" are achieved through "leadership" which drives the "policy and strategy," "people management," "resources," and "processes," leading to excellence in "business results." Each of the nine elements, therefore, is a criterion that can be used to assess the organization's progress along the path to excellence. The "results" indicate what the company has achieved and is achieving; the "enablers" indicate how those results are being achieved. The following table provides a top-level comparison of the EFQM Model requirements with those of the Baldrige Criteria. To receive a copy of the European Quality Award Self-Assessment 1998 Guidelines for Companies or the Self-Assessment Guidelines for the Public Sector contact European Quality Award Foundation at www.efqm.org. The e-mail address is info@efqm.org.

Comparing the European Quality Award Model with the Baldrige Criteria

European Quality Award Requirements	1.1	1.2	2.1	2.2	3.1	3.2	4.1	4.2	4.3	5.1	5.2	5.3	6.1	6.2	6.3	7.1	7.2	7.3	7.4	7.5
Leadership: How the behavior and actions of the executive team and all other leaders inspire, support, and promote a culture of Total Quality Management. Leaders:																				
1a. visibly demonstrate their commitment to a culture of Total Quality Management	•																			
1b. support improvement and involvement by providing appropriate resources and assistance	•								•											
1c. are involved with customers, suppliers, and other external organizations	•																			
1d. recognize and appreciate people's efforts and achievements	•									•										
Policy and Strategy: How the organization formulates, deploys, reviews its policy and strategy, and turns it into plans and actions. Policy and strategy are:																				
2a. based on information which is relevant and comprehensive			•				•		•											
2b. developed			•																	
2c. communicated and implemented	•			•																
2d. regularly updated and improved			•	•																
People Management: How the organization releases the full potential of its people. People:																				
3a. resources are planned and improved				•																
3b. capabilities are sustained and developed										•	•	•								
3c. agree on targets and continuously review performance	•			•						•		•						•		
3d. are involved, empowered, and recognized										•										
3e. and the organization have an effective dialogue	•									•										
3f. are cared for												•								
Resources: How the organization manages resources effectively and efficiently. How:																				
4a. financial resources are managed	•								•				•							
4b. information resources are managed				•										•						
4c. supplier relationships and materials are managed				•									•		•				•	
4d. buildings, equipment, and other assets are managed				•									•	•						
4e. technology and intellectual property are managed				•									•	•						
Processes: How the organization identifies, manages, reviews, and improves its processes. Processes:																				
5a. key to the success of the business are identified	•		•				•		•				•							
5b. are systematically managed	•												•	•	•					
5c. are reviewed and targets are set for improvement				•					•				•	•	•					
5d. are improved using innovation and creativity										•			•	•						
5e. are changed and the benefits evaluated										•			•	•						
Customer Satisfaction: What the organization is achieving in relation to the satisfaction of its external customers.																				
6a. the customers' perception of the organization's products, services, and customer relationships					•	•	•		•							•				
6b. additional measurements relating to the satisfaction of the organization's customers					•	•	•	•	•							•				
People Satisfaction: What the organization is achieving in relation to the satisfaction of its people.																				
7a. the people's perception of the organization							•		•			•						•		
7b. additional measurements relating to people satisfaction				•			•		•			•								
Impact on Society: What the organization is achieving in satisfying the needs and the expectations of the local, national, and international community at large (as appropriate). This includes the perception of the organization's approach to quality of life, the environment, the preservation of global resources, and the organization's own internal measures of effectiveness. It will include its relations with authorities and bodies which affect and regulate its business.																				
8a. society's perception of the organization		•																		
8b. additional measurements of the organization's impact on society		•					•													•
Business Result: What the organization is achieving in relation to its planned business objectives and in satisfying the needs and expectations of everyone with a financial interest or stake in the organization.																				
9a. financial measurements of the organization's performance																	•			
9b. additional measurements of the organization's performance																				•

Additional correlations between the Baldrige and European Quality Award criteria might exist, depending on the interpretation of where results of some support areas are reported.

Appendix B: 1999 Systems Required for Performance Excellence

The following section is intended for use by leaders of the organization and its units as a management tool. It defines responsibilities and management systems that are drawn from the 1999 Criteria for Performance Excellence. It can be used as a relatively simple way to focus on the Criteria requirements. Some organizations use this type of information to guide the work of management champions. Organizational leaders at various levels can use the following section for setting objectives and requirements rather than having to translate questions into statements. These statements can be used in conjunction with the Category Champion descriptions to further define the areas of responsibility and focus for each Category Champion.

1 Leadership

Senior leaders must address values and performance expectations, as well as focus on customers and other stakeholders, empowerment, innovation, learning, and organizational directions. Also your organization must address its responsibilities to the public and support its key communities.

1.1 Organizational Leadership

Senior leaders must effectively and systematically guide your organization and review organizational performance.

a. Senior Leadership Direction

Senior leaders must clearly set, communicate, and deploy organizational values, performance expectations, and focus on creating and balancing value for customers and other stakeholders through your leadership structure to all employees.

Senior leaders must establish and support employee empowerment and innovation, and organizational and employee learning.

Senior leaders must set clear directions and seek future opportunities for your organization.

b. Organizational Performance Review

Senior leaders must systematically review organizational performance and capabilities to assess organizational health, competitive performance, and progress relative to performance goals and changing organizational needs.

Key performance measures that are regularly reviewed by senior leaders must be defined.

Senior leaders must systematically translate organizational performance review findings into priorities for improvement and opportunities for innovation.

Key recent performance review findings, priorities for improvement, and opportunities for innovation must be known and documented. They must be understood throughout the organization and, as appropriate, by suppliers/partners and key customers to ensure organizational alignment.

Senior leaders must regularly use organizational performance review findings and employee feedback to improve their leadership effectiveness and the effectiveness of management throughout the organization.

1.2 Public Responsibility and Citizenship

Your organization must address its responsibilities to the public and practice good citizenship.

a. Responsibilities to the Public

The organization must systematically examine and address the impacts on society of your products, services, and operations. Key practices, measures, and targets must be identified for meeting or exceeding regulatory and legal requirements and for minimizing risks associated with all products, services, and operations.

The organization must have a system in place to anticipate public concerns with current and future products, services, and operations. It must address these concerns in a proactive manner.

The organization must have a system in place to ensure ethical business practices are followed in all stakeholder transactions and interactions.

b. Support of Key Communities

The organization, its senior leaders, and employees must actively support and strengthen the organization's key communities. A systematic process must be in place to identify key communities and determine appropriate areas of emphasis for organizational involvement and support, consistent with organizational business objectives.

2 Strategic Planning

Your organization must have a clear strategy development process, including a process to develop strategic objectives, action plans, and related human resource plans. Also your organization must deploy the plans and track performance.

2.1 Strategy Development

Your organization must have a strategy development process to strengthen your organizational performance and competitive position. Your key strategic objectives need to be clearly defined.

a. Strategy Development Process

A clear strategic planning process must be in place, including key steps and key participants in the process.

The strategic planning process considers relevant data and information for the following key factors as each relates to your organization:

- Customer and market needs/expectations, including new product/service opportunities;
- Competitive environment and capabilities, including use of new technology;
- Financial, societal, and other potential risks;
- Human resource capabilities and needs;
- Operational capabilities and needs, including resource availability; and
- Supplier and/or partner capabilities and needs.

b. Strategic Objectives

Your organization must have a timetable for accomplishing its key strategic objectives. Your organization must have a method to assess how well the strategic objectives respond to the factors in 2.1 above that are most important to your success.

2.2 Strategy Deployment

Your organization must have a strategy deployment process. Your organization's action plans and related performance measures must be clearly defined. Project the performance of these key measures into the future.

a. Action Plan Development and Deployment

Systematically develop action plans to implement key strategic objectives. List key short- and longer-term action plans. Identify key changes, if any, in your products/services and/or your customers/markets and be able to explain the reasons for the changes to employees throughout the organization.

Define key human resource requirements and plans, based on strategic objectives and action plans, the organization must implement to ensure it has the human resources to carry out the plan.

Develop a system to allocate resources throughout the organization to ensure they are aligned with strategic objectives, and that your overall action plan is achieved.

Define key performance measures and/or indicators for tracking progress relative to action plans.

Systematically communicate and deploy strategic objectives, action plans, and performance measures/indicators throughout the organization to achieve overall organizational alignment of work and resources.

b. Performance Projection
Define the two- to five-year projections for key performance measures and/or indicators. Include key performance targets and/or goals, as appropriate.

Determine the projected performance of competitors and key benchmarks, as appropriate, for the same time period as your projected goals. The basis for these comparisons must be clear.

3 Customer and Market Focus

Your organization must determine requirements, expectations, and preferences of customers and markets. Also your organization must build relationships with customers and determine their satisfaction.

3.1 Customer and Market Knowledge

Your organization must determine short- and longer-term requirements, expectations, and preferences of customers and markets to ensure the relevance of current products/services and to develop new opportunities.

a. Customer and Market Knowledge
Systematically determine target customers, customer groups, and/or market segments. Specifically consider the requirements of customers of competitors and other potential customers and/or markets in this determination.

Systematically listen and learn from current, former, and potential customers to determine key requirements and drivers of purchase decisions. If determination methods differ for different customers and/or customer groups, define the key differences and show how your techniques for learning about the requirements of these groups vary according to real differences among the customer groups.

Systematically determine and/or project key product/service features and identify their relative importance/value to customers for purposes of current and future marketing, product planning, and other business developments, as appropriate. Use relevant information from current and former customers, including marketing/sales information, customer retention, won/lost analysis, and complaints, in this determination.

Evaluate and improve your listening and learning methods to keep them current with changing business needs and directions.

3.2 Customer Satisfaction and Relationships

Your organization must determine the satisfaction of customers and build relationships to retain current business and to develop new opportunities.

a. Customer Relationships

Provide easy access to facilitate the ability of customers to conduct business, seek assistance and information, and complain. Document the key mechanisms used.

Determine key customer contact requirements and systematically ensure all employees involved in the customer response chain understand and adhere to these contact requirements.

Establish a systematic complaint management process to ensure that complaints are resolved effectively and promptly (ideally at the first point of contact). Ensure that all complaints received are aggregated and analyzed for use in overall organizational improvement.

Systematically build relationships with customers to ensure repeat business and/or positive referral.

Evaluate and improve approaches to provide customer access and build relationships to keep them current with changing business needs and directions.

b. Customer Satisfaction Determination

Implement systematic processes, take measurements, and collect data to determine customer satisfaction and dissatisfaction. Ensure that measurements capture actionable information that reflects customers' future business and/or potential for positive referral. Define any significant differences in processes or methods for different customer groups and/or market segments.

Systematically follow up with customers on products/services and recent transactions so your organization can receive prompt and actionable feedback for use in improving products and services and preventing future problems.

Obtain and use information on customer satisfaction relative to competitors and/or benchmarks, as appropriate, to improve your offerings and support strategic planning.

Evaluate and improve approaches to customer satisfaction determination to keep them current with changing business needs and directions.

4 Information and Analysis

Your organization must have a performance measurement system and a way to analyze performance data and information.

4.1 Measurement of Organizational Performance

Your organization must provide effective performance measurement systems for understanding, aligning, and improving performance at all levels and in all parts of your organization.

a. Measurement of Organizational Performance
Ensure the major components of the organization's performance measurement system, includes the following key factors:

- Select measures/indicators that examine the extent and effectiveness of daily operations;
- Select and integrate measures/indicators to ensure complete data are available to track overall organizational performance in areas key to business success;
- Select key comparative data and information and effectively use the data to set goals and improve work processes throughout the organization;
- Ensure the reliability of data and information used for decision making;
- Use information and data to improve the cost/financial understanding to help set priorities regarding improvement options;
- Use data and information to develop correlations/projections to support planning; and
- Evaluate and improve the performance measurement system to keep it current with changing business needs and directions.

4.2 Analysis of Organizational Performance

Your organization must analyze performance data and information to assess and understand overall organizational performance.

a. Analysis of Organizational Performance

Analyze data that examines the overall health of the organization, including key business results and strategic objectives, to support senior executives' organizational performance review and planning.

Systematically ensure that the results of organizational-level analysis are linked to work group and/or functional-level operations to enable effective support for decision making.

Ensure the analysis effectively supports daily operational decision making throughout the organization, and ensures that measures align with action plans.

5 Human Resource Focus

Your organization must enable employees to develop and utilize their full potential, aligned with the organization's objectives. Also your organization must build and maintain a work environment and an employee support climate conducive to performance excellence, full participation, and personal and organizational growth.

5.1 Work Systems

Your organization's work and job design, compensation, career progression, and related workforce practices must enable employees to achieve high performance in your operations.

a. Work Systems

Design, organize, and manage work and jobs to promote cooperation and collaboration, individual initiative, innovation, and flexibility, to keep current with business needs.

Ensure that managers and supervisors encourage and motivate employees to develop and utilize their full potential and encourage and support employees in job- and career-related development/learning objectives.

Ensure that the employee performance management system, including feedback to employees, supports high performance.

Ensure that compensation, recognition, and related reward/incentive practices systematically reinforce high performance.

Ensure effective communication, cooperation, and knowledge/skill sharing across work units, functions, and locations, as appropriate.

Systematically identify characteristics and skills needed by potential employees; and recruit and hire new employees to fill skill gaps consistent with fair workforce practices. When examining key performance requirements to identify needed skills mix, consider diversity within the organization's employee community.

5.2 Employee Education, Training, and Development

Your organization's education and training must support the achievement of your business objectives, build employee knowledge, skills, and capabilities, and contribute to improved employee performance.

a. Employee Education, Training, and Development

Ensure that the organization's system for education and training balances short- and longer-term organizational and employee needs, including development, learning, and career progression.

Design education and training to ensure it keeps current with business and individual needs. Include how job and organizational performance are used in education and training design and evaluation.

Seek and use input from employees and their supervisors/managers to design and set education and training needs and expectations.

Deliver, evaluate, and improve formal and informal education, training, and learning, as appropriate.

Systematically address key developmental and training needs of the entire workforce, including diversity training, management/leadership development, new employee orientation, and safety, as appropriate.

Ensure that training and education address the topics of performance excellence, such as ensuring that employees learn to use performance measurements, performance standards, skill standards, performance improvement, quality control methods, and benchmarking, as appropriate.

Systematically reinforce knowledge and skills on the job.

5.3 Employee Well-Being and Satisfaction

Your organization must maintain a work environment and an employee support climate that contribute to the well-being, satisfaction, and motivation of all employees.

a. Work Environment

Systematically assess and improve workplace health, safety, and ergonomics. Ensure employees take part in identifying these factors and in improving workplace safety. Ensure performance measures and/or targets are in place for each key environmental factor. Also identify significant differences in requirements, if any, based on different work environments for employee groups and/or work units.

b. Employee Support Climate

Enhance employees' work climate via services, benefits, and policies. Ensure these enhancements are selected and tailored to meet the needs of different categories and types of employees, and individuals, as appropriate.

Ensure that the work climate considers and supports the needs of a diverse workforce.

c. Employee Satisfaction

Systematically determine the key factors that affect employee well-being, satisfaction, and motivation.

Develop and implement formal and/or informal assessment methods and measures to determine employee well-being, satisfaction, and motivation systematically. Methods and measures should be tailored to examine the needs of a diverse workforce and to different categories and types of employees. In addition, use indicators such as employee turnover, absenteeism, grievances, and productivity to assess and improve employee well-being, satisfaction, and motivation.

Relate employee climate assessment findings to key business results to identify work environment and employee support climate improvement priorities.

6 Process Management

Your organization must have a process management system including customer focused design, product and service delivery, support, and supplier and partnering processes that involve all work units.

6.1 Product and Service Processes

Your organization must manage effectively key product and service design and delivery processes.

a. Design Processes

A clear design process for products/services and their related production/delivery processes must be in place.

Design processes must be capable of systematically incorporating changing customer/market requirements into product/service designs and production/delivery systems and processes.

Systematically incorporate new technology into products/services and into production/delivery systems and processes, as appropriate.

Ensure that design processes systematically and thoroughly address design quality and cycle time, transfer of learning from past projects and other parts of the organization, cost control, new design technology, productivity, and other efficiency/effectiveness factors.

Evaluate production/delivery process design to ensure it effectively accommodates all key operational performance requirements.

Systematically evaluate, coordinate, and test design and production/delivery processes to ensure capability for trouble-free and timely introduction of products/services.

b. Production/Delivery Processes
Key production/delivery processes and their key performance requirements are well known and clearly defined.

Day-to-day operation of key production/delivery processes consistently meet key performance requirements.

Key performance measures and/or indicators are used for the control and improvement of key work processes. Real-time customer input is used to improve work processes.

Evaluate and improve production/delivery processes to achieve better process performance and improvements to products/services, as appropriate. Improvements are consistently shared with other organizational units and processes, as appropriate, throughout the organization.

6.2 Support Processes
Your organization must manage effectively its key support processes.

a. Support Processes
A systematic process is in place to determine key support process requirements, incorporating input from internal and/or external customers, as appropriate. Key operational requirements (such as productivity and cycle time) for the processes are clearly defined.

Processes are designed to meet all the key requirements.

The day-to-day operation of key support processes consistently meet key performance requirements. How do you determine and use in-process measures and/or customer feedback in your support processes.

Evaluate and improve support processes to achieve better performance and to keep them current with business needs and directions, as appropriate. Improvements are routinely shared with other organizational units and processes, as appropriate.

6.3 Supplier and Partnering Processes

Your organization must manage effectively its key supplier and/or partnering interactions and processes.

a. Supplier and Partnering Processes

Key performance requirements your suppliers and/or partners must meet to fulfill your overall requirements are clearly defined. Systematically incorporate performance requirements into supplier and/or partner process management.

Develop a system to ensure that performance requirements are met. Systematically provide timely and actionable feedback to suppliers and/or partners to enable them to improve their performance quickly. Define key performance measures and/or indicators and any targets used for supplier and/or partner assessment.

Systematically and proactively minimize overall costs associated with inspections, tests, and process and/or performance audits.

Provide business assistance and/or incentives to suppliers and/or partners to help them improve their overall performance and to improve their abilities to contribute to your current and longer-term performance.

Evaluate and improve your supplier and/or partner processes, including processes to help customers and partners keep current with your business needs and directions. Improvements are systematically shared throughout your organization, as appropriate.

7 Business Results

Your organization's performance and improvement in key business areas must include customer satisfaction, product and service performance, financial and marketplace performance, human resource results, supplier and partner results, and operational performance. Also your organization must track and improve performance levels relative to competitors.

7.1 Customer Focused Results

Your organization's customer focused results must include customer satisfaction and product and service performance results. Your results must be segmented by customer groups and market segments, as appropriate and include appropriate comparative data.

a. Customer Focused Results

Display data regarding current levels and trends in key measures and/or indicators of customer satisfaction, dissatisfaction, and satisfaction relative to competitors.

Display data regarding current levels and trends in key measures and/or indicators of customer loyalty, positive referral, customer-perceived value, and/or customer relationship building, as appropriate.

Display data regarding current levels and trends in key measures and/or indicators of product and service performance.

7.2 Financial and Market Results

Your organization's key financial and marketplace performance results must be segmented by market segments, as appropriate, and include appropriate comparative data.

a. Financial and Market Results

Display data regarding current levels and trends in key measures and/or indicators of financial performance. Include aggregate measures of financial return and/or economic value, as appropriate.

Display data regarding current levels and trends in key measures and/or indicators of marketplace performance. Include market share/position, business growth, and new markets entered, as appropriate.

7.3 Human Resource Results

Your organization's human resource results must include employee well-being, satisfaction, development, and work system performance. Segment your results by types and categories of employees, as appropriate. Include appropriate comparative data.

a. Human Resource Results

Display data regarding current levels and trends in key measures and/or indicators of employee well-being, satisfaction and dissatisfaction, and development.

Display data regarding current levels and trends in key measures and/or indicators of work system performance and effectiveness.

7.4 Supplier and Partner Results

Your organization's key supplier and partner results must include appropriate comparative data.

a. Supplier and Partner Results

Display data regarding current levels and trends in key measures and/or indicators of supplier and partner performance. Display data regarding performance and/or cost improvements resulting from supplier and partner performance and performance management.

7.5 Organizational Effectiveness Results

Your organization's key operational performance results that contribute to the achievement of organizational effectiveness must be tracked and improved. Include appropriate comparative data.

a. Organizational Effectiveness Results

Display data regarding current levels and trends in key measures and/or indicators of key design, production, delivery, and support process performance. Include productivity, cycle time, and other appropriate measures of effectiveness and efficiency.

Display data regarding results for key measures and/or indicators of regulatory/legal compliance and citizenship. Display data regarding results for key measures and indicators of accomplishment of organizational strategy.

Index